PLANNING STRATEGIES FOR WORLD EVANGELIZATION

PLANNING STRATEGIES
FOR
WORLD EVANGELIZATION

by

Edward R. Dayton
and
David A. Fraser

Revised Edition

WILLIAM B. EERDMANS PUBLISHING COMPANY
GRAND RAPIDS, MICHIGAN

MARC
MONROVIA, CALIFORNIA

Copyright © 1990 by Wm. B. Eerdmans Publishing Co.
255 Jefferson Ave. S.E., Grand Rapids, MI   49503

First edition published 1980

This revised edition published 1990 jointly by Eerdmans and
Missions Advanced Research and Communication Center,
a division of World Vision International,
919 W. Huntington Dr., Monrovia, CA   91016

Library of Congress Cataloging-in-Publication Data

Dayton, Edward R.
   Planning strategies for world evangelization / by Edward R. Dayton
and David A. Fraser. — Rev. ed.
     p.   cm.
   Includes bibliographical references.
   ISBN 0-8028-0422-5
   1. Missions. 2. Evangelistic work. I. Fraser, David Allen,
1943–   . II. Title.
BV2061.D35   1990
266 — dc20   90-32558
                                                 CIP

*To the men and women of the Missions Advanced Research and
Communication Center without whom this book would not be possible
and
To all those who seek the challenges of first evangelization among
unreached peoples without whom this book would remain only words*

Contents

CONTENTS

x

CONTENTS

Preface

This is a book about the process of evangelization, what it is and how to go about it. Specifically, it is a book about cross-cultural evangelization. One might immediately question the need for another book on this topic. Are there not enough? Should we not get to work applying what we already know? Why *this* book?

For the past twenty-three years the focus of Missions Advanced Research and Communication Center (MARC) has been the task of world evangelization. Its goal is to bring that task into clearer focus. The founding of the Center coincided with the first modern conference on world evangelization held at Berlin in 1966. In many ways Berlin was a new beginning for evangelization. Berlin put down the biblical roots needed to regenerate the process. What a flowering of conferences and studies have followed that event!

The earlier founding of the Institute of Church Growth and its successor, the Fuller School of World Mission, by Donald McGavran brought new understanding of what God was doing in his world. The movement surrounding the Lausanne Committee for World Evangelization has encouraged hundreds of agencies and thousands of Christians to get newly involved. Hundreds of books on the theology of mission, mission and communication theory, and sociological and anthropological insight have been published. All this happened after a period of nearly forty years in which only minimal mission research was undertaken.

But there are few books written on the process of analyzing and planning a specific mission endeavor. This is precisely what this book is about: planning mission strategies. It places the entire mission enterprise within a framework that allows both individual and organization to approach their task with an overall understanding. It presents a ten-step planning model that can be applied to the process of thinking through any effort at cross-cultural evangelization.

We have placed a number of deliberately provocative considerations at the beginning of each of the major sections of the book. At the end we have posed a number of critical questions. We believe that questions are often more important than answers. There are already too many standard solutions and pat answers. Every situation we face is unique and our response must match the uniqueness of the situation. Our model is more a series of questions than a series of answers. At each of the ten steps in the planning process it is more important that we ask the right questions than come with what we already feel are the right answers. Much of the book is an attempt to demonstrate why those questions are important and useful.

While this book is written from a Western perspective, we have attempted to enter into the growing multicultural reality of the World Christian movement. We do not believe the day of Western missions is past. We do not believe the best strategy for the church in the West is to withdraw from the world scene and first get its own house in order. Part of the necessary corrective is for the church in the West to capture anew a sense of what God's kingdom is about in the present. It needs to recognize the magnitude of the task and to get on with that task in a significantly enhanced fashion. Millions of people still need to hear of the God who loves them in Jesus Christ.

We believe the planning model presented in this book is universally applicable *for planning strategies.* Yet it is true that we can speak only locally in English, to those who can read and understand English. Nevertheless, we have shared this model widely in various corners of our globe. We have reason to believe it is useful and adaptable even across the borders of language and culture.

Much of what we have to say builds on the work of others. We have tried to put their thousands of hours of research and experience into a comprehensive model. We have also benefitted from the comments and responses to the first edition of this book. Where we have failed to give adequate credit, we apologize. Much of our work happens within the larger fellowship of MARC. Many of the concepts, models, surveys, studies, and publications that we use come from discussion, dissection, and debate within that organization for over two decades. We knew that one day the very premise on which MARC was founded— seeking to understand God's strategy for world evangelization and becoming a part of it—would demand a more exhaustive formulation. We owe much to the staff and Fellows of MARC.

Neither MARC nor the two editions of this book would have

been possible if it were not for the confidence and encouragement of the leadership of MARC's parent organization, World Vision International. We salute its vision for the worldwide Christian movement and for those left out of the goods of this life and the knowledge of life eternal.

Monrovia, California   Edward R. Dayton
St. Davids, Pennsylvania   David A. Fraser
December 1989

INTRODUCTION

1. Beginnings

These are wondrous days for the church and world Christianity. When we compare our situation with the world that William Carey faced in 1790, we can rejoice. In his beautifully descriptive book, *An Enquiry Into the Obligation of Christians to Use Means for the Conversion of the Heathen,* Carey estimated that fewer than one-third of the countries of the world had any gospel witness. Today we are confident there are few if any countries in the world without a handful of believers.

Christianity has truly become the world's first universal religious movement. To many this has signaled an end to the Great Era of Missions. Mission efforts should end, they believe, especially from Western nations.

In many countries of the world the church has matured. Some churches now have the strength and the will to carry out the evangelization of their respective countries. The church is growing so rapidly in some areas that the only outside assistance needed is supportive rather than directive.

Yet an analysis that sees the world as evangelized because there is a Christian witness within every national boundary is faulty. Within many of these countries there are pockets of unreached people, whose culture is very different from that of their Christian neighbors. Thus, there is little human possibility of those Christians reaching those unreached without becoming cross-cultural missionaries. Further, some countries have very few Christians. Conservative estimates say that 65 to 70 percent of the world's non-Christians are reachable only by cross-cultural evangelism.

To understand what that means, imagine a circle representing the world of 5.1 billion people (the 1988 world population). We can

3

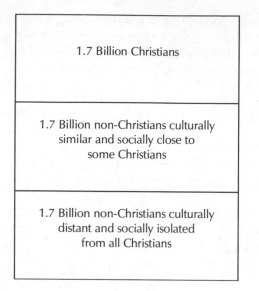

FIGURE 1.1   CHRISTIANS IN THE WORLD

divide the 5.1 billion into approximately equal thirds—1.7 billion each (see Figure 1.1). One third of these people name Jesus as Lord.

Another third are non-Christians living where they are reasonably mixed in with culturally similar Christians. We can hope for some witness here because of the social and cultural contact. Given adequate motivation, the churches can evangelize them in what we call near-neighbor evangelism. Missionaries from other countries choosing to serve in these areas should relate themselves to the churches in that country.

The last third is made up of non-Christians in areas where churches cannot evangelize them without crossing significant cultural and social barriers. In many of these countries Christians number less than 2 percent of the total population.

A few missiological notations help to clarify the general picture by assessing the relative difficulty of the job of evangelism. Using the notations E-0, E-1, E-2, and E-3,[1] we are better able to communicate the task that lies before us. When there are no cultural, denominational, or relational barriers to cross, evangelism is designated E-0. For example, not all members of a local community of Christians may have a personal

1. This notation, which has received widespread use, was first suggested by Dr. Ralph Winter.

relationship with Jesus Christ. Seeking to bring these to faith is a task that happens within the local congregation. Evangelism with people who are similar culturally and belong to one's own social group but not to the church is E-1. There is one barrier to cross (between the churched and the unchurched).

Once we begin to cross cultural boundaries—boundaries of language, of social class or caste, of ethnic difference—the task becomes more complicated. Here the evangelist spends much more time building trust and seeking to understand the people and their culture. The varying degrees of cultural distance between the evangelist and those being evangelized also correspond to differing degrees of difficulty. Situations of minimum difficulty are designated E-2; those with the maximum degree of cultural distance and difficulty are E-3.

In Figure 1.1, the first third, symbolizing Christians, includes many nominal Christians. They need E-0 evangelism. The second third, symbolizing non-Christians with significant numbers of Christians in their midst, requires at least E-1. The third group, non-Christians separated from Christians, requires E-2 and in most cases E-3 evangelism. Our major concern in this book is with E-2 and E-3 evangelism.

Those culturally and socially distant non-Christians will number about two billion people by the year 2000. If current growth rates continue, there will be about two billion Christians of all types. The current tragedy is that the vast majority of cross-cultural missionaries do not minister to the unreached peoples of this distant world. It is time to rethink missions—not in the direction of fewer pioneer or church planting missionaries, but more.

"But," some will reply, "should these missionaries be *North Americans?* Won't missionaries from the Two-Thirds countries do a much better job?" Perhaps. Yet in many areas of the world a North American or European will be more acceptable than someone from a Two-Thirds World country. No general principle can rule out any sector of the church. In some cases, however, Two-Thirds World missionaries will be better. We rejoice in the many non-Western missionaries that are active. We wish more resources were available so many more could venture forth. But it is premature to think the Western missionary a dinosaur.

This means three things: First, old and new mission agencies need to develop new strategies to reach the 1.7 billion culturally distant or unreached people. Second, missionary preparation must be rethought and replanned for a new thrust. Third, our strategies and plans will need to start with an understanding of the people we want to reach. Attention should be on strategies that attempt to meet them within the context of their need, rather than on the basis of preconceived means and methods.

5

INTRODUCTION

We believe God has given his church some new insights into how to think about reaching the "hidden" and unreached peoples. That is what this book is about.

WHAT DO WE MEAN BY A PEOPLE OR PEOPLE GROUP?

Many of us think of the world as made up of 220 nation-states, as defined by the United Nations. From a political viewpoint, this is very acceptable. From the viewpoint of world evangelization, thinking this way clouds the issue. We see the world more clearly as tens of thousands of groups within these national boundaries.

Research suggests there are over fifteen thousand different *ethnic* groups. Linguists have identified more than five thousand distinct languages. In addition, there are occupational groups, such as taxi drivers in Seoul, Korea, and whalers off the coast of South Africa. There are class and caste groups, such as the scheduled castes of India. There are people bound together by crisis situations such as famine and war refugees in Central Africa.

Each of these groups has a particular need and sense of identity. Our task is to show how the gospel makes sense to people with that need and group identity. Rather than think about 220 nation-states, we need to think about thousands of unreached peoples and people groups.

At first glance this may make the task seem almost insurmountable, yet there is a real advantage to thinking about it this way. Once a viable community of Christians is present in each of these socially and culturally distinct groups, the cultural barrier is broken. A cluster of churches planted by E-3 evangelism means the gospel then can spread by E-1 evangelism throughout the whole group.

Let's assume there are as many as twenty-five thousand unreached peoples who do not have a viable church in their midst. The task then is to establish a viable group of congregations in each of those peoples. If four cross-cultural missionaries from outside each group are needed to accomplish this frontier mission, only one hundred thousand missionaries are needed. The task of world evangelization is no longer overwhelming.

Doing this would only get the *process of evangelization* started. Yet that beginning would turn the distant unreached peoples into near neighbors of at least part of the Christian movement. Getting the process going is a much smaller task than actually reaching every single one of the 1.7 billion people.

A COMPREHENSIVE APPROACH IS NEEDED

One of our basic assumptions is that just as every individual is unique before God, so every people and people group is unique before God. This uniqueness implies that there are no universal *means and methods* of evangelism. Each group exists in a special context, with its special needs and special abilities. Given this fact, the only place to begin the evangelization of any people is with the people themselves. This is the basis of our strategy for evangelism. A comprehensive way to approach any unreached people grows out of this beginning point.

This is an *approach to thinking,* rather than doing. This book is about planning for action and thus about how to think through evangelism before and while it is happening. It includes much more than just means and methods. It focuses on unreached peoples and people groups as loved and sought by a compassionate God. His treasuring of them means they are worthy of all our thought, time, and energy.

This approach grows out of the work of the Missions Advanced Research and Communication Center, founded in 1966. Field testing this approach began in 1973. It was presented to the Lausanne Consultation on World Evangelization in 1974. The field workbook, *That Everyone May Hear—A Workbook* (Dayton), is now in its seventh edition, and has been translated into a number of languages. It is a basic working document of the Strategy Working Group of the Lausanne Committee for World Evangelization.

This book is a more comprehensive explanation of that planning workbook. It gives a more detailed account of what planning strategies for unreached peoples means. It deals with all the steps from defining a mission to the unreached to evaluating the results.

At the same time this book brings the task of cross-cultural missions into a comprehensive whole. It draws deeply upon the insights of a number of streams of thought: the Church Growth movement started by Dr. Donald McGavran and the School of World Mission at Fuller Theological Seminary; communications theory as represented by Wheaton Graduate School and Viggo Søgaard; the social and cultural sciences as exemplified in the Lausanne "Willowbank Report" of 1978; the various evangelical consultations of the past twenty years from Berlin 1966 to the second International Congress on World Evangelization in Manila, 1989; modern systems analysis and the adaptation of new psychological and sociological insights to management of human enterprises; and finally, the work of MARC and other research groups which have sought to clarify, classify, and identify peoples and people groups throughout the world who are unevangelized or underevangelized.

INTRODUCTION

The day of the Western missionary is not fading. There still is need for well-trained, culturally sensitive, Spirit-empowered men and women who are willing to share the good news of God's kingdom and salvation in foreign cultures. To give as much attention to the 1.7 billion distant unreached people as we now do to the 1.7 billion near neighbor non-Christians, we need about one hundred thousand more cross-cultural missionaries in 1990.

God calls us to contemplate the kind of world he desires for the future. Then we must follow the precepts of his word and the leading of his Spirit into that future. Let us begin.

2. Perspective

The last twenty-three years have taught us that there is a critical need for the process of *planning* strategies for evangelism. Some Christians still believe that the insights of the so-called secular world are not applicable to the missionary task. Yet planning was not always viewed with suspicion.

Many are unaware of the immense research and planning that typified the missionary enterprise in the late nineteenth and early twentieth centuries. Indeed, the information gathered for the Edinburgh Conference in 1910 was vast. At last report it is still uncollated.

We wrongly suppose that statistical summaries, analyses of population mix, studies on how to reach particular ethnic groups, and extensive mapping of the missionary enterprise are either new discoveries or applications of secular methodologies. Yet we are only now matching the depth of inquiry that typified the missionary movement from 1890 to the early 1920s.[1] That period ended with the issuing of the last Missionary Atlas in 1924.

Planning concerns the future. Christian planning deals with the future as God wants it. If you are comfortable with the idea of planning in missions, you may wish to turn to Chapter 3.

---

1. An excellent example of this is the American edition of the *World Survey* (Interchurch World Movement, 1920). One finds in the Table of Contents that thought has been given to all kinds of means and methods. Statistics have been plotted on the entire Christian movement within the USA with analyses of many types of social and ethnic groups. In our time David Barrett's *World Christian Encyclopedia* (Oxford University Press, 1982) commands even more information.

INTRODUCTION

THE FUTURE LIES IN THE FUTURE

Ecclesiastes asserts: "There is nothing new under the sun" (1:9). Solomon focused on the cyclical predictability of the processes of nature and human life. Yet other biblical authors, focusing on God's power, had the equally valid awareness that the future could and would be radically different from the past or the present. God would bring about a new covenant, a new heavens and earth. God could even give a person a new heart.

For centuries humans forecast the future on the basis of the past. Nature was regular in the rising and setting of the sun and the larger cycle of the seasons. Similarly, the changes from generation to generation seemed to move within narrow limits. Grandchildren lived very much as had their grandparents.

Modern industrial culture lives with a new idea of the future. History has become compressed. Time is marked off by a series of events, such as day and night.[2] The amount of history that occurs in any given chunk of clock time is rising significantly. With more people, increased technical capability and communication, more events occur and become important to us. With more events in shorter periods, it has become increasingly difficult to anticipate the future on the basis of the past. We have less and less time to make decisions about the future.

The impact of this increasing compression of history and novelty of events is known as "future shock."[3] People respond to it in various ways. Some do not plan at all. They say, "If God knows everything that is going to happen, there is no sense in our worrying about it. We cannot change a thing." Some attempt the futile path of planning a complete future as if God had no part. They say, "All of the future lies in our hands. We are completely responsible for it." Another approach is to plan the little things and "leave the big things to God."

None of these is adequate. Rather, we should plan *in paradox*. This means we plan as much and as carefully as possible, yet at the same time assume that God is at work in everything. We plan as though the future is our responsibility while believing God is the one who makes it happen. How we think about the future has much to do with how we think about evangelization.

2. For an interesting and thorough discussion on the whole concept of time, see Henri Yaker et al., *The Future of Time* (Doubleday, 1971).

3. Alvin Toffler (1970) was the first to popularize this awareness. Other futurists, such as Herman Kahn, have had a profound impact on the future simply by discussing it. Kahn and Weiner's *The Year 2000* (1967) was credited with changing government policy in Brazil because of the predictions it made about that country. More recently John Naisbitt's *Megatrends* (1982) has had major impact with his view of the future.

A THEOLOGY OF THE FUTURE

Christians view history as having direction and climax. We believe that a blessed hope lies ahead. Yet we also believe that God expects us to order our lives and our community in the light of that hope. We are responsible for the future of our own individual lives and our responses to the lives of others. When Paul deals with how we are to live in Romans 12, he is not talking about the past. He is concerned with how we are to live in the future.

The Bible also describes how God continually renews the individual. Past errors and sins are forgiven and forgotten: "as far as the east is from the west, so far has he separated our iniquities from us" (Ps. 103:12). God sustains only the positives in our lives. Yet both the good and bad *results* of the past are present in the future.

There are "laws" at work. At times God "interferes" with those laws and brings about results that are gracious and unmerited. For these reasons any statement about the future is, for the Christian, *a statement of faith.* A goal is a statement of faith. Plans are statements of faith.

Faithfulness to God includes making such statements of faith. As Christians, we begin with what we imagine is the sort of future God desires for humanity: a better life and future. Once we acknowledge that, we are responsible for individual and corporate action that will move toward that sort of future.

This should cause us to make statements (goals and plans) about what we, in faith, believe the future should be, and what we and others need to do about it. Even as we make these statements we must be ready to modify them as we gain new understanding. Proverbs says, "Humans plan their ways, but God directs their steps" (16:9). All of this requires that we live in the tension of a paradox. God is in control and is sovereign; yet humans are free and responsible.

We do not reject the past[4] and its lessons or the present with its continuing opportunity to learn from God's word and our fellow Christians. Yet we can no longer plan simply by extending the trends of the past into the future. History has become so compressed that we no longer have an adequate historical base for projection. Futher, our organizations often work against us in that they settle down into "the way we do things."

We have moved from an era of little and slow change to one of dramatic and rapid change. Even the rate of change is accelerating. If we can learn to think about the world and world evangelization in terms of

---

4. Robert E. Webber in *Common Roots* (1978) gives an excellent portrait of what happens when we seek to detach ourselves from our past.

what we believe the future should be, it will reduce future shock. At the same time, if we can better understand each other's plans, we can feel more comfortable about fitting into them.

In short: we need to manage the present in terms of the future. The only decisions we can make are decisions about the present. Although we can't avoid sketching a future history, we do it with Paul's motivation: "forgetting what lies behind, . . . we press on to the goal of the upward call in Christ Jesus" (Phil. 3:13, 14).

THE IMPORTANCE OF THE FUTURE

The idea of the future is important not only in our personal lives and our approach to missions, but also in the worldviews of the people we seek to reach. Many traditional societies are oriented more to the past than to the future. Ancestors and ancient customs have highest value. The future is a repetition of the past. All that is needed for living is already known. The assumption is that life will remain the same as it has for time immemorial.

Industrial societies operate from a completely different perspective. Inherent in modern industrial societies is the idea of change. Things will be different, and *therefore* better, tomorrow. Nothing is exempted from improvement and progress.

The very habits of carrying datebooks and planning diaries are ingrained in such societies. Parents plan for the education of their children, for their retirements and vacations. Yet as Peter Berger points out in *The Homeless Mind* (1974), planning for one's children is a new idea in history.[5] One hundred years ago most children died, even in the early industrializing societies. Today most children live. Two hundred years ago, children grew up to have the same vocation as their parents.

Today most people who participate in the industrialized sector of the world economy plan for the future. They are less and less surprised by the future because they have come to expect change. The future is no longer a question of "if" but of "when?"

As we progress in our study we will clarify the idea of imagining God's desirable future and designing plans to bring it about. As we do, the idea that the future lies in the future will become more significant.

5. For recent discussions of the impact of industrialization on North American culture see Lasch, *The Culture of Narcissism* (1979), and Bellah et al., *Habits of the Heart* (1985). See also Peter Berger, *Pyramids of Sacrifice* (1974) and *The Capitalist Revolution* (Basic Books, 1986).

3. Strategy

This is a book about the process of designing strategies, strategies for evangelism. It offers help to Christians at all levels who seek a strategy compatible with what they believe to be the will of God. Specifically, it is concerned with carrying out God's will to evangelize the unreached peoples of the earth.

What does *strategy* mean?

> Strategy differs from tactics. One has to do with the general plan of a campaign and the principles on which it is based; the other deals with the carrying out of the plan in its details, the various instrumentalities, agencies and methods. Tactics must be the constant study of those responsible for the conduct of the missionary enterprise. It is indispensable, but quite different from the study of the principles on which the world mission is built, the rationale of the enterprise as a whole. (Soper, 1943, p. 235)

In one sense everyone and every organization has a strategy, a way of approaching problems or achieving goals. Many organizations do this quite unconsciously. Others have developed their strategies into almost fixed, standard approaches.

The apostle Paul had a strategy. We read in Acts 17:2 that on the Sabbath he went into the synagogue *as was his custom*. Paul's strategy was to arrive at a major city, visit the synagogue if there was one, proclaim Jesus, and then let events take their course.

A strategy is an overall approach, plan, or way of describing how we will go about reaching our goal or solving our problem. Its concern is not with the small details. Paul's ultimate goal was to preach Christ throughout the world. His own calling motivated frontier evangelism, preaching Christ where there were no communities of Christians

(Rom. 15:20). His day-to-day plans would differ, but his strategy remained the same.

Strategy looks for a range of possible "means and methods" and various "operations" that will best accomplish an objective. Strategy is a way to reach an objective. It looks for a time and place when things will be different from what they are now. For the military it might be capturing a key town or city. For a business person it might mean achieving a desired volume in a particular market. For a Christian organization it may mean everything from deciding in what country to serve to the overall approach to reaching a particular group of people.

WHY HAVE A STRATEGY?

As Christians, a strategy forces us to seek the mind and will of God. Strategy is an attempt to anticipate the future God wants to bring about. It is a *statement of faith* as to what we believe that future to be and how we can go about bringing it into existence.

Strategy is also a means of communication to fellow Christians so they can know where we think we should concentrate our efforts. It thus gives us an overall sense of direction and helps to generate cohesiveness. Because it tells us and others what we *will* do, it tells others what we have decided *not* to do.

TYPES OF STRATEGIES

There are many different approaches to strategies for evangelism. Some are based on past success. That is, a particular way of doing things worked so well in the past that the pattern became a "Standard Solution Strategy." Standard Solution Strategies are assumed to be universally applicable. Their advocates use them in all parts of the earth with only cosmetic modifications.

The problem with these strategies is that they assume all people everywhere are basically the same. Cultural and social differences are not thought to play important roles in evangelism strategies.

Other strategies come from the notion that the Holy Spirit will provide serendipitous guidance in the moment of action. "Being-in-the-Way" strategies assume that Christian partnership with God's activity

14

does not require human planning. In fact, planning is sometimes seen as against the Holy Spirit.

The net effect of this approach eliminates failure. Whatever happens is God's responsibility. Anything that happens is God's will. But it runs into the problem that when two or more Christians appeal to the direct, inspired leading of the Holy Spirit "in-the-Way," they may be in each other's way. A hidden assumption of this approach is that proper spirituality cuts out the need for human forethought.

We are proponents of the "Unique Solution" approach to strategy. Like the Standard Solution approach, it recognizes that we learn from the way God has led people in the past. The successes of the Spirit are a real resource. We can and must learn as much as possible about what God has done and use it where it is indeed applicable.

But this approach argues that the differences between the situations and cultures of various people groups are also important. People and culture are not like standardized machines that have interchangeable parts. We cannot simply use an evangelism approach that has worked in one context in another and expect the same results. Strategies must be as unique as the peoples to whom they apply.

Further, the Unique Solution approach recognizes with the Being-in-the-Way Strategy that God has new surprises for us. Strategies must be open to new insight and new developments and cannot be rigidly standardized once and for all. Yet it also argues that we risk the sin of sloth (laziness) in not using all we have and are. We are to offer to God our best human efforts.

When God calls us to preach, we do not suppose we violate the leading of the Holy Spirit in carefully planning a sermon: researching the text until we have confidence we understand the author's intention, developing a clear outline to follow, praying for illustrations and examples that will communicate the point of God's word in contemporary terms. We *plan* the sermon carefully *because* we seek to speak about and for God. We can take the Lord's name in vain by invoking the Holy Spirit over our inattention, lack of discipline and forethought, or even laziness.

Just so, while remaining constantly open to God's surprises and extraordinary leadings, the Unique Solution approach believes that we can sketch the outline of a well-thought-out "Solution" to the question of how a given people could be effectively evangelized. We are not ruling out visions, dreams, or sudden convictions. Planning uses whatever resources are authentically given to us by the Spirit of God. The idea that the Holy Spirit does not use good human preparation in doing the work of the kingdom is inadequate to Scripture and experience.

The Unique Solution Strategy thus seeks to avoid what we see as the two extremes in some Christian approaches to strategy. On the one hand, the Standard Solution approach supposes we need only one basic strategy, that God has revealed the universal pattern once and for all, that success is "in the plan." The Being-in-the-Way approach, on the other hand, turns out to be an antistrategy dressed up in a rigid portrait of the Holy Spirit as guiding only when human beings do the least.

The Unique Solution approach argues that God has given us some universal *goals* and *guidance* as to what we are about in evangelism. Yet how and when and where and many other components are as variable as are the cultures and social groups God sends us out to evangelize. This is not to say that we do not use the experience of the past. Rather, we combine past experience with that which lies ahead.

IS OUR STRATEGY "WESTERN"?

If you are new to this idea of strategy, you may logically ask: "Isn't all this just a Western technological approach? Doesn't this substitute modern human methods for God's work?" These are valid questions.

We can never be complacent or arrogant about any of our approaches to doing God's will. There is a constant tension here. Often we do not know which ideas are purely our own and which indeed come from the wisdom of God. We never grow beyond the childlike dependence upon God, even when we have done our very best planning. However, childlike does not mean childish. When we act without forethought we risk the sin of tempting God (Matt. 4:7).

Planning and strategies, while greatly refined and strengthened in the modern industrial world, are not a modern or even Western invention. Joshua followed a strategy in his capture of the city of Ai. The building of the Great Wall of China or the pyramids of Egypt show the signs of careful planning and forethought.

However, in the most refined and technical sense of planning and strategy development (which we advocate in this book), we are following a pattern that has its roots and strength in Western developments. Yet it is also related to the Christian worldview. Because a loving and rational Creator created our world, early science was convinced it was a lawful world. And if the world is to some degree lawful, then we can anticipate it and plan for its future. The more we understand how the world and history works, the more we can plan for the future.

So on the one hand we must say: this is a Western approach.

Yet, on the other, we must say that developing strategies is not incompatible with the Christian mission. Planning is a way we can be "as wise as serpents, and as harmless as doves" (Matt. 10:16).

Strategies take God's commission and goals seriously. They do so by showing how we plan to carry out God's commission. They also show how we seek to be wise in our evangelism. They help us insure that we are not harmful to God's intentions or to the people he sends us to evangelize.

In the ten years since the concepts in this book were first developed, thousands of First- and Two-Thirds World missionaries have been exposed to them. Non-Western missionaries in Nepal, Indonesia, Chad, Taiwan, Singapore, Argentina, Chile, India, the Philippines, Kenya, Uganda, and a host of other countries have expressed joy in using them. They say that the Holy Spirit *focused* their thinking with these concepts and made them more effective for the Lord.

WHAT HAPPENS WHEN WE HAVE NO STRATEGY?

We have visited missionaries all over the world who seem to be in the business of doing, rather than getting things done. They appear not to have a strategy as to why they are there nor a clear idea of what God intends them to do. When asked for their goals and purposes, they often respond with answers that sound fine, such as: "to bring the Word to the people." One mission executive expressed his goal as "laying Japan at the feet of Christ." These are noble sentiments. Yet often we found that these sentiments were not supported by well-thought-through ideas as to *how* to do just that. Nor could they say *when* their task might be done. That will no longer do in the kind of world we live in nor for the kind of Lord we serve.

4. Management

As thinking, Spirit-led Christians, we need to consider how best to manage the mission enterprise. Proverbs 16:9 says: "In their minds people plan their courses of action, but God establishes their steps." We need to consider what God would have us do and the implications of that consideration.

Some years ago a mission agency discovered that the government of a small, predominantly Islamic country was willing to accept certain missionaries. This was startling news at the time. One of the leaders at the annual field conference gave an impassioned plea: "It is imperative that we reach this particular people now that God has opened the door."

A number of the missionaries responded to the appeal, leaving their current work and going to the new country. No apparent discussion or thought occurred about the reason the government had changed its stance or whether it might change its attitude again. No one thought about the particular type of missionary who would be most acceptable to the government. Unfortunately, as a result of a "change in government policy," all the missionaries had to leave after three years of residence. They had to begin their ministry all over again elsewhere.

We suspect this was an avoidable debacle. We cannot anticipate many shifts in the larger environment that might seriously weaken the progress we are making toward the goals God gives us for evangelism. Nevertheless, it is striking how *passive* Christian leadership can be about anticipating and planning for such changes. The level and number of failures in Christian work need not be as high as they are. One key is a more explicit recognition of the spiritual gift of administration/leadership (1 Cor. 12). Further, God's gift of leadership is expandable by training and experience. In modern terms we are talking about the arena of management and leadership.

WHAT DO WE MEAN BY MANAGEMENT?

Management, like strategy, is a much misunderstood term. Many associate it with manipulation. Some equate it with Machiavellianism. One well-worn definition is "the art or science of getting things done through and with other people."

In his book, *Professional Management: New Concepts and Proven Practices* (1973), Louis Allen differentiates between two kinds of work: *technical* and *management*. Most of us are familiar with technical work. When we conduct an evangelistic campaign or fly an aircraft, we are doing technical work. Management, however, is just as real *work* as is technical. Like many other management theorists, Allen sees the work of management as having four functions: planning, organizing, leading, and controlling. The management work of planning is, to a large extent, what this book is about.

Planning is setting a desirable objective, imagining many of the different ways of reaching that objective, and then laying out step-by-step programs for reaching that objective. Planning not only includes the means and methods for reaching goals; it also considers who will do the task, how much it will cost, and when it will be done.

Organizing is arranging the work in a way that is most likely to bring about the desired result. Organizing looks at the plans and asks questions, such as, "What would be the most effective way to relate people one to another to carry out the task?" Organizing deals with the relationships between individuals. It deals with what Paul described when he portrayed the ideal church as like a human body, with all the parts knit together and harmoniously working to produce health and vitality. Organizing takes energy and effort, as do all the other functions of management.

Leading describes the work of a manager: selecting and training people, delegating the necessary authority to carry out tasks, insuring that communication exists within the organization, and motivating members of the organization toward the goal.

Controlling refers to directing the work, not primarily the people. Good plans must have good measurement. Management focuses on discovering how well we are doing in reaching goals. Assigning someone the task of measuring progress helps an organization not to lose its way in the highways and byways of the future.

Management work is hard. Given the choice, Allen contends, most people will spend their time in technical work. There are a number of reasons for this. First, management work involves thinking, which is very difficult work. Second, most management work is not directly measurable. A bridge built is a result that is immediately obvious.

19

However, managing the process of planning and building the bridge may occur for years before the first person crosses it. And at that point the manager may get little credit for his or her work.

Bad management is very noticeable. Some indicators are low organizational morale, financial shortages, ineffective efforts, and a general feeling of confusion. Good management, on the other hand, is quiet and difficult to recognize. Management is like health—it is often easier to describe by its absence than by its presence. Good management is a learned skill. There seem to be "natural" or born leaders. There are no born managers.[1]

The complexity of the management task rises exponentially with the size of the organization. Most organizations begin with a natural leader, often one who has a strong "charismatic" personality—the ability to inspire others with his or her vision of what God would have them accomplish.

This type of leadership is effective so long as the leader has the time and energy to oversee the entire operation. As soon as the organization multiplies to the point where the natural leader cannot give day-to-day guidance, management skills are needed. Sometimes a natural leader can become a management leader. More often someone who understands that planning, organizing, leading, and contolling an organization are essential replaces the natural leader. Only then does an organization continue to prosper.

NEHEMIAH WAS A MANAGER

Management is a modern term, but the skills that it encompasses are very old. A good illustration is found in the Old Testament. Nehemiah was a highly placed and trusted official in the palace of the Persian king, acting as his "cupbearer." The account does not tell us how he got that position, but it tells us a great deal about how he carried out the task of urban renewal in Jerusalem.

When he first heard about the disgraceful condition of Jerusalem, the unrepaired walls and burned gates (Neh. 1:3), he wept, fasted, and prayed (1:4). This continued for *four months!* Yet in the midst of his intense prayers and fasting, he began planning.

---

1. For further discussion see Ted W. Engstrom, *The Making of a Christian Leader* (1976), as well as Edward R. Dayton and Ted W. Engstrom, *The Christian Executive* (1979), and Chua Wee Hian, *The Making of a Leader* (IVP, 1987).

By the time he showed his distress to the king (2:3-8), he had thought out answers to the questions the king might ask. He knew the material that would be needed and where he would live (2:8); the supplies and physical and moral support he would need (2:9-10). He had done some general, long-range planning.

When he arrived in Jerusalem (2:11), he immediately conducted a survey of the city. Short-range planning was his goal (2:12). Given what he found, he conceived an organization for the work (3:1-32). He put it into place after he had motivated the people of Jerusalem and the countryside into the work (2:17-18).

Nehemiah's enterprise met with a number of obstacles. The easiest task was the technical one of rebuilding the wall. The difficult job was dealing with enemies inside (4:1-2) as well as outside (6:10-14). Some Jews sought to use their economic power to further impoverish their fellow Jews, causing internal dissension (5:1-2). It was necessary to change plans to meet new attacks of the enemy (4:10-14, 21-23).

The distance between workers was great enough to create communication problems. So Nehemiah arranged for an alarm sounder to be at his side constantly (4:18). When Nehemiah finished the wall he moved on to the next phase and gave new assignments (11:1, 2). He was a skillful practitioner of "the art and science of getting things done with other people."

THE ROLE OF THE HOLY SPIRIT

Some years ago a missionary friend in Japan wrote to one of us, "With all of our well-oiled machinery and our well-laid plans, are we not in danger of attempting to do the work of the Holy Spirit?" Our response was a resounding, "Yes!"

With power comes the danger of misusing power. Power can be a tool used in the hands of God under the direction of the Holy Spirit. Or those who wield it can turn it inward to bring glory to themselves. The powers brought together and unleashed by good management bring with them a responsibility. The greater the responsibility, the greater the danger.

A Consultation on the Work of the Holy Spirit and Evangelization met in Oslo, Norway, in May 1985. It dealt with a wide range of issues that bear upon the Holy Spirit and the organizations and plans we use for evangelization. One of the issues it faced was this danger. Management in the West often pursues the secular goal of success at any price. Such an orientation can infect the Christian manager and organization as well:

> Success is the sacrament of a secular age. Its outward and visible signs are affluence, prestige, power, the ascent of the corporate ladder, the wider influence, the bigger church, the biggest audience. Its inward and invisible grace is its sense of having arrived, of being somebody . . . who is known, who has power. Somebody to be reckoned with.
>
> This motivation in the search for God's power is especially noticeable in societies where succeeding is important; in contrast, the search for God's power in the Bible is inseparable from suffering, humiliation, and the loss of those things that give us standing in the world. It is not for nothing that Jesus spoke of the disciple's cross, of losing limbs and eyes, of the hostility of the world. . . .
>
> [In these pages] we have encountered the Holy Spirit in his three major functions: he exhibits the truth, he engenders holiness, and he exercises divine power. These functions are also characteristics, for what he does expresses who he is. And the simple point that has to be rediscovered and should never have been lost is that the Spirit's power comes only in conjunction with his work of truth and holiness. Our obsession with his power is really an obsession with results. At its basest level, it is an admission that we will solicit converts on almost any terms and that gospel preaching can legitimately be carried on by almost anyone, regardless of how he or she lives. In thus seeking naked results we are dividing the Spirit's work of power from his work of truth (with respect to the convert) and of holiness (with respect to the evangelist). We are dividing what cannot be divided.[2]

Management for Christian mission aims at bringing about conditions on earth where God's kingdom comes, where people obey God's commands as they are obeyed in heaven. It aims at a "success" that happens only within the limits and by the power of God's Spirit, in conformity with the truth and claims of the gospel, and through the agency of people gifted by the Spirit whose lives exhibit the beauty of holiness.

Some might conclude that the best we can do is to pray and fast, seek the higher spiritual gifts, and move forward by a Being-in-the-Way Strategy (pp. 14-15). After all, if we generate none of our own plans, but attempt to follow the Spirit's leading in a day-by-day or moment-by-moment fashion, will we not be less likely to exercise power in the wrong way? Will not the Spirit have "more room" to go where he wants and accomplish his results?

2. David F. Wells, *God the Evangelist: How the Holy Spirit Works to Bring Men and Women to Faith* (Eerdmans, 1987), pp. 93-94.

We suspect that this is "dividing what cannot be divided." The work of the Spirit and the careful, prayerful, skillful planning and management of his people are not opponents. Nehemiah prayed and fasted and depended upon God *and* planned, organized, led, and controlled.

In many contexts the *absence* of planning inhibits the work of the Spirit. By making precise what we believe the Holy Spirit is gifting us to do and guiding us to undertake, we communicate to fellow Christians our understanding of the will of God. They can then respond appropriately.

Those who may be closer to the Spirit's moving can help correct our lack of understanding. Out of their common prayers and planning the body may well work and fit together more harmoniously and effectively. As the prophet Amos observed, "Can two walk together unless they be agreed?" (Amos 3:3).

The dangers in this area, as in most arenas of Christian life and thought, come from two directions. *Pride* pushes us to be independent, to suppose our solution to a problem is the one God must take. It leads us to think that our plans define the limits of effectiveness; that if we do not plan, God cannot work. In effect, we stop listening for new directions and possibilities. We compare what other Christians are doing unfavorably with what we are doing. Pride is the delusion that we are more than we are, that apart from us and our plans, God is not at work. It refuses God's responsibility and activity.

Sloth leads us to be less than we should be. It leads us to confuse our half-heartedness, our lack of prayer and wisdom, our refusal to consider and plan with "making room for the Spirit." Sloth tells us that the Spirit is more active in chaos and confusion than in disciplined, well-organized, skillfully executed plans. It refuses the human responsibility and activity.

However we put them together, a proper understanding of God's sovereignty and human freedom must not make more of humans and their plans or less of them than it is clear God's Word makes of them. God has commissioned the church to do the work of evangelization until the good news of the kingdom is "preached to all peoples" (Matt. 24:14). Management and planning are not everything in this task. Yet they are significant. They are tools that can express passionate dependence upon God and a clear understanding of what God is gifting and guiding us to do.

Experience in modern missions tells us that the Holy Spirit can and does use good management. For example, one group made a twenty-five-year plan for evangelizing Indonesia. In the light of what they thought God wanted accomplished, they established specific goals for different key cities within Indonesia. They worked with the local churches so they could participate in the detailed planning. They provided adequate resources based upon their projections as to what would be needed for the next five years. During the first phase of their effort they saw new churches appearing all over Indonesia. Such results are not uncommon. One can find many mission agencies that have reaped the benefits of good management.

RECAPTURING THE BIBLICAL BALANCE

We need to recapture the biblical balance between thinking and acting. Paul railed against the worldly-wise who did not factor in God's wisdom of saving the world through Jesus Christ. All of the best wisdom and strength of the world was inadequate to make humans right with God (1 Cor. 1:20ff.). God's "folly" is a wisdom that connects us to his power in Christ; it is a wisdom that *acts* (James 3:17).

Thinking is sub-biblical when it does not depend upon the Christ who seeks the lost and does not turn into action to find the lost. Thinking without acting and acting without thinking—both are inadequate responses to the demands for obedience.

The familiar verse we have twice used earlier says it well: "In their minds people plan their courses of action, but God establishes their steps." (Prov. 16:9).[3] We seek to bring about, by the Spirit, a concordance between our thoughts and actions and the thoughts and actions of God.

3. Compare this to Proverbs 16:1: "The plans of the mind belong to humans, but the reply of the tongue belongs to God." The point of these proverbs is that humans can plan to the last detail, but it is God who has final executive power. God has the last and the soundest direction for life. Our own plans, as proper as they are, are limited and will have kingdom-effects only so far as they correspond to God's will and Word.

5. Management for Mission

God's will is that every man and woman should have a valid opportunity to know Christ. God has chosen his people as the agents to spread that knowledge. What does carrying out that goal look like in the broad scheme of things? How might we apply management to the global task of introducing our generation to the power and person of Jesus Christ?

AN OVERVIEW OF THE TASK

The Lord Jesus Christ commands the church to make disciples of all peoples (Matt. 28:18, 19; 24:14). He calls every Christian to be a witness to his saving reality. No matter where we are or who we are, if we claim Christ as our Lord and Savior, God wants us to share our faith by what we are, say, and do.

The witness of the church is multiplying on all continents of the earth. Some are being sent from their home community to reach cities, villages, and towns where the witness is absent or almost absent. If the whole world is to know of Jesus Christ, there will be a need for cross-cultural evangelists and church planters. They will need to love and understand the people to whom they are sent. *Love will motivate* them to use the best strategy for reaching these people. They will develop plans for taking adept and attractive steps toward sharing Christ. *They will be sure his person and life makes sense to that new culture and social group.*

Yet we need to be more specific about what world evangelization means. So we will begin with a definition of the three parts of evangelization.[1] The following is from the Lausanne Committee for World Evangelization:

Nature: the nature of evangelization is the communication of the good news.

Purpose: the purpose of evangelization is to give individuals and groups a valid opportunity to accept Jesus Christ.

Goal: the measurable goal of evangelization is men and women who accept Jesus Christ as Lord and Savior, and serve him in the fellowship of his church.

Dividing evangelization into these three parts facilitates building a bridge between God's intention and our response. Only the Lord knows truthfully whether a particular person has given true allegiance to Jesus Christ. The only thing we can measure is a person's outward response. Goals must be measurable; so the goal of evangelization is men and women who name Christ in reverent submission to his claims on their lives. One way they show that submission is by becoming members of local communities of believers.

We believe that every person should have the opportunity to understand the good news in his or her own context. *Every man and woman and child in the world.* The task seems so enormous when we put it that way. Where do we begin in a world as large and as complex as ours is today?

We might begin with the world population. Its growth has been dramatic in recent centuries. Between the time of Christ and Martin Luther's challenge to the Roman Catholic Church the population doubled. It took fifteen hundred years to increase from 250 million to 500 million people. By 1793 when William Carey sailed for India, the population had doubled again. It had taken only three hundred years to do so. By the time of the Edinburgh Missionary Conference in 1910 it had again doubled and stood at over 2 billion. In 1989 it stands at 5.1 billion and by the year 2000 it will be 6 billion. How do we even begin to *think* about a world like that?

One way is in terms of countries or nation-states of various sizes. The 220 countries of the world vary in size from the mammoth 1.1 billion in China to the tiny 26 thousand of Liechtenstein. The variation between countries is so vast that a strategy cannot easily be developed that might be applicable for them all. Evangelizing the 150 million people of the many-islanded country of Indonesia is one thing; evangelizing the 26 thousand of Liechtenstein is another.

1. See David B. Barrett, *Evangelize: A Historical Survey of the Concept* (New Hope, 1987), for the most detailed analysis of the meaning of "evangelize."

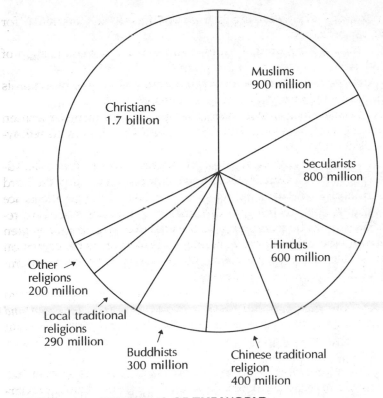

FIGURE 5.1   RELIGIONS OF THE WORLD

Another way to think about the world is in terms of its religions. The world population of 5.1 billion can be roughly divided up at present as in Figure 5.1.

The accuracy of the numbers is only approximate. What is important is that they show that about 67 percent of the world's population are not followers of Jesus Christ. But even this breakdown does not give us what we need to construct a workable strategy. For example, it does not distinguish between non-Christians who are in the same culture and social network as Christians and those who are not. Communicating to culturally and socially near-neighbors offers different sorts of opportunities and difficulties from conversing with distant unreached people. Evangelization must take that distinction into account.

So how do you evangelize a world like that? *Not one country at a time,* because countries vary so much. India, with its 1989 population nearing seven hundred million, has seventeen official languages (and nearly five hundred actual languages) with four hundred scheduled

27

castes. Certainly evangelizing India is a very different task than evangelizing Andorra with its thirty thousand people.

Not one person at a time. Even though each person must respond to Christ's claims on his or her life, individuals cannot easily reach every other individual. There are limits to their ability. More important than the limit of geography is that of culture and social relationships. Much of the non-Christian world is reachable only by cross-cultural means and methods.

Thus, *the way to evangelize the world is by taking it one people or people group at a time.* What do we mean by these terms?

David Barrett and Harley Schreck (1987) suggest that we might use the term *peoples* for the ethno-linguistic, church-planting target and the term *people groups* for the smaller, more finely defined groups within peoples.[2] In some cases the basic homogeneity within an ethno-linguistic group is such that no finer distinctions are necessary. Often this is true for relatively small, tightly knit tribal groups. In other cases, the ethno-linguistic group is so large and diverse that one can reasonably target only subgroups within it.

In 1982 the Lausanne Committee sponsored a meeting to discuss the terminology used for talking about world evangelization. From this came a workable definition for *people group:* a significantly large grouping of individuals who perceive themselves to have a common affinity for one another, because of their shared language, religion, ethnicity, residence, occupation, class or caste, situation or combinations of these.

This is a sociological definition. The intention is to focus on the largest groups within which the gospel can spread as a church-planting movement without meeting barriers of understanding and acceptance. Examples of such groups might be:

- Urdu-speaking Muslim farmers of the Punjab
- Cantonese-speaking Chinese refugees from Vietnam in Paris
- Welsh working-class miners
- Tamil-speaking Indian workers on Malaysian rubber plantations
- The gay community of San Francisco
- Nomadic Muslims moving into urban settings.

MARC Europe applied this principle to people groups in the United Kingdom. *Beyond the Churches,* edited by Peter Brierly (1984), de-

2. This book also has a registry of unreached peoples and people groups.

scribes hundreds of people groups in terms of their nature, present attempts to reach them, and possible strategic approaches.

There is no final answer in these matters of definition. The issue for strategy is to zero in on a particular group of people rather than an entire country. Because the particular individuals within peoples and people groups share a number of things in common, they have a sense of "we" over against other groups of people in their environment. Their cultural, linguistic, social, and ethnic distinctives set them off in their minds from others. They marry within their group. They spend their leisure time with each other. When they form partnerships it is usually within their own group. They are often suspicious of outsiders, who recognize them as different. They share a common worldview and tend to respond in similar ways to the events that come their way.

The reason we identify them and group them together is because of the task of sharing Christ with them. Because they form a long network of social relationships and share a common set of values and attitudes, they respond in similar ways. This is true of how they respond to Christ as presented by particular evangelists. When they are responsive, the growth of the church follows the natural lines of social relationships that bind the group together. When they are resistant to the gospel, most of the people in the same social network will resist it.

Each of the defining attributes characterizes a group more precisely. Thus, it makes sense to speak not only of the ethno-linguistic designation of Korean, but of the garbage collectors of Seoul. They live and work together in their own communal area. They are suspicious of outsiders.

Or we speak of bi-lingual Cantonese Chinese who live in New York City and work in restaurants. Their unusual working hours and conditions isolate them from other groups. They also bind them together as a distinct group with an affinity for each other.

Or we speak of the Kenyan Maasai who have lost all their cattle due to drought and are now in relief camps.

Now that we have defined *people* and *people group,* we need to ask what it means when we say an *unreached* people or people group. This refers to a group among whom there is no indigenous community of believing Christians with adequate numbers and resources to evangelize the group to its margins. This differs from the view that characterizes peoples by their *exposure to evangelism.* For example, David Barrett's *World Christian Encyclopedia* has a detailed scale for characterizing exposure. It runs from numbers of Bibles distributed to the presence of Christian themes on postage stamps.

What our definition highlights is Paul's concern in Romans 15 with the foundations of the church among all peoples, languages and tribes. Paul sought not simply to preach Christ, but by that preaching to establish communities where people name Christ in worship (15:11-12, 16, 18, 20).[3]

The presence or absence of a cluster of churches whose members have the potential to evangelize their group to the fringes is crucial. Paul considered his apostolic calling to frontier mission in a given place complete only when there were churches present. After he established churches in the northeastern provinces of the Roman world, Paul wrote that he was ready to go to Spain—where this had not yet happened (15:20-28).

In saying an "unreached" people or people group we mean a group still needing the foundations of a church planting movement in its midst. This usually calls for E-2 and E-3 evangelization. The group may be "evangelized" in the sense of exposure and remain "unreached" if a cluster of indigenous churches does not result. Thus, *the absence of a cluster of indigenous churches is the crucial defining characteristic of an unreached people.*

The world we live in has many groups that are unreached. Some of them are very large. Others are quite small. Many are in countries that severely restrict open evangelizing and the presence of foreign missionaries. Others are right next door to our churches in our own country. We need to discover strategies for reaching them that move with the current tides in the kingdom of God.

Certainly if the God of the universe is concerned with each *individual* in the world, he is also concerned with the *peoples* to which they belong. Psalm 87:6 says that God has a "register of the peoples"; in this he writes the names of unreached peoples as they become his people.

Revelation portrays the fulfillment of God's activity on earth as an immense group worshiping the Lamb, "a great multitude that no one could count, from every nation, tribe, people and language" (7:9). Our concern for the blessing "of all peoples on earth" (Gen. 12:3) finds expression in devising strategies to begin church planting movements among every one of them.

We need to give an important caveat here. It is not the concern of this book to determine the total number of all the people or people groups in the world. Our focus is on strategy, not on counting. For our

---

3. Note that the Greek in Romans 15:20 is "where Christ is not named." This is a technical phrase meaning "not named by people of faith in worship and hope." It is not simply the knowledge *about* Christ that concerned Paul; rather, it was *obedience* to God (15:18) so that the Gentiles would become an acceptable offering to God (15:16).

purposes the number of nations with a minimum gospel witness, the number of people or people groups without any witness is important only if we identify where they are and set about to reach them one by one.

THE BASIC APPROACH

Management for mission is best thought of as a process. In a short version of the overall process we should ask the following:

1. What people does God want us to reach?
2. What are they like?
3. Who should reach them?
4. How should they be reached?
5. What will be the result?

In short, we define the mission we are on by the need of the people to whom God is calling us. We plan the mission in a spirit of prayer and with the best information possible. We attempt to carry out our plans under the power and guidance of the Spirit. Then we evaluate it against the goals of evangelization with the mind of the Spirit.

We "cast a net into the future." When we haul it in, we check to see the fish we have caught. Our plans are our net and the fish are the results of acting upon our plan. What is indispensable is the risen Christ on the shore telling us when and where to let our nets down.

After we have attempted each part of our mission and evaluated the results, we need to replan. What have we learned? Do we now understand more clearly what the risen Christ is commanding us to do in evangelism? What is God leading us to do now? This is a circular model in which evaluation leads us into a new phase of action to reach the unreached.

A CIRCULAR MODEL

We have found it useful to expand these five steps into ten. This more detailed model of planning suggests more of the actual parts of the process. The division of the rest of this book follows the ten steps, as shown in Figure 5.2.

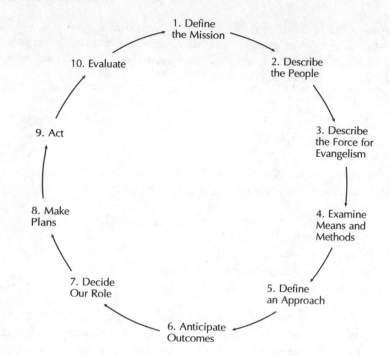

FIGURE 5.2   THE PLANNING MODEL

To illustrate the usefulness and commonsense nature of this model, we will illustrate it by the activity of farming.

God has called us to be sowers of the good seed of the message of the kingdom of God (1 Cor. 3:6-9; Ps. 126:6; 2 Cor. 9:10). Christ declares that the end of this age will come when the kingdom is preached to all peoples (Matt. 24:14). God has also called us to be reapers of the harvest. We are to look upon the peoples of the world as fields ripe for harvest (John 4:35). The harvest is to multiply "thirty-fold, sixty-fold, one-hundred fold." Seed is to produce more seed.

God can use the story of the farmer and the crops to help us understand how to prepare, sow, cultivate, reap, and multiply the harvest for him.

1. Define the Mission

Those of us who are not farmers do not understand the overall situation faced by a farmer. A farmer with land at his disposal does not face the question of where to plant crops. Yet every farmer faces the question of *what* crop to plant in which field. The government often steps in with regulations to insure that desired crops are grown. Costs also vary from crop to crop—costs for seed, soil preparation, sowing, irrigating, cultivating, and reaping.

Likewise, the evangelist must consider where the gospel needs to be sown. In some cases the mission agency may already have chosen the field. In others we may be like a farmer with many fields, each beckoning, each requiring a different labor and set of costs.

2. Describe the People

Our "field" is not merely a geographical location. In actuality it is people. Every field is made up of the "soil" of people. Each soil differs. Each has different capabilities for various crops. The fertility levels are not the same.

If Islam has permeated the field, the people will be very different from those of a field permeated by an animistic faith. Some soils are filled with stones that must be cleared. These can be the rocks of misunderstanding or cultural practices hostile to the kingdom. Other fields will be overgrown with weeds because no one has worked the field for years.

Every farmer learns as much as he or she can about the soil. Only then can the right fertilizers and pesticides be applied. The evangelist needs to understand the people to be reached with the gospel. Their economy, worldview, politics, working situation, and religion all affect their response to the kingdom of God.

3. Describe the Force for Evangelism

Who is to work the field? There is much to be done: clearing, tilling, fertilizing, sowing, cultivating, irrigating, reaping, processing, storing, and distributing the fruits of labor. Who will work alongside the farmer? Field hands? Neighbors? Veterinarians? Mechanics? Are there special agencies to help with expert advice in the event of difficulty?

The evangelist needs to consider all the range of skills and help needed to bring in the fullest harvest possible. Other Christians may be key in this process. Who has insight into this particular people? Are there others already at work in this field? How do we relate to them? Who has special skills in communications, translation, teaching, church development, follow-up, and a myriad of other tasks?

How can the Christians involved relate to each other as the body of Christ? What sorts of organizations and structures are necessary to sow and harvest? To train new farmers?

4. Examine Means and Methods

Tools can be very simple or enormously complex, inexpensive or almost priceless. In a certain field a farmer may be able to do all the work with a home-made hoe. As the field grows larger, a wooden plow pulled by an ox may suffice. Perhaps the day comes when a tractor-drawn harrow is preferred.

Or consider the problem of water. One farmer may depend on seasonal rains. Another has worked for years to set up an elaborate irrigation system. In high-tech agriculture there may be a maze of pipes and sprinklers.

Evangelistic tools and methods vary greatly. Some are as simple as distributing Bibles and praying for the reader to come to the truth. Others are based on modern mail systems and carefully developed correspondence courses. A whole community may be the target of a year-long campaign mobilizing the Christians of many denominations. A single person may be drawn to Christ by the friendship of a Christian neighbor. Which tools and methods are the most effective is a key consideration.

5. Define an Approach

All these elements—the crop desired, the soil available, the labor mobilized, and the tools utilized—are brought together in an integrated manner. An approach or strategy is the "glue" that holds them in place.

Part of the strategy has to do with what will *not* be done. If the ground is to be prepared by an ox-pulled plow and cultivated by hand, tractors and powered harvesters will not be needed. The strategy tells us how we are going to get the seed in contact with the soil and water and bring it to the point of harvest.

Similarly, if we decide our strategy is to use radio to offer a correspondence course, we commit to one set of activities. A different set will be necessary if we decide we will field a six-family group of missionaries for a minimum of six years. Our strategy may be to have them live in the community and spend three years in language and culture learning, followed by three years of initial church planting. At this point half the team will return home. The Bible translator, educator, and health expert will remain.

The approach integrates the people group, the force for evangelism, and the means and methods.

6. Anticipate Outcomes

Every farmer hopes for a good crop. Every wise farmer plans for what must be done when the crop is harvested. Part of the seed is retained for sowing the next crop. Part is sold. Part is consumed by the family and part by domesticated animals.

Every wise evangelist must also plan for results. If the seed of the gospel takes root, there will be new Christians needing support and training. Eventually there will be an indigenous community that will need to incarnate the meaning of the kingdom in ways meaningful in their own culture. Someday the cultural outsider will no longer be needed to bridge the gospel into a particular people. The gospel will reside at the very center of the life of that people.

7. Decide Our Role

Some farmers do all the tasks of farming by themselves: buying seed, preparing soil, planting, weeding, guarding, cultivating, and watering. Many, especially if the field is large, will do only some of them. Others are deeply involved in farming, but only as agricultural bankers or machinery salesmen or seed development researchers.

Evangelization requires not only those who are frontline, eyeball-to-eyeball evangelists, but also evangelization researchers, benefactors whose ability to make money is tied to financing church planting, experts in media production, and so on. We need to decide what our particular role might be in the evangelization of a particular people group.

8. Make Plans

With these first seven steps outlined, the specifics of action can be set forth. Every farmer knows in general the steps to follow in order to gain a harvest. For a small one-family farm the steps will be few and simple. When a number of people are involved, plans will be more complex. How and when will the seed be obtained? Who will prepare the soil, and when? What about fertilizer? Will the crop be insured? Where will it be stored when it is harvested? Who will coordinate the various jobs and assign responsibilities?

Plans that are to be used by many people need to be communicated. Jesus reminded the people of his day that one does not start building a tower without first counting the cost. Evangelism plans communicate the vision and the steps to all involved. They enable us to count the cost so that we can be sure we can complete the job to which we are called.

9. Act

Plans set us into motion. They aid us in changing our behavior so that we can change our world in the direction of our goals. Resources must be gathered and set into motion. The farmer's plans result in seed purchased, ground plowed, seed planted, weeds pulled, and finally harvest gathered. People are hired and put to work on specific days doing specific tasks.

How foolish to prepare and never act. We make plans because we care deeply for the goals we pursue. Plans enable us to act more thoughtfully and effectively. Planning without action is futile. The evangelist moves out and carries forward the plans. We plan our work and then we work our plan in the faith that the harvest will come.

10. Evaluate

The farmer is evaluating all the time. He compares last year's harvest with those of previous years in quantity and quality. He assesses the condition of the tools and makes repairs or purchases new ones. How neighbors are doing is common talk at the marketplace.

The farmer evaluates as the growing season marches on. Soil is tested, growth is measured, plant diseases are identified and countered. The invasion of insects is met with timely and proper measures. The weather is followed closely and the harvest dates changed as needed.

The evangelist also needs to evaluate what is happening in the process of evangelization. No one can fully predict the future. Yet we can see some of the results of our labor and discover how closely they match the goals God gives us. The feedback we gain helps us to adjust our behavior toward more effective and efficient approaches.

CONCLUSION

These ten steps are quite orderly and neat on paper. Real life is not so neat. Steps 1-8 are part of the thinking phase. Step 9 is the action. Step 10 is the evaluation. Yet as we focus on one step, we often are anticipating or rehearsing the others as well. All are interrelated.

Even as we act, we may well make piece-meal adjustments as certain elements of our plan show themselves to be unworkable. The model is helpful in forcing us to think about all of the elements together. Further, it reminds us that we are in a constant process of learning. New understandings develop into new plans.

Management for mission is a process requiring repetitive application. It "spirals" upward as we go around the circle of planning again and again. One hopes that Spirit-guided plans and Spirit-guided action will yield new depths of understanding. This new wisdom and insight, when built into our organizations, relationships, and plans will multiply the harvest.

There are no standard means and methods. Each situation and people is unique. Yet one approach can help us cope with the amazing diversity we find in the unstandardized social worlds. It is the approach of planning that centers its dynamic on *peoples and people groups* rather than on methods.

We begin with the fundamental assumptions that God has commissioned us to share Christ. Christ is the Way, the Truth, and the Life. Peoples everywhere need to be able to name his name in the midst of their hurts and hopes. To name his name in reverent submission is to receive God's fullness of salvation and life.

We also begin with the fundamental assumptions that we do not know God's wisdom or strategy for reaching a particular people. We do not have the answers. Because God has called us to a ministry and mission, we need to engage ourselves in the process of discovering his wisdom. Then we must devise a strategy in tune with that wisdom.

We assume that the most effective way to do that is to clarify the message, manner, and mission of God. At the same time we must clarify the identity, aspirations, and situation of a particular unreached people. By beginning with the God who sends and the people to whom he sends us, we believe we are on the path to discovering effectiveness and faithfulness in ministry.

STEP 1: DEFINING THE MISSION

Considerations

1. Mission has its source in the Triune God. The mission of God is the mission of the church. The intrinsic nature of the church is missionary because it is sent out by God.

2. Only a theology of the kingdom of God can overcome the polarizations that plague the church over mission. Conciliar and evangelical Christians both err by eliminating the tension between the kingdom as present and the kingdom as coming.

3. No abstract statement of mission priorities is possible. Priorities always relate to specific contexts. The road to Jericho sets its own agenda.

4. Mission is a broader reality than is evangelization. Yet the church no longer engages in mission when it ceases to evangelize. Jesus Christ is the permanent norm for evangelization. He is both the supreme evangelist and the content of the evangel. He never ceases being evangelistic in person or in work.

5. The good news can never be fully or finally expressed in a single statement or creed. It is a message with a unifying center in Jesus Christ. Yet it has innumerably diverse expressions. Its purity and authenticity can be preserved only by rephrasing. It is a word for all seasons, situations, and cultures. Too often its power and relevance lie hidden under rigid and culturally insensitive formulations.

6. Evangelization should be seen as a process to be enhanced, not a goal to be achieved.

7. By specifying the people or people group who are the target of our evangelization, we make our evangelistic mission concrete. When we realize there are three hundred thousand churches in North America with enormous resources, we can see how each currently unreached people group could be reached. If every twenty churches joined hands to send people and prayers to one such group, some fifteen thousand people groups could be reached with the gospel in the next decade.

6. *Mission and Evangelization*

Imagine a couple which has just received $10 million. They decide they don't want to put it in the bank. They want to invest it so it will be useful to our world and will make human as well as financial returns. So they begin thinking about various business ventures. Will it be bio-medical technology or genetic engineering? Or should they invest in developing efficient, small-scale solar energy mechanisms? Or what about enhancing entrepreneurship through leadership training?

The choices are infinite. Realizing that they know most about the food industry and wanting to help feed this generation, they decide to invest in farming. However, this decision only narrows the issue. There is no such thing as farming "in general." A farmer engages in wheat farming in Oregon, sugar cane cultivation in Cuba, wet rice farming in the Philippines, or orange growing in Israel.

Similarities exist between different types of farms. Farming everywhere involves plants and/or animals. Factors such as weather, soil fertility, disease, pests, tools, and market are all present. Yet farming can be radically different depending upon the crop being grown, the technology being used, and the social organization and size of the farm. The decision to go into farming inevitably requires more specific decisions before any food can be produced.

Likewise, what business shall we consider ourselves as Christians to be in? The resources of the Word of God and the power of the Spirit are vast. In addition, the combined financial resources of our fellow Christians equals $8,201 *billion*.[1] How shall we invest all of our magnificent gifts, energies, creativity, and time? What is it we will do to benefit our world?

1. David B. Barrett, "Annual Statistical Table on Global Missions: 1988," *International Bulletin of Missionary Research* 12 (January 1988): 17.

This book is about the "business" of evangelism. Only a clear idea of the nature and purpose of evangelism gives us a sense of what we are to do and be. Even then we will need to go beyond evangelism "in general." The task differs greatly depending upon where, how, and with whom we are evangelizing. Evangelizing illiterate farmers in a strongly Muslim country or nominal Christian graduate students at Oxford University are very different tasks.

When we set out "to evangelize" we need to have a sense of what such an activity entails. We also need to know the impact different target groups have on the process of evangelization.

This first section deals with defining and clarifying what we see ourselves doing when we say our mission is to evangelize. We will deal first with evangelism "in general." Here the questions are: *What is the mission of the church? What is evangelism?* Then we will deal with getting specific by focusing on a particular target group. There the major question is: *Whom are we going to evangelize?*

MISSION AND THE CHURCH

There are many answers to the question, "What is the mission of the church of Jesus Christ?" One article documents *five* alternative perspectives within the Roman Catholic Church (Ponsi, 1978). Similarly, Protestants have offered many answers.[2] This issue is not a simple one.

A statement of the mission of the church gives an overarching direction to all of the church's activities. It identifies its central meaning and purpose. Because it is so central to what the church should do, it remains a central topic of discussion among Christians. We do not propose to settle this issue here. Yet because we have a general perspective that influences the rest of the book, we must share our own definitions.

The Bible offers many models and commands to reveal what the church ought to be and do. Paul Minear (1960) has catalogued no less than ninety-six *analogies* that the New Testament uses for the church, three of the most familiar being a temple, the body of Christ, and the bride of Christ. Some of the *commands* that the Bible directs to Christians and the church are to care, nurture, witness, worship, give, study, pray, seek spiritual gifts, and be holy. Together these analogies and commands furnish the raw material from which to construct a definition of identity and mission.

2. Beyerhaus, 1971, 1972; McGavran, 1977; Stott, 1975; Krass, 1974; Braaten, 1977; Costas, 1974, 1977; Anderson, 1961; Verkuyl, 1978.

To do so we must identify the *primary* images or models of the church and the *controlling* commands given to it. Paul Minear considers the dominant images to be the church as a *people of God, a fellowship in faith, a new creation of the Spirit* and *the body of Christ.* Hans Küng's great study, *The Church* (1967), emphasized three images as fundamental: *the people of God, the creation of the Spirit* and *the body of Christ.* What these images do is offer metaphors and analogies that portray the way the various dimensions of the church are interrelated.

However, they do not exhaust the meaning and identity of the church. Rather, they suggest the central motives and framework within which the other images find their appropriate place. The church is also to be light, salt, leaven, a pillar of the truth, an ambassador for God, a good Samaritan, a temple of worship, a servant carrying a cross, a prophet denouncing evil. These less central images help give depth and breadth to the controlling metaphors of the church.

So too all the various commands fill in the meaning and nature of the Great Command: *to love God above all else and the neighbor as ourselves.* The commands to have no other gods, not to allow money to control us, to gather for worship, to pray and sing spiritual songs, to place our treasure in heaven, and to seek spiritual gifts show us concrete ways in which we can love God with all we are. The commands to witness, to feed the hungry, to be just, to be truthful and honest, to be faithful, not to allow room for pride and anger—these show us how to love the neighbor as ourself.

Some commands are clearly limited to a time and place and for specific circumstances. The covering or veiling of the head by women in worship is such an example (1 Cor. 11:3-16).[3] This is not as central to the identity and purpose of the church as are the last words of Christ to the apostles.

The Great Commission *to make disciples of all nations* also is a controlling and central command given to the church. The preaching of the good news and making of disciples is fundamental. Jesus repeated this command numbers of times. Its origins are found in the Old Testament promise to Abraham to "bless all nations" (Gen. 12:1-3). The whole narrative history of the Bible can be integrated around this divine intention to share God's salvation with all peoples.

The early church recognized this by confessing that the true church has a number of essential qualities. "We believe one holy catholic and apostolic Church" (Nicene Creed). The term *apostolic* means Christ

---

3. See Charles Talbert, *Reading Corinthians* (Crossroads, 1987), pp. 66-72; Gordon Fee, *The First Epistle to the Corinthians* (Eerdmans, 1987), pp. 491-530.

commissions and sends the church into the world. The term *catholic* means universal. No peoples are outside the sending impetus of the Holy Spirit. When the church ceases to reach out to all peoples, it ceases to be a true church. This is why the Great Commission is a controlling and central command.

All these metaphors and commands spring out of one profound reality: *the church is a result of and a participant in the mission of God.* God is acting redemptively in history. He is establishing his kingly reign over a rebellious and alienated creation. God has miraculously revealed himself by acting in history in the person of Jesus Christ and through his people. The church (and before it Israel) is the result of and a copartner with God in proclaiming the kingdom of God on earth.

Paul Minear has captured this well:

> Through all the analogies the New Testament writers were speaking of a single reality, a single realm of activity, a single magnitude. . . . Image after image points beyond itself to a realm in which God and Jesus Christ and the Spirit are at work. It was of that work and of that realm that the New Testament writer was thinking as he spoke of Kingdom or temple or body . . . the reality of the church is everywhere anchored in the reality of God, the Holy Spirit, Jesus Christ. (1960, pp. 222-23)

The church's mission is its participation in and cooperation with what God is graciously doing redemptively here on earth. The church is to be a sign and a sacrament of the presence of the kingdom in word and deed. It is to be a partial answer to the prayer, "Thy Kingdom come, thy will be done, on earth as it is in heaven" (Matt. 6:10).

The mission of the church is properly understood and defined in terms of the triune God. Wilhelm Andersen is right when he writes: "The basic and decisive recognition for a theology of missions consists in this: Mission has its source in the Triune God" (1961, p. 301).

Whatever images are used to portray mission, their dynamic grows out of a God who loves the world infinitely. He sent his unique Son to liberate us and open us up to the life of his kingly rule (John 3:16). The movement outward to seek and save the lost comes from the very action of God sending his Son. "As the Father sent me, so send I you" (John 20:21).

That is why we move out to feed the hungry, to clothe the naked, to set free the prisoners, to visit the sick. Because Jesus did those things we now do them (Luke 4:18-21). "The overall task of the missionary church is to interpret and translate, in its preaching, teaching and works of love, the will of God to salvation, as it is revealed in the eternal mission, the Father's sending of the Son" (Sundkler, 1965, p. 56).

45

This is why Emil Brunner is right in saying, "The Church exists by mission as fire exists by burning." The words of Carl Braaten capture it well:

> The very being of the church is shaped by its missionary calling to go into the uttermost parts of the world. This missionary structure of the church derives from its apostolic origin. . . . The church is sent by the Spirit; the Spirit is sent by the Son, and the Son is sent by the Father. Because church and mission belong together from the beginning, a church without mission or a mission without the church are both contradictions. (1977, p. 55)

The whole church, facing the whole world in the totality of its historical, social, and spiritual development, must embody all of the meanings connected with mission. Certain parts of the church may well specialize in only one facet of mission. Yet the church must be careful that these specializations do not limit the mission of the total church.

The body has many dimensions: seeing, hearing, walking, thinking, touching. They are combined in many activities, requiring more or less of one dimension or another. So also the body of Christ has many dimensions and engages in many activities. Somehow as a totality it must encompass all facets of mission.

EVANGELIZATION

The purpose of this book is to focus on that part of mission called "evangelization." In the contemporary debate over the meaning of mission and evangelization, we hold the view that evangelization is an indispensable and central component of the mission of the church. Mission includes all that the church is sent into the world to do. Evangelization refers to the specific process of spreading the good news about Jesus Christ as God's salvation so that men and women have a valid opportunity to accept him.

Evangelization is central because all the other activities of the church derive from it. Whatever else the church may do affects its ability to evangelize. Evangelization is indispensable because it is the process of offering salvation in its fullest meaning to people. This is the activity that calls people to faith and hope in Jesus Christ.

Our words *evangelism* and *evangelization* come from the Greek word, *euangelion* (Friedrich, 1964; Becker, 1976). Actually the Greek has four forms of the one word: two verbs meaning "to proclaim good news," and two nouns. One noun means "an evangelist." The other noun means the "good news" that the evangelist communicates. These original New Testament meanings provide a benchmark for evaluating contemporary definitions.[4]

The New Testament itself focuses on the saving events and person of the Lord Jesus Christ (Stott, 1975, pp. 44-54). The central topic of the gospels and the letters of the apostles is the nature and meaning of Jesus Christ. He is the incarnate God, the Jewish Messiah, the Lord of all the universe. Through him God has personally entered history and provided salvation for all. God's love has been manifested so fully and finally in him that all who put their trust in him receive eternal life and the gift of the Holy Spirit. God has made the rule of his kingdom available and present in Jesus Christ.

The Greek words centering on *euangelion* and its cognates stress *a message to communicate. Euangelion* is derived from the Greek word *angelos*, which means angel or messenger of God. The message of the events and meaning that surround Jesus Christ is to be shared with all peoples. Jesus Christ himself announces this gospel: "The right time has come . . . and the Kingdom of God is near! Turn away from your sins and believe the Good News!" (Mark 1:15). "Jesus went all over Galilee, teaching in the synagogues, preaching the Good News about the Kingdom . . ." (Matt. 4:23).

Jesus is the first evangelist in the New Testament. He continues and fulfills the ministry of the prophet, John the Baptist. Evangelism has its origin, pattern, and basis in the activity and message of Jesus Christ. We proclaim the kingly rule of God that he proclaimed and manifested.

According to Jesus, the kingdom of God, promised in the Old Testament, is now dynamically present. It overcomes evil, delivers humans from the power of sin and death. It ushers people into the blessings of the reign of God himself. The fulfillment of the prophecies of God no longer await the apocalyptic events of the end of the age. They are already being anticipated by his own ministry and miracles. Those present for his ministry, says Jesus, are blessed because their "eyes see and . . . their ears hear" (Matt. 13:16).

Although the kingdom will not reach its full expression until

4. David Barrett in *Evangelize! A Historical Survey of the Concept* (New Hope, 1987) gives the most complete summary of the concept. He concludes that biblical specialists see its meaning as encompassing six notions: preach, bring, tell, proclaim, announce, and declare (good news). He writes, "From the standpoint of biblical exegesis, the best brief summary of the overall meaning of 'evangelize' and cognates is probably 'obedience to the Great Commission', this being subdivided into the Commission's 7 basic mandates: Receive! Go! Witness! Proclaim! Disciple! Baptize! Train!" (p. 78).

Jesus comes on the clouds with the angels (Matt. 24:30-31), God is not waiting for the initiative of humans to submit to his kingdom. He is invading human history in new and unexpected ways. His kingdom is invisible except to those who have the eyes of faith. We cannot create or control it; we can only submit to its dynamic presence in our midst.

Jesus commits the message of the kingdom to his apostles as the ones chosen to carry it to all peoples. "This Good News about the Kingdom will be preached through all the world for a witness to all mankind; and then the end will come" (Matt. 24:14). "This is what is written: the Messiah must suffer and must rise from death three days later, and in his name the message about repentance and the forgiveness of sins must be preached to all nations, beginning in Jerusalem. You are witnesses of these things" (Luke 24:46-48).

This message has so much of the power of God that it brings God's salvation when accepted. When rejected it brings God's condemnation (John 3:16-21). It produces peace between traditional enemies such as the Jews and Gentiles (Eph. 2). It makes the person a completely new self (2 Cor. 5:17; Gal. 2:20).

To evangelize in the New Testament sense is to declare the salvation available through Jesus Christ. Such declaration involves more than just a simple, single form of communication. We often think of evangelism as proclamation from a pulpit. The New Testament associates it with a wide range of communication settings. *We proclaim (kērussō) the* good news like a herald declaring a military victory. It is a word we *declare with enthusiasm (apophthengesthai), speak freely and openly (parrēsiadzesthai),* even *call out in a loud voice (krazō).* Or it can be a matter of everyday *speaking (legō, laleō)* or *conversing (homileō)* with another. We can *discuss (dialegesthai), explain* or *interpret (diermēneuō), transmit (paradidomai),* or *announce (angellō)* it.

The evangelist who relates this message acts not as one dispassionately relaying one message among others. Rather, the gospel communicates something that concerns his or her own deepest being. It is a message that is *confessed (homologeō),* a reality to which the evangelist gives *witness (martureō)* as one who personally knows the power and dynamic of the good news. We can *describe (diēgeisthai, ekdiēgeisthai, exēgeisthai)* this word from God. We can express it with such conviction that its recipients are *entreated (parakaleō), admonished (elenchō),* seriously *warned (epitimaō),* and *persuaded (peithō).* The apostles declare the gospel not only to those who have never heard of the kingdom in Jesus Christ but also to Christians. They *teach (didaskō)* the good news, and it is *revealed (gnōrizō)* to them (Friedrich, 1965, pp. 683-718, esp. p. 703).

In sum, the New Testament sees evangelism as involving an

important message. This message comes from God in the person of Jesus Christ. He is an evangelist *par excellence.* He is also the one who embodies the good news in dynamic works of power, signs, and authoritative teachings. This message is so important it has the power to convey the abundant life of the kingdom of God to those who welcome it.

THE MEANING OF EVANGELISM

Paul describes the good news as a sacred trust (2 Tim. 4:17). He held it as a gift from God that he must proclaim at every opportunity. His basic attitude was that those without knowledge of the gospel have a right to hear it. He felt obliged to share it:

> I want to win converts among you also, as I have among other Gentiles. For I have an obligation to all peoples, to the civilized and the savage, to the educated and the ignorant. So then, I am eager to preach the Good News to you also who live in Rome. (Rom. 1:13-15)

> I have no right to boast just because I preach the gospel. After all, I am under orders to do so. And how terrible it would be for me if I did not preach the gospel! (1 Cor. 9:16)

Paul was an apostle and, as an apostle, also an evangelist. The word for evangelist, unlike the other Greek terms dealing with evangelizing, appears only three times in the New Testament. It refers to Philip (Acts 21:8), Timothy (2 Tim. 4:5), and evangelists as gifts to the church (Eph. 4:11). The custom of calling the writers of the gospels evangelists arose only after their writings were labeled "gospels."

Why this reticence to use the word for evangelist? There are several explanations. First, everyone in the church is to proclaim the gospel. Through casual contact, preaching in the synagogues and marketplaces, and acts of charity and love, all members of the body of Christ are to share his reality. In that sense all Christians are evangelists. Yet the New Testament recognizes that some are specially gifted. These are given the formal title of evangelist. It signals the awareness that

> although evangelism is a prime responsibility of the whole Church and to that extent all Christians are to be involved in evangelism, not all Christians are called to be evangelists. All Christians belong to the Church, which is inescapably involved in evangelism, but many Christians will find their primary sphere of service *within* the Body of Christ. (Watson, 1976, p. 35)

Second, the New Testament shows little concern with the details of ecclesiastical order and office. Rather, the Lord and his message are of prime concern. We know there were those with the special calling of evangelism by the third and fourth decade after the birth of the church. We also know that evangelism involved all members of the Christian community even when they were not officially designated as evangelists. Their new life and loyalty motivated them to share Christ naturally and continuously in the Roman world (Green, 1970).

The apostles are singled out as the primary evangelists. After all, their primary witness to the life, death, and resurrection of Jesus Christ makes up the New Testament. Their words and lives serve as a model for evangelism. Modern-day evangelists link themselves to the apostles whenever they seek to engage in evangelism.

The content of the apostles' message is so definite that Paul describes it as a "pattern of sound words" (2 Tim. 1:13). He urges Timothy to hold firmly to it in a spirit of love and faith. To evangelize means to make *this* message known in the power of the Holy Spirit. There is a substitute gospel that is subversive of the kingdom of God (Gal. 1:6-9). Care to conform to the meaning and intent of the gospel is essential.

Yet it is also clear that the message is *expressed* in a variety of ways. The message finds its unity in a common witness to Jesus Christ. It is, however, "varied in its presentation of his relevance to the varied needs of the listeners, urgent in its demand for decision" (Green, 1970, p. 66). The "pattern of sound words" is not a straitjacket, rigidly requiring only one set of words. Yet it is substantive enough that we can gauge the faithfulness of the varied expressions.

What is the nature and content of this message that evangelism shares? If we are to understand evangelization, we must understand it by the evangel. The meaning and character of the gospel motivates the activity of evangelization and serves as its content, basis, form, and emphasis. We must define this "pattern of sound words." What is the shared commonness to which all the varied expressions serve as faithful witness? What is the core of the early proclamation of the gospel against which all other proclamations are measured?

Paul sought to summarize the gospel:

> And now I want to remind you . . . of the Good News which I preached to you, which you received, and on which your faith stands firm. That is the gospel, the message that I preached to you. You are saved by the gospel if you hold firmly to it—unless it was for nothing that you believed.
>
> I passed on to you what I received, which is of the greatest im-

portance: that Christ died for our sins, as written in the Scriptures; that he was buried and that he was raised to new life three days later, as written in the Scriptures; that he appeared to Peter and then to all the apostles. (1 Cor. 15:1-5)

The essential content of the gospel finds its center in a verbalized content about Jesus Christ.

> To evangelize is to spread the good news that Jesus Christ died for our sins and was raised from the dead according to the Scriptures, and that as the reigning Lord he now offers the forgiveness of sins and the liberating gift of the Spirit to all who repent and believe. (Douglas, 1974, p. 4)

> The message is first and foremost a declaration. It is good news about God. It is the story of what God has done in and through His Son Jesus Christ, our Lord and Saviour. He has established His Kingdom. True, the full manifestation of the Kingdom is yet to come. We await the final consummation. But the Kingdom of God has been inaugurated. The time has been fulfilled. (Stott, 1964, p. 176)

The crux of the evangelistic message is that God has acted decisively in Jesus of Nazareth. Christ inaugurates an age of salvation in which all who call upon him in faith and confess him as Lord are made right with God. God offers reconciliation with himself and with an alienated world through his Son. We who were far from God are now able to come near. We who were enslaved to a variety of "powers" are now set free.

Because the gospel is more than a formula to recite or believe (though it is a pattern of sound words), because it is more than a fixed kerygma that must be mimicked, because it is a Living Word, it cannot be fully or finally expressed in a single statement or creed. Statements that vary according to their audience and purpose can only approximate the gospel. There is an identifiable gospel, but it is a unity that exists in diversity, a single message that retains its essential meaning in its many valid and varying expressions.

The gospel must be lived as well as verbalized. Those who follow the One who submitted to the cruel death of the cross have their own cross to carry. They also will face suffering and sacrifice as they seek to evangelize the world. The evangel is not simply the message Jesus proclaimed. It is also the reality that Jesus lived, the kingdom that he brought. The evangelist must live the evangel if it is to have any credibility or authenticity.

51

STEP 1: DEFINING THE MISSION

DEFINING EVANGELISM WHEN DEVELOPING A STRATEGY

Given the meaning of the gospel, we want to define evangelism in a way useful for planning strategies. Strategies exist to generate skillful, intelligent, persistent action. A strategic definition of evangelism must allow us to state what *actions and results* are essential to the business of evangelization.

There are many good definitions of evangelism. The Evanston Assembly of 1954 described evangelism as "the bringing of persons to Christ as Saviour and Lord that they may share in his eternal life" (Stott, 1975, p. 39). The Anglican Archbishops' "Committee of Enquiry into the Evangelistic Work of the Church" of 1919 in England produced a well-known definition: "to so present Christ Jesus in the power of the Holy Spirit that men shall come to put their trust in God through Him, to accept Him as their Saviour, and serve Him as their King in the Fellowship of His Church." The Lausanne Congress on World Evangelism (1974) gave a more detailed definition:

> To evangelize is to spread the good news that Jesus Christ died for our sins and was raised from the dead according to the Scriptures, and that as the reigning Lord he now offers the forgiveness of sins and the liberating gift of the Spirit to all who repent and believe. Our Christian presence in the world is indispensable to evangelism and so is that kind of dialogue whose purpose is to listen sensitively in order to understand. But evangelism itself is the proclamation of the historical, biblical Christ as Savior and Lord, with a view to persuading people to come to him personally and so be reconciled to God. In issuing the Gospel invitation we have no liberty to conceal the cost of Discipleship. Jesus still calls all who would follow him to deny themselves, take up their cross, and identify themselves with his new community. The results of evangelism include obedience to Christ, incorporation into his church, and responsible service to the world. (Douglas, 1975, p. 4)

Each of these is a good definition. Each brings into focus certain clear elements that are a part of evangelism. Our problem is to be biblically responsible and at the same time offer a definition that is useful for strategy. Here's our definition:

To evangelize is to communicate the gospel in such a way that men and women have a valid opportunity to accept Jesus Christ as Lord and Savior and become responsible members of his church.

This definition captures what we believe to be the heart of the evangelistic intention. It also provides ways to designate evangelistic action and to measure the results. Any definition of the mission of evangelization must have these characteristics if it is to be used to plan a strategy.

Note some of the features of our definition. Evangelization is offering knowledge ("to communicate the gospel") that will change attitudes and lead to new behavior ("to accept Jesus Christ"). It will also generate new relationships ("responsible members of his church"). Each of these elements can be spelled out in greater detail and evaluated.

This definition is intentionally silent on the specific phrasing of the content of the communicated gospel. The message must lead to an authentic encounter with the biblical Christ. Yet how the gospel is phrased depends for the most part upon the audience being addressed. Because the communicator must consider what people already know and think, sharing the gospel will vary. What to say first and what to emphasize depends on the target group.

Including in our definition a commitment to Christ as the intended outcome gives us a way of measuring mission accomplishment. When Christ is presented, people can respond in a number of ways:

1. People can accept Christ and become an active part of a Christian community.
2. People can accept Christ without publicly aligning themselves with some specific Christian community. David Barrett (1982) has documented millions of "secret Christians."
3. People may understand the elements of the gospel in clear terms and know its implications. Yet they may not be ready for commitment. They have had a valid opportunity to accept Christ but rejected it or put it off.
4. People may hear the gospel but find its terms and agent alien and strange. It may not make sense within their own worldview. It may appear grotesque and seem like a foreign cultural imperialism. Rejection may be the response.

We are assuming that an authentic gospel is being communicated in each case. Thus, those in the first three have had a valid opportunity to accept Christ.

Yet measurement of the outcome of evangelism is not easy. The easiest to measure is the number of those who commit themselves to Christ and join a Christian church. It is more difficult to estimate secret believers. It is even more difficult to distinguish those who understand and reject or delay commitment from those who still misunderstand and reject. (Of course we can also speak of those who misunderstand and "accept Christ" and join a church. But that is another problem.)

So the *purpose* of evangelism is to give people a valid opportunity to accept Christ. However, the *measurable goal* is to see that acceptance manifested by people identifying themselves with Christ and with some community of Christians. This is the clearest indicator that our evangelistic activity is fulfilling its intended purpose.

We could argue that repeated exposure to the gospel means a people is evangelized. They know or should know enough to make an intelligent decision for or against Christ. That they remain unchurched and uncommitted is an indication that they are in category 3 above. Yet it is not this simple. A "valid opportunity" involves more than just exposure. Communication studies show that exposure is not equivalent to either understanding or even motivation to make a decision about the information.

We would suggest a number of ways to assess the validity of the opportunity to respond to Jesus Christ:

1. The gospel, not some substitute, must be the communication.
2. The messengers who bring the good news must themselves be disciples of Jesus Christ.
3. The message must be in the idiom and thought forms of the audience to whom it is communicated.
4. The means of communication must be suited to the target group. The illiterate must receive an oral presentation. The agents of communication must be acceptable to the target group. The accustomed channels of communication should be followed.
5. The witness to Jesus Christ must be sustained long enough for its content to become comprehensible to the average person. One exposure simply may not be enough.
6. Ultimately, a valid opportunity implies the presence and work of the Holy Spirit. The Holy Spirit takes the messengers, message, media, and manner of communication and makes them effective.

A person may need to hear the gospel dozens of times before it "clicks" and makes sense. Even Paul, speaking in one of his native languages, was misunderstood in the market at Athens (Acts 17:18). Some thought he was preaching about foreign gods—one named "Jesus" and the other the female goddess "Resurrection" (in the Greek *resurrection* is a feminine noun).

A valid opportunity means enough time and content, enough clarity and clarification that we are confident *Jesus Christ* is the one accepted or rejected.

How much exposure, what use of traditional channels of communication, what rephrasing of the authentic gospel message will be necessary will vary. Such matters are only definable in terms of the particular qualities and background of the messengers and their target group.

What can we say then about the status of world evangelization? We can obviously *surmise* that more than one third of the world who call themselves Christians have been evangelized. But to our way of thinking it is impossible to establish consistent and measurable criteria as to whether the task of evangelization has been completed for any people or people group short of each person indicating that they indeed believe they have heard the message and accepted it or rejected it. To put it another way, each generation needs to be evangelized, including those generations that have been brought up within the Christian faith.

EVANGELIZATION AS A PROCESS

Some distinctions are important for understanding how we use several key terms. *Evangelization* is the *total* process of announcing the gospel and bringing people into discipleship. In this sense evangelization is a process to enhance rather than an event or goal to happen.

In contrast, *evangelism* refers to specific actions or methods associated with the process of evangelization. In speaking of evangelization we mean the total context of circumstances, evangelism events and approaches, personal contacts and media programs that move individuals and people groups through a decision-making process that confronts them with Jesus Christ.

Most of our goals deal with evangelism. It is easier to measure specific evangelistic events than the total process of evangelization. Such an event is the telemarketing strategy "The Phone's for You." In one church one hundred volunteers called 17,177 homes to discover people who were not currently active in a local church and wouldn't mind hearing from theirs. It took four weeks. A mailing list of 1,486 resulted. On Open House Sunday some 140 first-time visitors attended. Now some months later several dozen of them are attending worship regularly and nearly 20 have joined the church.

The various steps in this process were measurable. Unchurched people heard the gospel and joined the church. Those were countable results. But the steps and results of "The Phone's for You" are only one facet of evangelization happening in that church. There is also a ministry to pre-school children and their mothers. A number of church members are working to evangelize the women prisoners of a local jail. Couples who seek weddings in the beautiful sanctuary are counseled with the gospel. Witnessing goes on in the workplace by a number of church members. The process of evangelization is much larger than just the events of the telemarketing strategy.

It is one thing to register the activity levels of an evangelism strategy and the decisions made. It is another thing to enhance the process of evangelization so that dozens of once passive Christians become active in evangelism.

While a given event of evangelism can be completed and put behind us, the process of evangelization continues until Christ returns. Jesus has told us that when the kingdom was preached to all nations he would return. Yet none of us knows when the gospel is so widely and so thoroughly available that the end of this era will come (Matt. 24:14).

Our task is to continue to be preoccupied with the communication and spread of his salvation while we pray and hope for his return. In acts of evangelism and social action, in special programs of compassion and nurture, we must prepare ourselves and help others prepare for the coming of the King.

Here we would depart from many of the current efforts to "evangelize the world by A.D. 2000." We admire the faith of those who believe the task can be accomplished, while separating ourselves from the view that we can set a date. To put it in the words of an earlier generation, we all have the responsibility to evangelize our generation, but the final results are up to God.

7. Defining Your Mission

Now that we know the general "business" we are in, we are ready to make specific *how* we are in that business. Two choices set the shape of activity: deciding what activity we will undertake and what group to target.

Biblical and theological reflection tell us the nature of our activity. They specify the nature and purpose of evangelization. They also tell us that our final objective is the evangelizing of all peoples of the earth. Yet each of us and each of our organizations cannot fulfill that total goal. Rather, we must narrow it down to a part of the whole. That means targeting certain peoples and people groups as our share in fulfilling the Great Commission.

Paul was an apostle to the Gentiles. His own sense of calling and identity within the world of his day sent him on a path around the Mediterranean. He did not attempt to go east into the Parthian Empire and beyond to India, or northeast into central Asia and China. Nor did he stay in Palestine to evangelize the Gentiles in that area. His strategy was to go in a circle starting in the eastern provinces of Rome and circumscribing the Mediterranean Sea (Rom. 15:19, note the Greek). Had he lived, Paul would have evangelized in what is now Spain. With congregations there, he would have crossed over into northern Africa on his way back in the circle to Jerusalem. We too need to define our mission by naming *whom* we seek to evangelize.

STEP 1: DEFINING THE MISSION

ASSUMPTIONS FOR MISSION DEFINITION

How do we decide whom and where to evangelize? What sorts of information and questions lead us to narrowing the task down to God's will for us?

We follow a number of assumptions in answering those questions. We state them here though we will explain and justify them later in the book.

1. Human beings can be most meaningfully perceived when divided into subcultural social groupings of various types.
2. The communication of a message or expression of compassion is most effective when aimed at these subdivided social groupings. Their particular social and cultural characteristics provide both the barriers and the bridges for effective ministry (Engel, 1979, p. 32).
3. The specification of particular peoples and people groups is the beginning point for the development of a strategy for evangelization.

These assumptions have become more widely accepted in missions and evangelization in the last fifteen years. Yet they are not obvious nor uncontroversial. In the past, many missions came into existence to evangelize a given *geographical* area: West Indies Mission, China Inland Mission, Red Sea Mission, Afghan Border Mission.

In 1886 A. T. Pierson issued his call at D. L. Moody's Mt. Hermon conference that "all should go and go to all." The Student Volunteer Movement was born at that meeting. Yet it was not clear what it meant to "go to all." It is still not unambiguous.

Much current mission practice focuses on reaching a *region* by the use of a trade language. Trade-language approaches have a number of advantages. Practically speaking, cross-cultural evangelists have paled at the prospect of learning many languages. A missionary from Germany going to the Turkana in northwest Kenya faces learning English (the colonial language), Swahili (the *lingua franca* of East Africa), and Turkana (many nomadic Turkana know neither English nor Swahili).

Pastoral training faces a practical problem when faced with dozens or hundreds of languages in a single country. In which language should Bible school or seminary training be conducted? Often the problem of leadership training and seminaries is solved by adopting a single, trade-language approach. Furthermore, the colonial heritage in many areas means Western languages are commonly used in education. Commentaries, dictionaries, theological works, and curriculum are already available in those trade languages. Educational structures do not have to be duplicated in each separate language group.

Bible translation faces this same problem. We do not want to make pronouncements here on vernacular versus trade-language translations. However, the decision to function in a trade language defines one's mission and target group in a given way. It narrows the potential audience in sometimes unanticipated ways (Wonderly, 1968, chaps. 1-5). A trade-language approach usually means:

1. Only those who are bi-lingual can hear or read the good news. Most frequently this discriminates against women in traditional cultures.

2. Often the bi-lingual are the modernizing sector of a people, those assimilating to the dominant surrounding culture. For example, in Central America the descendants of Mayan Indians who are adopting a Spanish life-style want Spanish Bibles and Spanish worship services. Their interest in the vernacular Bible or worship services is limited. This usually leads to the neglect or exclusion of mono-lingual sectors of a people.

3. The training of the leadership by using the trade language leaves gaps in incorporating the gospel into the indigenous culture. Church leaders learn the concepts of Christian faith in a trade language. How they transfer this into their vernacular often is not clear. Often "standard solutions" for handling various pastoral and evangelistic issues make up the curriculum. Yet these may have little to do with the central pressure points of the traditional cultures.

4. Mono-lingual individuals with leadership qualities are passed over in favor of young people who are in the educational pipeline. Community leadership patterns are bypassed in favor of those that depend upon use of the trade language. Experience comes to mean experience in the formal school settings developed by Western models.

5. The cross-cultural evangelist in effect remains an outsider. The bypassing of the vernacular language means the gospel is not bridged into that language (and often not incarnated in that culture).

Our conviction is that mission definition cannot stop at the point of selecting a country or even a trade language. *Evangelization must focus on a specific people or people group within its larger context. Only then is the target suitable for designing a plan to engage in evangelism.*[1]

1. David J. Hesselgrave, *Today's Choices for Tomorrow's Mission: An Evangelical Perspective on Trends and Issues in Missions* (Zondervan, 1988), p. 55: *"And so, over the years since World War II both the vision and the plan . . . for world evangelization have slowly emerged. The slogan 'the evangelization of the world in this generation' has taken on new meaning. People groups must be identified, described, and targeted. Then the gospel must be proclaimed with a view to establishing viable churches among them."* (Italics in original.)

STEP 1: DEFINING THE MISSION

THE NEED FOR MISSION DEFINITION

How complex is the world we live in! We know there are more than five thousand distinct languages and over two hundred nation states. Hundreds of thousands of villages go about daily life with no Christian church in their midst. How do we decide where Christian workers should go? How do we decide which people we should evangelize and which we will not? These are crucial and difficult questions.

We define our mission first by choosing the activity that will occupy our thought and time, then by indicating our target group, the specific audience our activity seeks to influence. Communication studies are unequivocal here. Communication is most effective when aimed at specific, limited audiences.

This is what we see happening in the New Testament. The early church carefully adjusted the form of its message to relate more directly to the distinct audiences it faced. It did not send the same message in the same form to all comers in the vague hope that someone somewhere might understand it.

Paul's practice is an excellent example. He approached the Jewish synagogue as a place where there were Jews by both birth and conversion as well as Gentile godfearers. All accepted the Old Testament as God's Word. He tailored his message so as to be understandable and appealing to them (Acts 13:16-43). He quoted the Old Testament extensively and showed how it pointed to Jesus as the Messiah. But in Athens, when addressing Greeks with little or no contact with the Jewish Scriptures, he changed his approach. He knew they were saturated with current Epicurean and Stoic philosophies. So he preached Jesus Christ, but filled his message with allusions and quotations from these philosophies (Acts 17:22-34). He was bridging his message to a different audience and so restated the gospel in the way most understandable to them.

Often this step of planning is called "field selection." Field secretaries and planning committees constantly engage in overseeing present mission fields and selecting new ones. Could we assemble them all, we might hear them echo the words of one executive whose agency entered twenty-five countries from 1973–1979: "The problem of field selection is a very knotty issue. In most cases it's very, very subjective." Even with new technologies and information, it is still risky and difficult to decide where to place the priority in evangelization.

A survey of missiologists and eleven mission agencies (with a total of four thousand missionaries) has shown that none was satisfied that this process was being handled well. Most agencies and missionaries had no criteria by which to guide their decision. Daniel C. Hardin of the Churches of Christ characterizes the frustration here:

> The fact is that many missionaries use little objective judgment in selecting their fields. When this writer is asked what influenced him to go to Korea, he usually replies that it was God's guidance. That answer seems necessary because the only other alternative is to call it a matter of pure chance. He did not search for the best place, ask the advice of responsible elders, study the literature, or use any of the tools and resources available but merely accepted an invitation to go to Korea and trusted that it was God's will. He is not ashamed of that decision to go to Korea because it was honest and based upon all that he knew back in 1957. Today, however, he feels it would be extremely rash to ignore the many avenues of help that are open and blunder into a field without any preparation or selective planning. (1978, p. 22)

FIELD SELECTION PRACTICES

"Field selection" refers to the events that bring Christian and non-Christian into an evangelistic relationship. These events are as diverse as they are many. The conscious, carefully planned choice to evangelize a specific group is only one type of event that leads to evangelism. Our primary interest is in enhancing such deliberate choices because many unreached peoples will be reached only in this way. Our tendency is to avoid the strange and the unknown. Often we reach out to engage in difficult evangelism only by conscious choice.

Of course, God has his own timetables and uses very unusual circumstances to spread the gospel. When his people do not voluntarily take the good news, he may bring people to them who need the good news. For example, the Queen of Sheba came to Jerusalem to see the glory of Solomon. She returned home impressed with the God of Israel. American black churches started in the brutal and tragic institution of slavery. Ripped from their homelands, blacks became Christians as well as slaves. The United States currently has an ongoing "Pentecost" of foreign students flocking to its shores, many from so-called closed countries. They are voluntarily within the church's reach.

Sometimes God disperses his ingrown people. Israel and Judah were dispersed into the Assyrian and Babylonian kingdoms. There they lived and there Gentiles came to know of the God of Israel for four hundred years before Christ came. The Vikings were evangelized by the Christians they captured and made wives and slaves in their cruel raids in Europe. Christian tentmakers are found all over the world at present. They make a living as construction workers, technical experts, bankers, and so on. But they also share their faith.

A study of the rationale and process of field selection in modern times is revealing. It shows a number of overlapping and incompatible principles in use. At least five distinguishable sorts of procedure lead to the action of evangelizing a particular group.

Charismatic field selection is the result of a vision, dream, prophecy, or intuitive impulse seen as sent by God. Paul's night vision of the man from Macedonia (Acts 16:9) is an example of this. So too is the prophetic utterance at Antioch that selected Paul and Barnabas for their work (Acts 13:1-3). Hudson Taylor experienced this when he was only seventeen:

> Never shall I forget . . . the feeling that came over me then. Words can never describe it. I felt I was in the presence of God, entering into covenant with the Almighty. I felt as though I wished to withdraw my promise, but could not. Something seemed to say, "Your prayer is answered, your conditions are accepted." And from that time the conviction has never left me that I was called to China. (Taylor and Taylor, 1911, p. 78)

Traditional field selection is a choice made on the basis of long-standing practice. Often this is no more than the decision to continue to evangelize the peoples a mission agency has evangelized in the past. The early church never questioned the choice to evangelize the Palestinian Jews. They were the ones Jesus himself evangelized. No special deliberation or choice needed to happen for evangelization to continue.

Ecclesio-political field selection is a choice based on relationships with other church bodies. A mission agency may not enter a given country or seek to evangelize a particular people because of comity arrangements.[2] Or it may hold extensive discussion with churches and agencies already in an area. The concern is to determine whether it would be welcome and could fill a unique role. Some churches look upon most other denominations as inadequate and so go wherever their own brand of Christianity is not yet planted. "Church politics" is a strong factor in guiding the choice of entry.

Situational field selection is actually a rather nonintentional sort of choice. Circumstances are critical in determining where an evangelist

2. A comity arrangement is an agreement between various agencies or denominations. It divides a region or set of peoples so that each region has only one church in its midst. This limits competition and overlapping effort.

winds up, almost more than conscious choice. Paul evangelized the highest leaders of Palestine and Rome because of his imprisonment. So far as we know he had not planned to evangelize Caesar's household or King Agrippa. Yet he did.

Sometimes the circumstances are unfortunate. Missionaries may not be able to get along (similar to Paul and Barnabas in Acts 15:36-41) and must go separate ways. Even the famous Lottie Moon experienced this with an abrasive missionary who drove many younger workers away:

> His insistence, as mission chief, on dictating even how [younger missionaries] spent their own salaries was taken by most as a personal insult.
>
> The result was that the younger people all moved rapidly to interior locations. Life with T. P. Crawford, Lottie Moon wrote, had become too much a "constant matter of humiliation," as he tried to make all around him "stultify themselves by absolute submission." (Hyatt, 1976, p. 50)

Rational field selection is a choice governed principally by a consciously rational process. This involves gathering information and experience and weighing alternatives in the light of given goals. An intellectually demonstrated need and opportunity matrix determines the choice. Here a mission agency may commission a study to help make the decision.

The Conservative Baptists entered eastern Mindanao in the Philippines as a result of a survey done in doctoral work.[3] The China Inland Mission (now Overseas Missionary Fellowship) used this principle when forced out of mainland China.

> When we were compelled to leave China, we sent research teams through East Asia to different countries to discover where there were opportunities of ministry and service. At that time we were particularly committed to the Chinese people, but as a result of the research of these teams it became clear that there was a major need in other communities as well, and in fact our work is now more amongst such communities than amongst the Chinese people themselves. (Lane, 1979)

Field selection needs more study. Too often it turns out to be a rather difficult, often arbitrary decision. Colonialism in the past and the difficulties of gaining visas for missionaries sometimes have more to do with the result than other selection factors.

In what follows, we will suggest a number of considerations

---

3. Bob Skivington, *Mission to Mindanao* (1978).

basic to a more rational field selection process. We begin with theological principles and end with a perspective on this whole issue.

THEOLOGY AND FIELD SELECTION

Field selection should be congruent with our understanding of the priorities that come from the Word of God. The early Reformers believed the Great Commission was no longer in effect. The apostolic church, they said, completed that commission. They concluded that the contemporary church had no remaining foreign mission obligation. Congruent with this theology, Protestants mounted no major cross-cultural mission efforts for several centuries.

But careful study of the Scriptures shows a continuing obligation to evangelize. We can express this in three basic principles.

First, *the church is to evangelize everyone*. This is a clear implication of all the statements of the Great Commission. We are to "Go, then to *all* peoples everywhere" (Matt. 28:19); to "Go throughout the whole world and preach the Gospel to *all* creation" (Mark 16:15). "The message about repentance and forgiveness of sins must be preached to *all* nations, beginning in Jerusalem" (Luke 24:47). Jesus is the light of the *world* (John 4:42) who shines on all (John 1:9). His life was a sacrifice for the whole world (John 6:51).

Recently, some theologies of mission have challenged this principle. The dismal history of Christian treatment of Jews, the connections between colonialism and mission, and the questions of cultural integrity of other peoples and their indigenous religion are issues that have contributed to this challenge. A few theologians and missiologists have developed a "bad conscience" about cross-cultural evangelism.

Some argue that Christ is anonymously present already in all human religions. Each local and ethnic religion already possesses qualities that can save. People who participate in the religions not connected with the Christ of the Bible are saved *without* any direct contact with the distinctive Christian gospel. Traditional religions are the "ordinary ways of salvation." Explicit Christian commitment is God's "extra-ordinary way of salvation."

Others argue that Christ's atonement on the cross is primarily an objective event. Everyone is already reconciled to God, even if they do not know it, understand it, or accept it. People are "born again" irrespective of their knowledge or attitude toward the historical saving activity of God in Israel or the Messiah, Jesus of Nazareth. The universality of the gospel (that it is necessary for and applicable to all humans) is made into the universality of salvation (that it has already been applied to all humans).

The net effect of these approaches is to deny the urgency of evangelization or the gravity of the decision to accept or reject the historic Christ. The apostolic church in the midst of a religiously pluralistic world, however, took a very different approach.

The apostles believed all *could* become the children of God. The apostolic offer of salvation is directed to all people without exception who are not yet bound in conscious faith to Christ. There is salvation in no other name, religious or secular, than Jesus Christ. The universality of the gospel in the New Testament was not a basis for banishing conversion missions from the acts of the church. Rather, it was a spur to continue reaching out to ever new and distant peoples with the offer of faith.

Whatever other theological principles may guide our field selection, we must never lose sight of the fundamental goal: everyone, everywhere. John Wesley was right: the world is our parish. No one is excluded for social, cultural, political, religious, or racial reasons. Nor can any be excluded for so-called theological reasons, as though the twentieth-century church is wiser in this matter than its Lord.

Second, *those without Christian churches in their midst are to be given high priority.* Field selection is not settled with a slogan: to everyone, everywhere, at any cost. Once we accept the universal scope of evangelization, we must set priorities for making that happen. The New Testament example of Paul, the apostle to the Gentiles, suggests a basic ordering principle.

Paul gave highest priority to expanding the spread of the gospel into places where Christ was not already named in Christian worship.[4] He saw his task as one of founding congregations that could evangelize their region. He laid foundations on which others built. Once he laid those foundations, Paul went elsewhere; he saw his work as finished (Rom. 15:19, 23).

In modern terms, Paul sought to extend the gospel to "unreached" or "hidden" peoples. Insofar as he serves as a model for evangelization today, he tells us to go to peoples and places where the foundations of Christian churches need building.

---

4. Romans 15:20: "It has always been my ambition to preach the gospel where Christ is not named *(onomazo)*." To name Christ is to call upon his name in faith. This occurs when people invoke his name in worship or use it for healing and encounters with demonic powers. Paul does not seek only places with absolutely no knowledge of Christ. Rather, the issue is (contrary to the Good News Bible translation, "where Christ has not been heard of") places where Christ "is not heard" (i.e., where he is not yet obeyed).

The easily misused slogan, "Why should anyone hear twice before everyone has heard once?" has a basic element of truth to it. We ought to be concerned in field selection with a more evenly shared opportunity for the peoples of the world to hear. We ought to be concerned with "penetrating the last frontiers"—as was Paul.

Third, *those relatively more responsive to Christ should receive high priority.* The Church Growth movement has made this a basic theme: winning the winnable.[5] Their essential point is that while God loves all equally, there is a selectivity to God's activity. On the one hand, those who resist God's call and warnings eventually face his judgment. God's Spirit no longer strives with them. Their own passions and evil ways have free reign (Rom. 1:21, 24, 26). If they turn from the light they have, even that light is removed (Hos. 4:17; Amos 8:11; Matt. 11:11-12; Rom. 11:7-8). On the other hand, God elects a people from the midst of sinfully rebellious humanity to be his people (Rom. 9:10-12). Many are called but few are chosen. Those whom God draws to himself come (John 6:44, 65; 15:16). Jesus put it this way:

> The knowledge about the secrets of the Kingdom of heaven has been give to you, but not to them. For the person who has something will be given more, so that he will have more than enough; but the person who has nothing will have taken away from him even the little he has. (Matt. 13:11-12)

The response to the light people already have becomes the door to further or even less light. No one ever lives up to the light they have. Yet there is a difference between those who stubbornly resist and those who seek more. Cornelius was a seeker for more light (Acts 10–11). God sent Peter to him so he and his household could be saved.

Furthermore, Jesus commanded his disciples to be discerning in their use of evangelistic energies (Matt. 10:14, 23). The twelve were told to turn from those cities and households that rejected them. Paul and his team apparently obeyed that command (Acts 13:46, 51). He literally shook the dust from his shoes upon leaving the resisting synagogue. Where there was a large response (as in Corinth and Ephesus), Paul extended his stay for ministry (Acts 18:8-11; 1 Cor. 16:8-9).

Both theology and practice show examples of the priority of ministry and time in ministry being set in part by responsiveness. There are good reasons for this principle. First, we are stewards of the gospel. Good stewardship not only preserves the gospel but also invests it where

5. McGavran (1970), pp. 49, 256; (1979), pp. 239-40; Tippett (1970), pp. 30-31, 46, 52-54); Wagner (1971), pp. 44-47; McQuilkin (1973), pp. 26-31.

it shows the greatest return. As copartners with God (1 Cor. 3–4; 2 Cor. 4–6) in sharing the good news, we need to align our activity with his. Receptivity to the work of the Spirit is a *prima facie* evidence that God is at work among a people for their salvation.

Second, Jesus sends us to the *harvest* fields (John 4:35, 38). The farmers of Jesus' day understood this imagery. Crops have different seasons: seasons of planting, weeding, cultivation. The harvest season is a crisis time of opportunity. A crop not gathered quickly is lost.

In its particular use in the New Testament the Greek notion of "a favorable time of opportunity" *(kairos)* captures this idea.[6] Particular peoples find themselves in crisis because God is "visiting" them. Cornelius found himself in this position when confronted with Peter.

Social groups pass through periods of unusual readiness and responsiveness. They will consider Christian faith carefully if approached during this time and many will commit themselves to Christ. Receptivity is evidence that the time is strategically right for evangelization among a given people.[7]

Finally, it is often true that the least receptive are won to Christ most effectively by concentrating on the most receptive. This is the implied argument in Romans 9–11. Israel's hardening is temporary. By concentrating on the responsive Gentiles, eventually Israel will itself turn to God again.

Many missions have had this experience. Peoples have different periods of responsiveness and the best long-run strategy is to concentrate (though not exclusively) on the most receptive. Paul clearly states that his motivation is the winning of more: "I make myself everybody's slave in order to win as many people as possible" (1 Cor. 9:19).

We need to acknowledge a few qualifications here. Turning away from the resistant happens only in a clearly defined situation. Jesus left his home territory because the Jews there were not receptive (Mark 6:4-6; John 7:11-12). Paul turned away from the resistant synagogues in a Roman city without leaving the city. He left Roman cities only when the civic officials (Gentiles) turned against his ministry. In other words, he turned away from those who had *every reason to understand* the truth but rejected it. This principle holds only in that situation. It does not hold when resistance is to a misunderstood, culturally inappropriate gospel, or to a perceived cultural imperialism and a distorted picture of Jesus that we ourselves would reject.

Those who judged receptivity and resistance were native to the

6. Luke 19:44 is an example of this particular use.
7. See Recker's essay in Harvey Conn (1976), pp. 82-86.

culture of the people they were assessing. Jesus and the Twelve dealt with Palestinian Jews. Paul was bicultural and moved easily in the Roman world. Because they knew the people they evangelized from within, they could make clear assessments of responsiveness and resistance. As cross-cultural evangelists, our own assessments need to be very tentative and open to correction.[8]

Finally, this principle of concentrating on the responsive is relative. Long-term residents of a city who were Christians apparently stayed, even when Paul or the apostles left due to resistance. A Christian community continued to live in and evangelize Jerusalem long after its leadership persecuted Christians.

Furthermore, not all in a city are equally resistant. Often winnable people are within a larger population that is resistant. Those whom Paul won in the Roman cities remained to evangelize after he was forced to leave due to resistance. They could continue to share Christ when he could not. So resistance to one agent of the gospel may only mean that we must look for others more acceptable to the people we believe God wants reached.

In conclusion, we believe that the biblical material gives us direction for field selection. The largest goal is the evangelization of *all peoples,* without regard to religion, culture, race, or social constitution. No one is exempt from the imperative to be discipled.

Within that goal we are to give priority to those *peoples without an indigenous cluster of Christian congregations* in their midst. Frontier (or foundational) missions should be stressed if the ultimate goal of evangelization is to be accomplished. Energies and resources are to be distributed according to the *responsiveness of people groups.* These three principles give us direction to guide our search among all peoples of the earth.

One might logically ask, "Where do we find information about the unreached?" Since 1974, MARC has been building a computerized database on such people and people groups. After the first rather crude directory was produced for the International Congress on World Evangelization at Lausanne, Switzerland, in 1974, an *Unreached Peoples Directory* was produced each year from 1979 to 1984. Today MARC, Global Mapping International, the Foreign Mission Board of the Southern Baptist Convention, and a growing number of First and Two-Thirds World agencies share a vast amount of specific information about the unreached.

---

8. See David Liao, *The Unresponsive: Resistant or Neglected?* (Moody Press, 1972).

FIELD SELECTION CRITERIA

Those who must make the field selection, individual missionaries and mission agencies, do so from two different perspectives. Usually the mission organization will concern itself with a wider range of issues than does the individual. The individual usually does not have as wide a range of contacts or resources for gathering information for such a decision. Yet the actual operation of mission agencies is such that the initiative and concerns of individual missionaries carries great weight.

The informal survey of Protestant mission agencies referred to earlier uncovered a number of specific criteria for making a field selection.

1. We must have a *mandate,* a mission that God has commissioned us to do. From that mandate we ought to be able to state the basic objectives or purposes that govern our existence as an agency or missionary.

2. We must have *knowledge* about peoples who can be targeted for evangelization. How can a messenger be sent to a people Christians do not know about (Rom. 10:14-15)?

3. We must see them as having *priority.* If the people are already well evangelized, if they already have a dynamic cluster of Christian congregations, we may well conclude there is little need for us.

4. We must have *personnel and resources.* If our people and resources are already fully engaged, it is futile to strategize about new outreach.

5. We must be *able to enter* the field. If we cannot get in and we know of no others we can support who can, then we can do little more than pray or develop methods (such as radio or mail) that can begin the process. We may have to become nonresident missionaries (see below).

6. We must be *able to evangelize.* If the people are at war or under such strict proselytism laws that we cannot evangelize, we either have to change our mission to them or seek another people at present. We must ask: Can the church be planted among this people?

7. We must sense *God's call.* In and with all the information and discussion must come a sense that God is saying, "This people, now." Only such a conviction can surmount many of the unanticipated problems that invariably arise in such a project.

These are easy to list; they are difficult to use. That is because those who use them have differing philosophies of ministry, differing ideas about what should be decisive in making this decision. The facts are never self-interpreting or unambiguous. The call of God is seldom heard as clearly by all concerned. The resources and people are never fully adequate to the task envisioned. Yet faith, hope, and love motivate us to move forward to the completion of the task our Lord has given us.

Furthermore, church traditions lead people to look at this process in very divergent ways. For some, an inner calling and even a revelation from the Lord is the only way to define a mission and select a people. They fear that all the rational procedures or research and discussion may be a substitute for the urgings of the Spirit.

Yet others advocate greater stress on orderliness and stewardship. Careful pre-field preparation and research is central. Detailed reports are submitted and argued over until consensus occurs. Their fear is that individual emotions may be confused with the calling of God. They hear his call mainly through a rationally demonstrated need-opportunity matrix.

Traditional commitments also weigh heavily. Arab World Ministries (formerly North Africa Mission) is unlikely suddenly to see its ministry as Bible translation among tribal peoples in Asia. The Church Missionary Society in England ministers in particular countries. When a candidate comes forward the possibilities of field selection are already limited. Church hierarchy and previously established commitments define most possibilities of ministry.

These are expressions of organizational specialization. Just as individuals have certain gifts and not others, so organizations also have particular gifts and competencies. Wycliffe Bible Translators is skilled at reducing tribal languages to writing. It knows how to do this under technologically primitive conditions. Its personnel have years of linguistic and cultural training. Its mission is not focused on urban literate populations.

When the Vietnamese came to the shores of the USA, the Christian and Missionary Alliance went right to work. They had a number of former missionaries who knew the languages of Vietnam and even some of the refugees themselves. Field selection is guided by the particular constellation of gifts and competencies that make up a missionary and a mission agency.

Church groups vary widely in their successes and failures around the world. Little strategic attention has been paid to this. Yet it might hold significance for future plans. Presbyterians can point to very vital churches in Korea, Taiwan, and Pakistan. Methodists dominate the mission scene in Fiji. Pentecostals are growing at high rates in Latin America, Baptists in Burma and Nagaland in India, and Roman Catholics in Uganda. Somehow the denominational ethos and the peoples they evangelize fit.

Does it make sense to ask, given what we know about a denomination or mission as well as a given people group, if this is likely to succeed? Does the outlook, theological twist, and cultural baggage of a given agency make it a good candidate for evangelizing this particular people?

Finally, another important consideration is geopolitical. Fewer countries are "open" to Western missionaries now than were twenty-five years ago. Mainland China is unlikely to open its doors to professional Western missionaries in the near future. The number of Islamic countries restricting access has increased in recent years. It is still difficult for Westerners to get visas for India and a number of other countries.

Two-Thirds World missionaries are on the upswing. So too are "tentmakers."[9] Many of the Two-Thirds World missionaries engage in "diaspora evangelization" and pastoring. That is, they are seeking to follow the migrations of their own socio-culturally similar peoples into new areas of the world. This is an essential part of the larger picture. The Koreans of southern New Jersey need to be evangelized. Likewise, the Chinese diaspora in some seventy countries of the world, the Vietnamese in Paris, the Gujarati in London—all need Christ.

What we must acknowledge is the reality of the worldwide church. While Western professional missionaries may not be able to enter many countries, other Christians can. Some may be nonprofessional missionaries engaged in technical or service occupations. Others may be cross-cultural professional missionaries. Syrian, Korean, Chilean, and Nigerian missionaries can find entry and receptivity where the American missionary may not. Field selection must recognize the complex situation we are in.

The nonresidential missionary is a new notion meant to cope with the difficulty of countries denying residence to Western missionaries. In this situation, an agency appoints a missionary to a particular unreached people or people groups. His or her assignment is to do everything possible to see that the gospel somehow reaches them.

Research is the beginning point in this process. What are these people like? Who has the best legal, cultural, and/or possible access to them? Who is currently thinking about them? Are there strategies for reaching some of their members who are outside their boundaries, as in the case of the hundreds of thousands of international university students? This may well be the wave of the future, particularly if such agen-

---

9. Tetsunao Yamamori, *God's New Envoys: A Bold Strategy for Penetrating "Closed Countries"* (Multnomah Press, 1987), and J. Christy Wilson, *Today's Tentmakers* (Tyndale House, 1979). For further information on tentmaking ministry, write Tentmakers International, c/o Ron Miller, P.O. Box 33836, Seattle, WA 98133, or Global Opportunities, c/o Ruth Siemens, 1600 Elizabeth St., Pasadena, CA 91104.

cies commit themselves to enable others to go who *can* go. It combines the research and planning skills of the outsider with the cultural and communication skills of the insider. It forces us to enter into strategic partnerships in radio, literature, education, and every form of Christian witness.

UNREACHED PEOPLE DEFINED

What we need is more agreement as to how precisely to define an unreached people group. The best and most widely used definition emerged out of a 1982 meeting of forty mission leaders: "*A people group within which there is no indigenous community of believing Christians able to evangelize this group.*"

This definition is based on the notion that evangelization must be concerned with more than the degree to which people in the world are exposed to the gospel. David Barrett's massive surveys of evangelization are based on considerations of exposure to the gospel. Evangelized non-Christians are "persons who are not Christians in any recognized sense but who have become aware of Christianity, Christ, and the gospel and yet have not, or not yet, responded positively by accepting them" (Barrett, 1982).

On that basis Barrett argues that the twentieth century has seen a dramatic increase in the percentage of the world's population which has been exposed to the gospel. The percentage of the world's people who are "unevangelized" has dropped from about 48.7 percent in 1900 to 25.8 percent in 1988 (Barrett, 1988, pp. 16-17). This is good news indeed! Every Christian should rejoice that some knowledge of Christ and the church is being extended to more and more.

However, the unreached peoples perspective focuses less on the extension of *minimum levels of knowledge about Christ* than on the establishment of the *minimum level of Christian presence* for the continuing evangelization of a people. A people group that has had minimal levels of exposure to the gospel would be classified as evangelized by Barrett's definition, yet they may be unreached. They are not considered reached until a cluster of indigenous communities of Christians are present with the capacity to complete the evangelization of that people group.

The difference between an approach based on exposure to the good news and one based on the existence of worshiping Christians may seem small at first glance. Yet the results for strategy and planning are dramatic.

An exposure approach tends to focus on the activity of the

evangelizing agent. How many gospel messages are sent on the radio? How many Bibles are in print? How many Christian meetings are held? The assumption is that the higher the activity level, the wider the exposure level. The problem with this assumption is that it does not reckon with audience segregation and segmentation. It tends to overestimate the number of those actually evangelized and to underestimate the number who still need significantly more knowledge in order to respond positively to Christ.

The unreached peoples approach is based on Paul's goals as given in Romans 10 and 15. In both situations his focus was on more than levels of evangelizing activity. He was concerned with what was *heard*, not just with how many were exposed to the gospel (Rom. 10). His conclusion that the gospel had been preached and his work was completed was based on *the existence of worshiping Christian communities* (Rom. 15).

With exposure as a strategy focus the evangelist will conclude that the job is finished much sooner than the evangelist with a church planting focus. However, an exposure focus is not unconcerned with establishing Christian congregations. Nor is the church planting focus unconcerned with increasing the exposure of the gospel. Rather, the question is which approach provides the better long-term enhancement for the process of evangelization. We are convinced that the church planting focus of the unreached people approach captures more of the apostolic goals. Furthermore, it includes the exposure goals in a way the exposure approach does not include the goal of church planting.

Hence, we consider a people as unreached *until* there are worshiping groups of Christians in sufficient numbers with enough resources to complete the task of evangelization within their own kind without outside help. Our mission is to identify not only the unevangelized of our world but also the unreached peoples who still need outside help in laying the foundations of Christian communities able to do the job themselves.[10]

The bottom line in defining our mission is the selection of a specific people or a more precisely defined people group within a people as our target audience. Field selection and mission definition is not

---

10. "Unreached" can become confusing if we consider a people or people group who *have* an indigenous community of believing Christians that is able to evangelize this group as being a "*reached* group." Since in everyday English usage when we speak of a "reached" individual we normally mean someone who has accepted Christ, if we apply "reached" and "unreached" equally we will miss the point. Since the introduction of "unreached people" by the Lausanne Strategy Working Group, the word "unreached" has gained such common usage that we would probably be better off to talk about people groups that were "unreached" or "not reached."

complete for strategy purposes until we have reached this point. If we follow the priorities of Scripture, then we will seek a people group that is not only unevangelized but unreached. We must then develop and carry out a strategy that will enable them to respond authentically to the offer of God's salvation.

PERSPECTIVE

In all of this we need to remember that God is with us. This is the mission he has been on since our original parents were expelled from the garden. We can have hope and patience in the midst of the complexities and ambiguities. We are part of a dynamic, growing body of Christ that continues to surprise us. While we cannot take the whole burden on our shoulders, we can share it with many other churches and Christians.

It is possible to reach every one of the remaining hidden and unreached peoples of the earth. Some have said it can be done by the year 2000. Given the resources and vitality of the Christian church, this is a real possibility. Yet it will not happen by then or even by 2100 if we do not identify the hidden peoples and give them priority in our strategies. We must adopt a long-range vision and begin going after the unreached peoples one at a time.

While we may not see the evangelization of some peoples of the earth in our time, we can help build organizations and visions that will carry world evangelization strongly into the next century. We need to be building bridges into the future.

Thus, this is not a single step, but a process. Changes constantly modify the factors we must deal with in evangelization. So we must select a people or people group, come to understand them, devise a plan for evangelizing them, carry it out as best we can, and then evaluate what has happened. Then we re-think, revise, and re-plan. In faith we need to think as far as we can into the future God has for us and then move forward.

Questions

1. What is the mission of God on planet earth? What is his plan for the universe? How does the mission of the church fit into what God is doing?

2. How does the alleviation of suffering and injustice relate to the priorities of the kingdom of God? How does evangelization (in the sense of gospel proclamation) relate to the priorities of the kingdom of God?

3. In what ways can a theology of the kingdom of God overcome some of the contemporary polarizations in the contemporary debate over the proper mission of the church?

4. What is evangelism? How does the Bible define it? How do you define evangelism?

5. What is the essential content of the gospel? What must a person (a) know and (b) believe in order to be rightly related to God? What are the minimum requirements for a person to be saved?

6. What types of diversity in expression are permissible in the presentation of the good news? How can the various presentations of the gospel be evaluated so as to identify the authenticity and faithfulness of new expressions?

7. What relationship exists between the evangelical message, the evangelist, and the demands of the evangel on everyday life?

8. How do we define *evangelistic need*? What must be true of a group if we are to identify it as "unreached" or "unevangelized"? When does a group no longer need help from groups outside itself in the process of evangelization?

9. How do we go about finding the information we could use to discover the peoples or people groups who might most benefit from the evangelization help we can provide?

STEP 2: THE PEOPLE TO BE REACHED

Considerations

1. The single most important element in planning strategies for evangelism is an understanding of the people to be evangelized.

2. Standard solutions to evangelize nonstandard peoples violate the humanity of those being evangelized. They also make an offensive confusion of the kingdom of God. Evangelism that attempts to ignore the social and cultural differences that exist in human society quickly becomes misevangelism and may unnecessarily drive people away from Christ.

3. A people is definable by those common attributes that make them either reachable by a given means or difficult to reach by any known means.

4. Each distinct people group is worthy of a special strategy and its own indigenous church institutions. The crucial matter in considering any group as a distinct people is their subjective sense of group identity, not the objectively provable fact of homogeneity or a given set of characteristics.

5. The kingdom of God must be understandable within a people's meaning system, relevant to felt needs, and viable within their institutions if it is to encounter the inner soul of a people.

6. The real choice that faces us in evangelization is contextualization or confusion.

7. Evangelism begins with need as a people defines it. The felt needs of a people group are intimately related to the spiritual dimensions of the kingdom of God. The hungers of the body as well as those of the soul are addressed by God's purposes.

8. To understand the culture of a people is to understand both the glory of how the gospel can find new expression and the agony of a new confrontation with unique forms of human evil. Because culture is a mixture of good and evil, there is always an ambivalent, ambiguous relationship between it and Christianity.

79

STEP 2: THE PEOPLE TO BE REACHED

9. In attempting to evangelize across cultural boundaries, most of us do not need more education. We need complete re-education.

10. The political, social, and economic contexts sometimes can be so overbearing that they become the primary definers of the life of a people.

8. A People-Centered Approach

The people or people group to be evangelized are like the soil into which the farmer of Jesus' parable sows his seed (Matt. 13:1-23). Not all soils are alike; neither are all peoples alike. Each will bear a different harvest. Some will yield no harvest at all. Intelligent sowing of the seed is crucial to the eventual fruit. A good harvest depends in part on understanding the condition of the soil.

Pedologists (scientists who study soils) tell us there are many types of soil. When combined with the various climates, they support hundreds of thousands of different plants and animals. Each soil developed under different conditions from different parent materials. Each has distinctive nutrients and qualities that help the growth of certain plants and retard the growth of others. The pedologist tests the soil to determine the proper fertilizers, weed controls, crop rotation, and pest control measures necessary to produce a good crop.

In like manner peoples have developed from different parents under different conditions. Each people has its own particular language and culture, its own economic and religious institutions. Some have the "rocks" of misunderstanding about Christianity. Others are lush with the crops of Islam or Hinduism. The evangelist will want to understand the soil conditions into which the Word of God is to be sown. Even the hardiest of seeds will remain dormant if sown in the wrong place or at the wrong time.

The farmer accepts the needs and conditions of the soil. So the Christian also accepts as a given the particular characteristics of the target group to be evangelized. The evangelist accepts a people group where it is and in its need. Evangelization meets people where they are, not where we would like them to be.

When we say "peoples" we refer to an enormous variety of social and cultural groupings. Each has its own beauty and strength, its own weaknesses and sinfulness. No one knows exactly how many distinctive peoples and people groups exist, but the figure is in the thousands. There are Gypsies in Spain, Boston Brahmins of Nob Hill, Cantonese restaurant workers in Vienna, Arabs of Saudi Arabia, Dinka cattle herders of the Sudan, Mennonite Germans in Russia, cooperative peasant farmers in the Hunan province in China, and copper miners in Chile.

Persons do not exist as isolated individuals. All of us live in a network of social relationships and cultural notions. Some of the groups we belong to are as large as a nation such as Japan. Some are as small as the face-to-face hunting and gathering bands of the !Kung Bushman in Namibia.

The reality of the diversity of groups is the single most important fact in strategies for evangelism. Once we have our definition of mission, we must understand the people or people group we are setting out to evangelize. Understanding the target group is the second step in this planning cycle because everything else grows out of it. In the pages that follow we seek to make a case for a people-centered approach to evangelization.

THE IMPORTANCE OF A PEOPLE-CENTERED APPROACH

Alwyne Wheeler's *Fishes of the World: An Illustrated Dictionary* (1975) lists thousands of fish: fresh and salt water, denizens of the deep and occupants of the top inches of the sea, whales and dolphins, trout and tuna, extravagantly colored tropical reef dwellers and mammoth white sharks. Modern science has classified some twenty-two thousand different species. Each has its own size and shape, its own location, and its own way of living that allows it to survive in the wild.

Fishing is one of the oldest of human pursuits. A four-thousand-year-old Egyptian tomb picture depicts fishermen pulling their nets from reed boats. Today more than five million people make their living harvesting the bounty of the seven seas. Sophisticated sonar devices help to locate fish in the water. Large-scale research institutes advance our understanding. Fish farms employ graduates of advanced programs for ichthyologists.

Seven of Jesus' twelve disciples were fishermen by trade. He told them, "Don't be afraid; from now on you will be catching people" (Luke 5:10). He meant that they would persuade individuals, families, and groups to become his disciples. Fishing was to be a picture in their minds that would help them understand what evangelization would require in their lives.

In one of his parables Jesus spoke of the large dragnets or seine that fishermen used (Matt. 13:47-50). It catches all kinds of fish. Some they considered edible, like the tilapia and sardines of Lake Galilee. Some they considered inedible, like the catfish that the Jews labeled unclean (McCullough, 1962; Cansdale, 1970, chap. 17). Sorting took place on the shore and the unclean were returned to the lake. The parable taught that only the angels could sort the good and the bad in the kingdom at the end of time.

Jesus' disciples knew various techniques to catch fish since different fish required different techniques. They would have seen the connection to people. Like fish, peoples and people groups live in many different communities, each with its own location and habits. Some are catchable by the "cast nets" of evangelism, designed to take those close to shore in shallow water. Others need a deep water dragnet far from shore. Still others are caught only by the patient night fisherman, one at a time.

Each distinctive people group is like a species of fish. The more we understand it, the more skillful and effective will we be in our mission of "catching people." The methods we use, the timing and location we choose for gospel communication, the evangelists we commission— all relate to the distinctives of the target group. It is absurd to try to catch a tuna with a fly fisher's rod and reel. It is just as absurd to harvest trout from a small mountain stream with a large seine two hundred feet in length!

Unfortunately, this is not an obvious point to many engaged in evangelism. It is often overshadowed by the "standard solution" approach, which builds on the notion that people are really more alike than different. Beneath the differences of language, customs, and clothing, which make others seem exotic, there is a deeper commonness. Pride, loneliness, fear, hungers for security and happiness, and the struggle for survival are part of all cultures. Theft, adultery, envy, and violence mar the daily life of all peoples. Religious customs everywhere witness to the desire for knowledge of the unknown and control over the mysteries of life.

The standard solution approach assumes that the differences that make peoples, people groups, and cultures distinct are not terribly significant. So long as one can use another language, a standard methodology and strategy will work in virtually all cultures. An approach that works well in Philadelphia will work well in Peking or Pago Pago. It is not difficult to find examples of the problems that occur by following this line of thinking.

The skillful use of "magic" and illusion is one approach used in the USA to attract an audience and communicate Christ. Some of the premier entertaining magicians are Christian. Western audiences understand that the tricks are all illusions and skillful manipulations. Yet when one such person went to Kenya to present the gospel in this way, misunderstandings developed. There "magic" also means real spiritual powers. Some people had never seen Western entertainment magic and illusion. Seeing the astounding tricks led them to believe Christianity is simply a more powerful form of the witchcraft practices of their traditional culture.

Sometimes the use of standard solution approaches creates this sort of confusion and hinders future evangelism. Frank S. Khair-Ullah tells of the effects of such an approach in his homeland of Pakistan:

> A "scripture distribution" program was launched from Wheaton, Illinois. Every name listed in the telephone directory of some city or cities in Pakistan was sent a copy of the New Testament in Urdu by mail. Some addresses were changed by the time the packets arrived, some people refused to accept these unsolicited packets of the Christian Scriptures. Tons of these got accumulated in the post office, which had to be disposed of by auction as "waste paper." Some of us discovered this when some small merchandise was purveyed to people in envelopes made out of the pages of the Bible. Anyone who is familiar with our culture would have been horrified, for the greatest respect is accorded to all scriptures in the East whether it be the Quran or the Bible. You can imagine the chagrin of our Muslim friends who could not understand why such mass desecration of our Holy Book was carried out by the American Christians.
>
> Pakistan Bible Society, I am told, did make a protest. But they were told that some letters of appreciation did arrive at their office appreciating the distribution. How many? That we were not told. (1979, p. 570)

Confusion and offense are high risks when standard solutions are carried across cultural barriers. That is why *both* the differences and the commonness of humans must be respected. The problem with standard solutions is that they respect only human commonness. Yet it is the differences in cultural traits, world-views, felt needs, lifestyle, modal personality, and responsiveness that create problems. To maximize the meaningful hearing of the gospel, the evangelist will tailor a strategy that respects the distinctives of a people or a people group. We call this a people-centered approach.

Standard solutions do not work well for unstandard peoples. People-centered approaches seek to tailor a strategy to fit a distinctive people or people group. One difference between the two approaches is what each considers to be an appropriate target group. The standard solution sees its target group as large sectors of the world across many cultural and language barriers. It may be all people with a telephone or all who read. The people-centered approach sees its target as a much smaller group, a socially and culturally bounded one. It is small enough so that the gospel can spread without requiring major modifications in form or presentation because of problems of understanding. This means that the effective accomplishment of world evangelization will take as many distinctive approaches as there are distinctive peoples or people groups.

What is standard in our approach is the set of steps or questions used for planning. Following those steps creates distinctive plans, tailored to fit the evangelistic activity to the social and cultural shape of the target group. Because such evangelism respects the peoples' culture, it is more likely to communicate Christ fairly and effectively. Yet beyond the higher likelihood of successful communication, we believe this to be a biblical approach.

PEOPLES AND PEOPLE GROUPS IN THE BIBLE

The Old Testament displays a clear awareness of peoples, acknowledging various human groups based on various principles that unify their members (Bietenhard, 1976). It draws the most dramatic distinction between the holy people (*'am*) of God and the Gentiles (*goy*) (Schmidt, 1961, p. 6). The main emphasis in the Old Testament falls on the two-fold movement found in the Abrahamic covenant. On the one hand, God is creating a people for himself. He called out Abraham and made of him a great nation (Gen. 12:2). Yet he also dispersed the human population into separate language groups (Gen. 11). God now seeks to reach them through one of those peoples whom he will create over time. The purpose of creating a holy people is to reach all the other peoples with the blessings of God. So it is through Abraham's seed that the world is to be blessed (Gen. 12:3). All through the Old Testament there is a tension between Israel as blessed by God and Israel as a blessing to all peoples.

Old Testament terminology is relatively simple in characterizing people groups.[1] The term for "lands" (*'eretz*) recognizes that people

---

1. Norman Gottwald, *The Tribes of Yahweh* (Orbis, 1979), Part IV, speculates on various sociologically relevant terms within Israel's pre-monarchic organization.

who share a common territory often also come to share a common way of life. The term for "tongues" *(lashon)* stresses the importance of shared communication in creating distinct people groups (Behm, 1964). Most evangelism and church planting strategies admit that this is a legitimate basis for distinct congregations and even strategies. In addition, the term for "tribes" or "clans" *(mishpachah)* highlights the integrating power of kinship and marriage as a basis for creating solidarity groups. Over time family traditions can become the basis for subcultures and distinguish tribe from tribe (Maurer, 1974).

New Testament terms are more comprehensive and set within a different phase of God's redemptive activity. The Old Testament accent is on achieving a cultural uniformity in a single, holy people set apart to serve Yahweh. The New Testament accent falls on a unity that incorporates great cultural diversity.

Pentecost is a sign that the new people of God will include the vast array of tribes, tongues, castes, clans, and subcultures. The miracle of tongues signals that each language group is to have the good news in its own tongue. The church does not reduce the people of God to one culture or people in the same sense that Israel was a single culture. The people of God are now a community of many cultures sharing a common loyalty to the same Lord, confessing the same faith, yet retaining distinctive ethnic and cultural ways of life.

A number of verses in Revelation envision the end of time as climaxing in all languages and peoples worshiping God (5:9; 7:9; 10:11; 11:9; 13:7; 14:6; 17:15). The end of history in "heaven" does not erase the rich social, racial, and cultural differences between the peoples. All they are and have become is brought to the Lord in tribute.

New Testament terminology for the various peoples and people groups does not employ modern scientific terms. Nonetheless, a clear awareness of people groups based on a variety of principles exists. Unity and solidarity are achieved in social groups because of several factors. The most general term is that of *ethnos,* translated as nation, Gentile, or people. It refers to peoples bound together by the same manners, customs, or other distinctive features (Schmidt, *"ethnos, ethnikos"*). This Greek word comes the closest to modern anthropological terms for labeling people groups. About 40 percent of its usage, however, is in passages that contrast the Jews or Christians with the "Gentiles," that is, the pagan nations. Yet such passages as Matthew 28:19 and Luke 24:47 use the term to include Jews as well as Gentiles.

The church's commission is to evangelize all the *ethnē,* Jews as well as Gentiles. This commission goes back to the Abrahamic promise that God would bless all peoples through the children of Abraham. Some argue that *ethnos* does not refer to "ethnic units," but rather to the whole of humanity from which God is gathering a people (Verkuyl, 1978, p. 107). This ignores the range of meaning and usage of the Greek term. As Schmidt notes: "In most cases, *ethnos* is used of men in the sense of a 'people.' . . . [It] is the most general and therefore the weakest [term for people], having simply an ethnographical sense and denoting the natural cohesion of people in general" (*"ethnos, ethnikos,"* p. 369).

The Great Commission's goal is not simply to organize Christian communities within the political units currently recognized as nation-states. It aims at all peoples and people groups which exist in various states of natural cohesion because of shared language and life. However we classify them (as tribe, caste, class, clan, language-group, status group, etc.), all peoples and people groups are to be given the gospel.

It is probably preferable to translate Matthew 28:19 as "Go, then, to all *peoples* everywhere and make them my disciples . . . ," as does the *Good News Bible*. Most other translations render it as "nations." The problem is that the English term *nation* has the connotation of a geographically bounded political state. Such a state has many *ethnē* in the New Testament sense of the word. This is especially true in the United States, with its Puerto Ricans, southern Blacks, Cantonese-speaking Chinese, Navajo Indians, New England Italian Catholics, Vietnamese refugees, midwestern farmers, and so on.

Jesus gives the full meaning to *ethnē* by sending forth the seventy-two (Luke 10:1-20). The table of nations in Genesis 10 sees the world after Babel as divided into seventy (Hebrew text) or seventy-two (Septuagint text) "nations." The Jews viewed the world as having seventy-two princes and seventy-two languages.[2] The sending out of the seventy-two was a foreshadowing of the "Gentile mission" of the church. In sending out the twelve (Luke 9:1-11), Jesus indicated that evangelization sends us to the twelve tribes of Israel. In sending out seventy-two others he showed that all peoples of the earth are recipients of the message of the kingdom. The Book of Acts displays the beginning of that process.

The point of the New Testament's use of *ethnē* is not to provide a precise term for the sociological groupings of humanity. Nor is the number of "nations" from Genesis 10 meant to map the world precisely.

---

2. See the pseudepigrapha 1 En. 89:59ff.; 3 En. 17:8; 18:2-3; 30:2. Joseph A. Fitzmeyer, *The Gospel According to Luke X–XXIV* (Doubleday, 1985), pp. 841-50; I. Howard Marshall, *The Gospel of Luke: A Commentary on the Greek Text* (Eerdmans, 1978), pp. 412-16; Charles H. Talbert, *Reading Luke: A Literary and Theological Commentary on the Third Gospel* (Crossroad, 1982), p. 115.

It points to the diversity of the world after Babel. However many "nations" there are, all are to be reached with the gospel.

The realities of linguistic change and social divergence means that new peoples are emerging every century, in some cases every decade. The impact of industrial societies upon less technologically advanced societies means that peoples are also vanishing. The task is not simpler now. It is more complex.

Other Greek terms recognize other sorts of principles that organize people groups. *Phulē* stresses the notion of a national or political unity. It is normally translated "tribe" (Maurer, 1974). Yet it refers to a range of different groups from a clan to a large chieftainship or tribe with centralized political authority. What holds the *phulē* together is common descent, leadership, and law.

Glossa, usually translated as "language" or "tongue," refers to a people as a group bound together by virtue of speaking and understanding the same language or dialect (Behm, 1964). Wycliffe Bible Translators as well as modern linguistics have made us keenly aware of the "babel" of over five thousand languages (Grimes, 1984). Each language has its distinctive way of labeling and categorizing the world and its experience as a people. By its distinctive use of words and concepts as well as grammar, it creates its own world of meaning. Such linguistic worlds include only those who understand the language and exclude all others.

Language is a powerful and important factor in creating a distinct people group. Language riots in such polyglot nations as India and Iran are examples of how important language can be to peoples. Yet a single language may encompass so large a population and be found in so many localities that it may be composed of dozens of smaller subgroups identifiable as people groups.

Laos, often translated "nation," "race," or "people," views groups or populations as bound together as a political unity. A *laos* is gathered together under a common history and constitution, such as the citizens of the same city (Strathmann, 1967).

The New Testament uses a variety of other terms as well. *Dēmos* refers to people as residents of a single city or community (Grundmann, 1964). *Diaspora* describes the situation of an exiled or dispersed people, living in many places among other peoples (Schmidt, "*diaspora*"). Because of their common history and identity (such as the Jews in the Roman world), they retain a sense of unity. Their sense of pride keeps them distinctive in their way of life. *Patria* describes a group of people who see themselves as one because of common descent from a single father (Schrenk, 1967). They might be a single nuclear family, a lineage or kindred, an extended family with servants in a household, or a caste or tribe. *Ochlos* normally denotes a people who have grouped together because of some common situation or need (but not because of a permanent principle or condition) (Meyer, 1967). A crowd at a football game is one example of the *ochlos*. A mass of people temporarily unified because of a natural disaster such as an earthquake is another example.

Thus, apparently there is an awareness of people groups in the Bible. While the Bible does not use the precise terms we do, it recognizes various degrees and types of solidarity in society.

People develop their own communication patterns and life-styles as a result of living together. Whether it be geography, language, family connections, or political commonality, the world of humanity out of which God is calling a single "people" is highly diverse. Evangelization does not result in the erasing of that diversity. Each people can become a "disciple" of Jesus Christ, learning to follow him within its own language and life-style.

Revelation tells us of a book of life in which the names of those individuals who follow Christ are written (20:15). So also is there a register of peoples, in which the names of discipled peoples are written:

> Indeed, of Zion it will be said, "This one and that one were born in her, and the Most High himself will establish her." The Lord will write in the register of the peoples: "This one was born in Zion." (Ps. 87:5-6)

EVANGELISM AND PEOPLES OF THE NEW TESTAMENT WORLD

Evangelism in the early church took place in a world with many social and cultural groups. Much of Acts deals with the way in which various peoples were brought into the church by the guidance of the Spirit. It also chronicles some of the controversies over the changes surrounding this expanding circle of peoples. Paul's letters frequently deal with the relationships between Christians from Jewish and Gentile backgrounds.

Scholars recognize at least three major groupings of peoples and several subgroups. Jesus and his disciples were part of the Palestinian Jewish people (Aramaic-speaking, insistent on rigorous observance of Mosaic law, centered in Jerusalem). Hellenistic Jews became Christians at an early date. Their native tongue was Greek. They were less rigorous in observance of Jewish laws. Stephen is symbolic of them (Acts 6–7). The Samaritans were half-Jewish outcasts who did not participate in the worship at Jerusalem. In addition, there were Hellenistic Gentile peoples who became Christians. Some were part of the Jewish synagogues and knew the Old Testament Scriptures; others were pagans with little knowledge of Jewish traditions. Within the Gentile Christian movement various differences in values and worldview are discernible.[3]

The early chapters of Acts tell the story of the movement of the message of the kingdom and Jesus out from the Palestinian Jews to Gentile groups. One of the Greek-speaking Hellenistic Jewish Christians took the first step. Philip proclaimed Christ in Samaria (Acts 8). Then the Gentile God-fearer, Cornelius, came into the church (Acts 10–11). Finally, there is the story of the first congregation whose members were predominantly from Gentile backgrounds with no affiliation with Jewish synagogues (Acts 11).

The picture being painted is the dramatic shift from Israel to the church as God's instrument and community. Israel was a relatively monocultural, ethnically based people. The church is a multicultural, multi-ethnic universal people without a center in a geographically limited nation-state.

The diversity faced by the apostolic church was almost as complicated as the diversity found in many modern societies.[4] Among the Jews there were many schools of thought: the Pharisees, Sadducees, Zealots, and Essenes.[5] The peasants and poorer sectors of Palestine were known as the 'A ha-aretz, the people of the land. They were despised by the Pharisees because they could not keep the law strictly.

Judean Jews looked down on the Galilean Jews who spoke with an accent. Hellenistic Jews lived in Palestine as well as Gentiles. Samaritans and Idumeans were present and excluded from the social gatherings of strict Jews.[6]

The Roman world was even more diverse[7] with its many social classes. At the top were the elite Senatorial families and the equestrians. Municipal bureaucrats and veterans of the Roman armies were also privileged populations with special rights. Freeborn citizens (plebeians),

---

3. F. F. Bruce, *The Defense of the Gospel in the New Testament,* rev. ed. (Eerdmans, 1977).

4. John Stambaugh and David Balch, *The New Testament in Its Social Environment* (Westminster, 1986); Wayne Meeks, *The First Urban Christians: The Social World of the Apostle Paul* (Yale, 1983).

5. Richard Horsley and John Hanson, *Bandits, Prophets and Messiahs* (Seabury/Winston, 1985).

6. Jeremias, 1969; Safrai and Stern, 1974, 1976; Schürer, 1973–1987; Hengel, 1974; Freyne, 1980.

7. Rostovtzeff, 1957; M. Grant, 1960; Judge, 1960; Benko, 1971.

freed slaves, "peregrini" (working class and peasantry not citizens of Rome), and slaves made up the lower classes. They did most of the work and made Rome prosperous. Then there were the conquered and border-land peoples: Lasitanians, Celtiberians, Lystrans, Ethiopians, Aedui, Suebi, Turdetani, and so on. Occupational groups and guilds lived to-gether and formed cohesive groups in cities (such as the silversmiths at Ephesus—Acts 19:23ff.).

The early church did not grow among all of these peoples and people groups. Many of them are not even mentioned in the New Testa-ment. This seems to be because the majority of converts came from only a few of the social and cultural levels of the Roman world. It would take the church several centuries to begin to penetrate them all. The evidence for this is not entirely clear or decisive. The sociology of early Christian-ity is still in its early stages of development.[8] Our own view is that there was a social class axis to the movement.

Early Christianity was a congregational religion carried by charismatic followers of Jesus Christ. They were enthusiastic in their faith and came mainly from the anonymous petite bourgeoisie. These were the artisans or small business people of the towns and cities of the eastern provinces of the Roman world. From its start Christianity was shaped by its petite bourgeoisie origins. Jesus was a carpenter. Peter, James, and John were self-employed fishermen. Matthew was a minor tax collector. Paul was a tent-maker. Lydia sold dyed cloth to the upper classes.

Social classes were not highly bounded in Roman times. Slaves, former slaves, the poor, and the middle status people were linked with the powerful and wealthy through networks of clientage. People

8. The sociology of early Christianity upon which much of this analysis is based has seen rapid development in recent years (Judge, 1960; Theissen, 1977; Gager, 1975; Malherbe, 1977; Hengel, *Judaism* and *Property*; Nock, 1964; Sherwin-White, 1963; R. Grant, 1977; Benko, 1971; Meeks, 1983; Osiek, 1984; Verner, 1983; Balch, 1981; Elliott, 1981; Kee, 1980; Malina, 1981; Tidball, 1984). So far as we can tell, Christianity in apostolic years did not grow well among the rural peasantry (who were more attuned to magic), members of the upper levels of the military (who had a tendency to be negative toward salvation re-ligions), the civic bureaucrats (who used religion for civic control but tended to be skepti-cal of its truth-claims), the commercial patriciate (who were strongly this-worldly), or the economically dispossessed (including the lower levels of slavery whose lives were too dis-organized and marginal to permit much preoccupation with anything but survival) (cf. Max Weber, 1968, pp. 468-517). Most of the minority ethnic and tribal groups of the Roman world were not touched. Consequently, the Christian movement was concentrated at the end of the first century in cities in the Hellenized parts of the eastern and central provinces of the Roman empire. These conclusions merit more detailed support than can be given here. Yet this outline expresses the major conclusions that guide our analysis of the early church and its relationship to the peoples and people groups of its day.

would fan out in the mornings to visit their patrons and receive a small dole from them. In exchange they provided services and support in the struggles that invariably pitted the powerful against each other.

The slaves mentioned in the New Testament were city slaves. They were parts of households whose masters had become Christian. The large numbers of slaves on farms and mines do not appear in the New Testament. This probably means the slaves mentioned were among the better educated, carried off to slavery as a result of Roman wars.

Within the ranks of Palestinian Judaism we find the 'Am ha-aretz most responsive to Jesus' proclamation of the kingdom of God. Pharisees and priests also became Christians, but apparently in fewer numbers. Acts 11, 15, and 21 indicate that the strict pharisaic Jewish Christian was influential within the Jerusalem church.

In spite of its inability to triumph over the broader Jewish Christian viewpoint, the early church sent Judaizers all over the Roman world. Paul was hounded by them and they are represented in the later Ebionite movement from the second to the seventh centuries. The treatment of Hellenistic Jewish Christians (Acts 7) and the triumph of the broader Christian view at the Jerusalem Council (Acts 15) offers the best evidence of the Jewish Christian make-up. It appears the 'Am ha-aretz and the Hellenistic Jewish Christians appear dominant.

Outside Palestine, Christianity appears to have grown around the nucleus of converted Hellenistic Jews and Gentile God-fearers. The God-fearers found Paul's message of full status with God without circumcision attractive. His message denied the religious value of Jewish food taboos and its strict social rules for Gentiles.

When we imagine the fabric of client relations as well as the ties of collegia (associations of trade guilds, corporations, and clubs) and familia (extended family households) that existed in the Roman world, we have some idea of who was in the early church. The petite bourgeoisie with its social network was an identifiable social segment of the Roman world.

In sum, the early church grew as a congregational religion. It was located in the cities where Judaism was strong, primarily in the Hellenized and Romanized sectors of the eastern and central provinces of the Roman world. Socially, the petite bourgeoisie and their clients and families were the most numerous adherents. The slaves found in the Christian movement were most likely the domestic and artisan slaves connected with this social stratum.

As it grew, the Christian movement experienced a number of crises over how Christians from various backgrounds and convictions were to interrelate. This was especially true of Jews and Gentiles, though other issues such as slave and free, male and female were also addressed.

Frontier and peripheral regions of Rome yield no evidence of Christian presence in the first century. Only those who spoke Greek or Aramaic appear in the New Testament movement. Whether this limitation of the social character of early Christianity was intentional cannot be answered at this distance in time. The New Testament records the various ways in which the gospel was contextualized to deal with the social diversity faced by the apostolic movement. We can only discover what was done in hope that it will aid us as we seek to be as powerful a movement in the hands of God in our generation.

PAUL'S PEOPLE-CENTERED APPROACH

Paul never called himself an apostle of a city or province. He was an apostle to the Gentiles, just as Peter was an apostle to the Jews. Paul's strategy was designed to encircle the Mediterranean with Christian congregations. To accomplish that he followed the paths already well used by the Jewish diaspora. He went to cities where Jewish synagogues existed. There he found Gentiles already attracted to the God and Father of Jesus Christ. His strategy included provinces and cities, but only because he saw himself as an evangelist of a given set of peoples and people groups (contra Liefield, 1978, pp. 179-80; Verkuyl, 1978, p. 51).

Paul's strategy included adjustments based upon the distinctives of the group he was seeking to bring to faith. In his first letter to the Corinthians (9:1-23, esp. 22b) he shows this: "I have become all things to all people so that by all possible means I might save some." Paul mentions four groups to whom he sought the clearest way to make Christ known. He did not compromise the content of the gospel. He did compromise his own cultural preferences so nothing would be an issue except Christ himself. Thus, when he was with Jews he followed their customs and food laws. When he was with those not under the law, he set aside the scruples of the law. He lived consistently within his commitment to Christ but did not ask the Gentile to keep the details of the Mosaic law. The Gentile was not required to adopt circumcision or the food taboos of the Jews in order to follow Christ.

Paul's point was that winning "as many as possible" (1 Cor. 9:19) involved avoiding things that offend or confuse the target group. Without moral compromise or syncretism in the message Paul reshaped his life-style, message presentation, and methodology. His goal was to maximize the impact of the kingdom of God so more rather than less would be obedient.

Such a procedure is people-centered. To avoid the offensive and the confusing we must understand a people from within their own viewpoint. We must know their scruples, customs, and ways of thinking. To become a Jew to the Jews, we must understand their way of life. To become a Motilone to the Motilones, a Sawi to the Sawis, an Algerian to Algerians, and so on requires sympathetic understanding.[9]

Paul's example is a challenging one. He was bicultural. He spent many years of life in Tarsus, a Gentile city. He knew the habits and jokes, the principles and prejudices of Gentiles. He could quote from their poets and philosophers and make the message of the kingdom compelling to them (Acts 14:15-17; 17:22-31). Yet he had lived for years as a rabbinical student in Jerusalem and knew Jewish ways from the inside (Acts 22:3-5; Phil. 3:4-6). His strategy of working first with Jews in a city and then turning to Gentiles was based on his biculturalism. He could authentically and effectively enter both worlds.

Underlying this approach was his theology of salvation. He was convinced that God's salvation comes by *hearing*. People must truly hear the Lord's voice in their own context if they are to be saved. Salvation comes by calling upon the name of the Lord. Paul's words in Romans 10:10-17 capture this conviction:

> For it is by our faith that we are put right with God; it is by our confession that we are saved.... As the scripture says, "Everyone who calls out to the Lord for help will be saved."
>
> But how can they call to him for help if they have not believed? And how can they believe if they have not heard the message? And how can they hear if the message is not proclaimed? And how can the message be proclaimed if the messengers are not sent out? ... So then, faith comes from hearing the message, and the message comes through preaching Christ.

The implications of these convictions are revolutionary for much evangelistic practice in our time. Here is a summary of a few of the implications.

1. People cannot obtain salvation through their own efforts or through religious activities. Salvation is an act of God that happens when people put their faith in Christ. To do this they must have knowledge of the gospel.

9. Bruce Olsen, *Bruchko* (Strang Communications, 1989); Don Richardson, *Peace Child* (1974).

2. The ability of people to respond appropriately to God's offer of salvation comes about when messengers bring the gospel to them. If no one is sent to them, there is no opportunity to hear. How many messengers need to be sent? According to Christ's symbolism of the sending of the twelve and the seventy-two, at least one to each tribe of Israel and one to each of the peoples of the world. Each group that is different enough in culture and self-identity to need a specifically tailored act of preaching will need a messenger. Each will need a unique strategy.

3. "Hearing" has a special meaning in Romans 10:14, 17. Hearing includes the idea of "hearing *and* understanding." The mere recitation of the words of the gospel or the handing out of a piece of literature is not "hearing" unless it generates understanding. The crucial question for Paul was not the amount of preaching, but the amount of hearing.

Communication is much more than simply the sending of a message. The target audience must be listening. The message must be clear and attractive. It must be comprehensible within the audience's own patterns of meaning. Because of differences between groups, the message will have to be presented in different ways, using different languages, illustrations, media, and spokespersons.

4. Hearing and understanding the message is no guarantee that it will be accepted. Preaching Christ is not an act of propaganda or coercion. Even in this passage Paul indicates sadly that "not all have accepted the Good News" (v. 16). Nevertheless, Paul made every effort to be sure rejection was willful rejection of an understood offer of God's gracious salvation.

Too often rejection comes because the message and the messenger are insensitive to the cultural barriers involved in the communication. What is rejected is a confusing and offensive mixture of the good news and the foreign cultural trappings of the messenger.

This is far too brief to do justice to Paul's people-centered approach. It is enough, however, to suggest how important this was in his evangelism. God himself gave us the most challenging example. He incarnated himself in the person of a Jewish boy in a small marginal village of Palestine. For nearly thirty years Jesus lived among the people. He spoke their language, ate their food, and learned their customs. He watched people live and die. He heard their questions and struggles. Only after learning about the inner soul of the Palestinian Jews did he begin to proclaim the kingdom of God. He was God's anointed messenger and apostle to the people of God. Yet he spent thirty years of apprenticeship before he began apostleship. He understood them so well that his words penetrated to the very heart of their motivations and the meanings they gave to their lives.

STEP 2: THE PEOPLE TO BE REACHED

Having finished his task, he then turned to his disciples and said, "Peace be with you. As the Father sent me, so send I you" (John 20:21). They now became God's sent ones. They too must live and learn the inner soul of the people to whom they are sent. We who continue that same mission cannot act as though we are greater than our Lord. We too must incarnate a strong and patient love that is sensitive to the people to whom we are sent.

We must communicate Christ in as clear and compelling a fashion as possible. This message will vary in its form with each messenger and with each distinctive people group. The Spirit of Christ alive within us will enable us to live and speak as Christ himself did. The Spirit will be our strength, peace, and counselor in the midst of the difficulties and ambiguities of ministry.

9. Defining and Describing Peoples and People Groups

Accepting a people-centered approach leads to a logical question. How do we decide that a collection of individuals or families is a *people or a people group?*

In other words, how do we put boundaries around a human population and say, "This is a valid target group—to it we need to send a specific messenger employing a unique strategy"? How dissimilar must two people groups be before they each need a specially tailored contexualization of the gospel or their own separate indigenous church institutions? Does a people-centered approach foster divisions that are contrary to the unity of the body of Christ?

THE DEBATE ABOUT MONO-ETHNIC CHURCHES

These are not easy questions to answer. Almost no one would dispute the idea that separate language groups require separate institutions and worship services. It does not make sense to force the Kikuyu to learn Luo, or vice versa, in order to become Christian. The miracle of Pentecost shows that God wants his kingdom message put into all languages.

The question gets far more controversial when the differences between people are within a so-called single language group. These differences are matters of education, social class or caste, race or life-style. There is a significant controversy over the legitimacy of mono-ethnic (or mono-class, mono-racial) churches that result from people-oriented evangelism. This leads to a tension between indigeneity and self-determination on the one side and the unity of the church on the other.[1]

One problem is the different meanings mono-ethnic churches have in different social contexts. In South Africa they reinforce and express the dreadful system of apartheid. Separation sustains the power and privileges of the white minority. In other contexts, such as the Korean language churches of Southern California, they are voluntary in nature. They provide a place where the Korean immigrant can worship in his or her native language. Leadership is indigenous and the issues dealt with are related to the immigrant life situation. They are effective centers for evangelizing other Koreans who might never think of attending an Anglo-American congregation.

There is a very real dilemma here. The Bible registers strong concern for the demonstrable unity of the people of God across cultural prejudices and social distinctions. At the same time it does not seek to efface those distinctions. The church is a unity with diversity, a spiritual unity that enriches rather than erases cultural diversity. The gospel preserves the rich variety of culture. It does not destroy it.

Yet the very preservation of cultural differences often also preserves attitudes of cultural superiority and exclusiveness. The attempt to transcend or ignore the cultural differences leads to a nonindigenous, artificial church without power to evangelize its own group. A truly indigenous church is rooted in the soil of the local culture of its own people.

There is no widely accepted answer to this dilemma. It may be that giving priority to one side or the other depends on the particular context. Unity is imperative. Love and justice require mutual respect and trust across social and cultural distinctions within the church. Christ's atonement means reconciliation at the human level, not just between God and human beings. Every Christian is called upon to give up social and cultural arrogance and superiority without surrendering social solidarity and cultural distinctiveness. How to do that in multi-cultural settings is a difficult matter.

The Church Growth movement stresses the empirical fact that mono-ethnic churches on average grow more rapidly than multi-ethnic ones. David Barrett's survey of churches worldwide shows "that people join mono-ethnic churches everywhere; and only join [multi-ethnic] conglomerates where there is no mono-ethnic alternative" (1979, p. 276). Issues of leadership do not get entangled with the larger social struggle

---

1. Lausanne Committee, *Pasadena Consultation;* Wagner, 1978; McGavran, 1979; Shenk, 1973; Conn, 1976; Dubose, 1978.

between social groups. People feel comfortable because they can use their own native language and govern themselves.

The critics of the Church Growth movement argue from the theological point of reconciliation. If the church does not reconcile people on the horizontal level, it is hard to see that their vertical reconciliation with God is authentic. If we cannot love the person we can see, how can we love God whom we have not seen (1 John 4:19-21)? How can one have genuine church growth if it does not mean reconciliation? Church growth that does not go beyond numbers counted on membership lists is defective. The quality of discipleship is crucial and cannot be ignored in evaluating various sorts of church growth.

This is not an issue we can settle in a few pages. There are thousands of people groups who need indigenous churches in their midst. Only then can we begin to hope that the barriers between peoples might have a chance at being pulled down. We must not hide the demands of the gospel when we proclaim its benefits and blessings. Yet neither can we insist that the barriers come down first before we offer the gospel to peoples not previously discipled.

THE HOMOGENEOUS UNIT AND PEOPLE GROUP EVANGELIZATION

Perhaps the sharpest way in which this issue appears is in the criticism of the homogeneous unit principle (HUP). David Bosch claims that the HUP is based on the same theological justifications as the theology that buttresses the racially segregated churches of South Africa. René Padilla claims that the HUP has no biblical justification. Some see it as reinforcing sinful distinctions and divisions in human communities. We must ask if these criticisms apply also to the people group approach. Does people group evangelization lead to a fragmented and divided church? Does it reinforce social divisiveness rather than reconcile social groups at odds with one another?

We have already attempted to provide some of the biblical foundations for a people group approach. However, we have done little to deal with the objection that it leads to or at least reinforces racism, classism, and other forms of structural injustice.

The Pasadena Consultation—Homogeneous Units (LCWE, 1978) offers the most balanced account of the HUP and its application. Stated simply, the principle is that the church grows best when planted in social groups that are ethnically and socially homogeneous. In church planting we are to *allow* (not require) people to be gathered into congregations that are homogeneous in their cultural and social characteristics. Donald McGavran and his colleagues at Fuller Theological Seminary have been the chief advocates of this principle.

The problem with the principle is how to reconcile it with the theological imperative of reconciliation within the church. One of the marks of the authentic church is oneness. The Nicene Creed states: "we believe one holy catholic and apostolic Church." Paul constantly worked for reconciliation and accommodation between Christians of Jewish and Gentile origins in his congregations.

While we have not chosen to base our approach on the HUP, there are obvious affinities. People groups are sociologically bounded groups of people whose perceptions, understandings, and response to the gospel are relatively uniform. There are certain dimensions of experience and existence in which there is perceived homogeneity. From this point of view they can be called "homogeneous units."

Yet our definition (see Chap. 5, p. 28) stresses the subjective sense of groupness rather than an objective set of shared characteristics. As McGavran classically defined it, a homogeneous unit is "a section of society in which all members have some characteristic in common" (1970, p. 85). We stress the subjective sense of peoplehood or identity that is derived from shared characteristics. So our people group approach is somewhat differently focused than the classic HUP.

Nonetheless, what about the charge that these similar approaches share the same defect: they reinforce a divided church that simply reflects the tensions and divisions that are present in society because of sin?

The realities of communication and ministry are that we never communicate Christ except in a cultural and social context. People perceive or hear the gospel only within their context. God brought about the original linguistic and cultural diversity that led to the contemporary variety and multiplicity of social divisions (Gen. 11). The people group approach acknowledges this reality and builds upon it. It seeks to meet people where they are, not where we would like them to be.

Yet it seeks to meet them where they are with all of the gospel. Sin has tainted the legitimate differences in language, culture, and ethnicity—yet the gospel will challenge those patterns. It will address ethnocentrism, racism, classism, and institutional and structural injustices. Christ's reality is a transforming reality. He comes to us as we are, but he does not leave us as we are.

Furthermore, the people group approach may lead to evangelization strategies that encompass nonhomogeneous units. Schreck and Barrett have put it well:

> People groups are not necessarily homogeneous units. To evangelize, to bring the good news of Jesus Christ to all, might mean that the people group most appropriately defined for the purposes of evangelism would include class divisions or other forms of divisions due to structural injustices. It might be multiethnic. It might be multilingual (a trade language could be the most appropriate linguistic medium of the Church). . . . Fast changing realignments of ethnicity or institutionalized patterns of injustices might require non-homogeneous peoples to be our concern for ministry. In the former case, effective evangelization would be to an audience which is multiethnic. In the latter, the need to confront injustice and evangelize in a way that allows people to see Jesus Christ in his full truth would require ministering to a people group fractured by class or other types of division. The most appropriate people groups for the purposes of evangelism are often, but not always, "homogeneous." (1987, pp. 27-28)

MEMBERSHIP IN GROUPS

Throughout our lifetime we spend much of our time in groups with other people. We are born into a family. As we grow older, we become part of play groups and school classes. Later we are members of clubs and associations. We form cliques and groups of friends. We work in organizations that put us into many different work groups.

Out of these group experiences we develop into the kind of people we are. The majority of what we know we learn in groups. We are conditioned to understand and conform to a set of customs and ideas. Our personalities are formed by the way people relate to us, especially in families and friendships. Groups are crucial to the way we become adults.

The church is a group. It is a fellowship of sharing, a *koinonia*. Its solidarity comes from the unifying effects of the Spirit of God. Because he is active we are able to express and experience love and commonness. Paul's image of the body of Christ portrays the interconnection of fellow Christians.

Social scientists have devised a large number of terms to classify the fantastic range of human groups. Some of them are: the nuclear family, the extended family, moiety, deme, sib, clan, kindred, and lineage. Other terms are: social class, caste, status group, voluntary association, primary group, secondary group, and reference groups. Some of the residential clusters are: villages, hamlets, towns, cities, mega-cities, and suburbs. Still other terms describe whole societies: band, tribe, chieftainship, and nation. The full list is much longer than these examples. Which of these or others are a people group? What is a people group?

WHAT ARE PEOPLES AND PEOPLE GROUPS?

We have already suggested a simple definition (see p. 28). Here we must explore the question more fully. It is helpful to approach it as broadly as possible. Harley Schreck and David Barrett suggest a distinction between a global and a particularistic focus.[2]

The global focus considers the whole world and classifies individuals in terms of ethnicity, language, and political boundaries. Each person is considered as belonging to one and only one group. The particularistic focus is concerned with a group of individuals in the context of their social and cultural life. Individuals may belong to several overlapping groups that influence their identity and response patterns.

When we consider the world in global focus we tend to classify individuals in terms of *peoples:* "a human population with a common language, shared ethnicity, and significant pattern of social interaction."[3] There are ethnolinguistic peoples such as the Moroccan Arabs in France, the Hispanics of New York City, the Chinese of Canada, the Armenians of the Soviet Union. There may be a great deal of sociocultural diversity within these groups. But they are grouped together because of broadly shared ethnic bonds and linguistic-cultural traditions.

When we consider the world in particularistic focus we classify individuals in terms of *people groups:*

> a significantly large sociological grouping of individuals who perceive themselves to have a common affinity for one another. From the viewpoint of evangelization this is the largest group within which the gospel can spread without encountering barriers of understanding or acceptance.

These are more finely defined groups such as Moroccan university students in Lyon, France, Guatemalan refugees in Manhattan, Cantonese restaurant workers in Toronto, and Armenian factory workers in Azer-

---

2. *Unreached Peoples: Clarifying the Task* (MARC, 1987), pp. 6ff.
3. Ibid., p. 6.

baijan. People groups are bound together by a variety of forces including residence, class, occupation, ideology, education, political status, and so on.

We can illustrate the difference by considering mainland China. We often speak of "the Chinese," meaning the population that inhabits the political territory of China proper. Yet we also are aware that China is divided between the Han Chinese (ethnically Chinese) and the so-called minority peoples who are ethnically distinct. Even within the Han Chinese there are dozens of dialects of spoken Chinese: Mandarin, Cantonese, Teo-Chiu, Wu, Hakka, Amoy, and so on. Many of these spoken dialects are as different as English is from German. The written characters used by the dialects are basically the same. This enables the country to be unified at the written level. Increasingly the Beijing dialect of Mandarin is becoming the standard spoken language.

If we are speaking at the ethno-linguistic *people* level, then we speak of the Chinese as though their subdivisions and sociogeographical differences were not important. If we are speaking at the *people group* level, then the differences of dialect, geography, and internal social distinctions that the Chinese themselves make become crucial.

The picture is even more complex when we consider the Chinese worldwide. Those who are ethnically Chinese live in more than ninety countries. There are 3.6 million in Indonesia who no longer speak any Chinese dialect. An equally large number live in Thailand. Many have intermarried with the Thai and taken Thai names, nationality, and language.

The Chinese as an ethnic people are divided into numerous people groups with strikingly different social customs and attitudes. They would have as much difficulty being socially intimate with one another as an American with a Russian or as an Oxford educated industrialist with a semi-literate dockworker.

Schreck and Barrett (1987) give examples from ten different sorts of sociologically defined people groups. We list some of them here as examples of the sorts of groups whose life situation and social identity are such that they are good subjects for evangelization strategies:

1. Sociolinguistic groups (which may subsume several ethnic groups): English speakers in Guadalajara.
2. Sociogeographical groups: Aborigines in Brisbane, Japanese in Kenya, Bengalis in London.
3. Sociopolitical groups: Hmong refugees in Thailand, Sudanese repatriates, USSR Kirghiz refugee shepherds in Afghanistan.

4. Socioreligious groups: Bengali Sufis, Druzes in Israel, Jews in Winnipeg, Parsis in India, rural Vodun believers in Haiti.
5. Socioeducational groups: Chinese students in Australia, pension students in Madrid, youth in Toronto Peanut District.
6. Socioeconomic groups, specifically the poor: Favelados in Rio de Janeiro, squatters in Manila, street people in Victoria, slum dwellers in Madras.
7. Socioeconomic groups, specifically the elite: Copacabana apartment dwellers, Patels (a commercial caste in India), Cebu (Philippines) middle class.
8. Sociomedical groups: the blind of the Philippines, deaf Japanese, lepers of central Thailand, the handicapped of Singapore.
9. Sociodeviant groups: dead-end kids in Amsterdam, prostitutes in Abidjan, drug addicts in São Paulo, gays in San Francisco.
10. Socio-occupational groups: Becak drivers in Bandung (Indonesia), Chinese restaurant workers in France, factory workers in Manila, bus girls in Seoul, Korean army personnel, Turkana fishing community, Hong Kong police.

What is distinctive about these groups is that they all have various social, cultural, and political boundaries about them that often act as barriers to the communication of the gospel. Only by exploring the nature of their "groupness" can we devise a strategy. In some cases this strategy may be a bridge from pre-existing churches that aims at bringing them into those congregations. In other cases it may mean establishing a new, indigenous congregation, specially designed and suited to the people group in question.

10. *Understanding Peoples and People Groups*

To describe a people is one thing. To understand them is another. We can define a people group quickly, but it takes years to penetrate its secrets.

Understanding is the chief currency of successful evangelism. It enables us to touch the inner springs that motivate and sustain a people group. Understanding enables us to dramatize how Christ cares about the deepest hopes and highest aspirations of a group.

The greatest parable of such understanding is Christ himself. So thoroughly did he know his people and its various people groups after thirty years that he could say the right things at the right time. He opened channels of communication his own people did not know existed. They said of him, "No one teaches like him." He could read their body language so well that he knew what individuals around him were thinking. His understanding was the result of acute listening, questioning, observing, living, and absorbing life about him for thirty years. We who claim to be his disciples can do no better than to follow his example.

THREE-DIMENSIONAL UNDERSTANDING

To probe deeply into the heart of a people is to go far beyond the objective questions that describe a people group. It is to reach the foundational meanings and motivations that make them live the way they do. It is to see the world the way they see it. Understanding a people group means discovering their answer to the question: What is life all about? Charles Taber has written:

The evangelist, before planning his approach, must discover what assumptions the hearer holds about reality, truth, and value; and more important, must be keenly aware of what problems deeply trouble the hearer, so that he can maximize the fit of the Gospel presentation to the hearer's needs. This is what Jacob A. Loewen has called "scratching where it itches." Such an adaptation presupposes on the part of the evangelist more or less extended, more or less intimate contact with the hearer in a variety of social situations, and a keen sensitivity and awareness of what social scientists call the paramessage of the situation. True evangelism rarely flourishes in isolation from the whole of life, it rarely succeeds in reaching and transforming a man by operating in a vacuum or at a distance. (1973, pp. 121-22)

No simple scheme can provide all the elements needed in searching for an answer. Yet it is helpful to have places to begin the search for understanding. We find it useful to stress three dimensions of a people group's life: meanings, needs, and behaviors. As evangelists we are looking for ways to bridge the gospel into a culture different from our own (McGavran, 1955).

There are several bridges that we can use. "Bridging concepts and symbols" within the language and lore of a people can serve as conduits of Christian reality (Richardson, 1974). "Bridging needs" are close to the inner psycho-social-emotional core of a people. These are needs that the claims and promises of the kingdom can meet. There are also "bridging customs, behaviors and relationships," in which the gospel can be embodied in a culturally authentic way.

Each of these dimensions is crucial because of its significance to the task of communicating Christ. The first deals with what a people thinks and how they think. Their perceptions and interpretations of the world and life are the filters through which they will understand Christian communication. Their language and patterns of reasoning are the only tools they have to make sense of this "new religion." If it does not make sense, they will reject it.

The second deals with the matter of relevance. People who see the kingdom of God as peripheral to their basic issues will ignore or reject it. They experience the kingdom as vital when it meets important needs as the people group defines and feels those needs. If the way we present Christ makes him *appear* unrelated to their hurts and hopes, they will perceive him as unrelated.

The third deals with the matter of cultural appearance. Behavior patterns, social roles and structures, and social relationships pattern the external texture of everyday life. Christianity is always incarnated

106

through certain external patterns of roles and actions. If it appears only in Western garb, it will be no surprise that people will treat it as alien. Cultural authenticity happens when Christianity is no longer a stranger in the land.

Christianity must be incarnated in these three ways (meanings, needs, and behavior patterns) in each distinct people of the world. *If Christianity is not culturally authentic, it can never gain the vitality it needs to transform a culture from within.* We will briefly examine each of these three dimensions in this chapter.

THE MEANING SYSTEM OF PEOPLES AND PEOPLE GROUPS

People continually attempt to make sense of their world. Deep anxiety strikes when everyday living loses its meaningfulness. All peoples develop systems of meanings to give order to the experiences they have of the world. They explain what the universe is like, what sorts of things exist, why they exist, what they can expect from life, how to understand death. They even tell a people how to communicate with others about common and uncommon events.

Symbols and cognitive maps make up meaning systems. These provide labels, perspectives, interpretations, and explanations of experience. When effective they provide coherence to life. Such systems are learned. Children are surrounded by them so that when they are adults they perceive and understand the world by those systems. They find other systems of meanings obscure, difficult, absurd, even evil.

It is as though we were born extremely nearsighted. Until we receive a pair of glasses, we cannot bring anything into clear focus. Our culture provides us with the lenses by which to see. But once our eyes grow accustomed to the lenses, it is difficult to put on another pair. When we do, the world seems akilter and askew. Wearers of cultural lenses feel there is no other way to see the world. Each people assumes the way they see the world is the way the world really is.

Putting on the lenses of another culture is the lifelong task of the cross-cultural evangelist. It is not easy. Looking at things long enough through those new lenses will surprise us. We will see aspects of reality and the gospel we never saw with our first pair of glasses.

STEP 2: THE PEOPLE TO BE REACHED

Making Sense of Things

There are a number of components that together make up the meaning systems in which we all participate.[1]

1. Language

Each language is a symbolic system of codes. It labels the world and thus assigns meaning to it. Through these verbal symbols people can communicate with one another. Each language labels the world differently from other languages. People do not live in the same world with different labels. Rather, because their labels differ, they live in different worlds.

Language is fundamental to every people's identity and ability to survive as a relatively unified group that cooperates in common ventures.[2] Apart from an understanding of the actual verbal communication patterns of a people, it is doubtful that an evangelist can enter into their mind and communicate the gospel effectively.[3]

1. Hesselgrave, *Communicating*, pp. 121-271; Hiebert, 1985, pp. 141-69.
2. Some excellent examples on language and communication are works by Brewster (1977), Larson and Smalley (1972), and Eugene Nida (1957, 1964, 1974).
3. Language learning and the use of the vernacular is crucial to missions. Yet there is still a great deal of inertia and resistance to the full mastery of languages. At the 1979 meeting of the American Society of Missiology, Dr. Nida summed up more than thirty year's experience. Through acquaintance with nearly three thousand missionaries, Dr. Nida reached these conclusions:

> Despite the valiant efforts of numerous missionaries to master strange unwritten languages and the considerable success which a few persons have had in doing so, verbal communication for the most part has been poor and often seriously misleading. Almost all early Bible translations in so-called "new languages" have been found to be seriously deficient. Many of them are so literal that people have found them difficult to understand. In Africa, for example, many persons have had to read the Scriptures in English, French, or Portuguese first in order to know what they meant in their own native languages. . . .
>
> In comparison with the level of linguistic adequacy in the Scriptures, the level of missionaries' proficiency in oral use of Third World languages has been even worse. Despite the fact that most of the languages in Africa south of the Sahara have tonal distinctions which are extremely important, not only in distinguishing words but in marking grammatical relationships, very few missionaries have ever learned to use the tones correctly. . . .
>
> Though for the most part missionaries were often conscious of their linguistic handicaps and desired more time and help in learning local languages, the mission boards which sent them to the field were usually far less sensitive to the problems of verbal communication. . . . On numerous occasions I have pled with missionary leaders to take more seriously the problems of verbal communication, but only rarely have I experienced a positive response. ("Why Are Foreigners So Queer?" pp. 2-3)

2. Hermeneutics

Languages are codes to label experience and identify its components. The hermeneutics of a people refers to its system for *interpreting* and understanding the significance of that labeled experience. It has to do with how people think, the processes by which they interpret, explain, and understand the basic information received by the senses and labeled by their language.

Hermeneutics deals with how they formulate conclusions. What roles do syllogistic reasoning, proverbs, intuitive leaps play? What is considered adequate evidence and what counts as factual? The hermeneutical procedures of a people give them ways to understand new ideas and new practices. Hermeneutics concerns the way language is used in order to secure the principles and patterns that guide life and thought.

3. Worldview

When we consider a people's *total response* to their universe, we touch their basic assumptions about experience (Hiebert, 1976, p. 356). A worldview is "the central governing set of conceptions and presuppositions that [a] society lives by" (M. Kraft, 1978, p. 4). It is the framework into which all other thoughts and concepts are placed. It is made up of a set of themes that pattern the perceptions of what is real or unreal, what is possible and impossible (C. Kraft, 1979, p. 53).

The worldview is a *gestalt* within which all understanding of the world takes place. Normally the hermeneutical and linguistic systems of a people reflect and give expression to the worldview. The result is a self-sustaining, mutually reinforcing system of beliefs and perspectives that give meaning to almost all of life.

Peoples hold very different worldviews and consequently come to very different conclusions from the "same facts." When Paul was bitten by a poisonous snake (Acts 28:1-6), the people of Mileta concluded he was a god because he did not die. Had a modern Western scientist been present, he or she probably would have concluded that the snake was not poisonous. Differences in assumptions about the reality of the spirit world, the appearance of gods in human forms, and the existence of microscopic toxins would all produce different ways of explaining the event.

These three components are all deeply involved with the religious system of a people. The distinctive philosophy and religious outlook of a group give specific content to the worldview and the hermeneutic processes at work. This content is carried in myths, stories, folk tales, or scriptures. Here are found explanations as to who God is, what the spirit realm is like, and how these relate to the human realm.

Even the various rituals contain implicit if not explicit notions of the basic nature of the universe and the place of human beings in it. What is evil and how human beings can avoid it or neutralize it are dramatized by religious beliefs and rituals. Religion is one of the key systems of meaning that expresses how language, hermeneutics, and worldview shape people in their quest for significance.

Beginning with a People Group's Understandings

Meaning systems are important because they serve to make sense or nonsense of Christian communication. We all learn by moving from the known to the unknown. For an unreached people the gospel is the unknown. The known is made up of what is already present in their meaning systems.

People come to the gospel with prior concepts of justice, love, mercy, evil, and law. They already have sophisticated and thoughtful ways of explaining common events. They can tell you why people get ill and how the spirits or God help in healing. They have schemes about space and time, marriage and child-rearing, honesty and sharing. They have definite ideas about how God speaks to humans and what he or she is likely to say. All of these influence the way they hear and interpret the gospel.

Bible translation has to deal with meaning systems all the time.[4] Employing just the right words, phrases, and grammatical ordering is important for conveying the original sense of biblical passages.

The problems of Bible translation are symptomatic of the larger problem of the transculturation of Christian faith into new cultural contexts. The gospel is to be translated not only in word, but also in deed. If we are to make known "all things whatsoever he has commanded," then we must have a good mastery of meaning systems.[5]

Concern with the essential meaning of Christian faith as expressed in particular cultures is natural, given the importance of the goal. The validity or nonvalidity of communicating Christ is at stake. Ambiguous choices that could change the course of evangelization face the evan-

---

4. Nida, 1964, 1974; Wonderly, 1968; Kasdorf, 1978.
5. There is a large number of books dealing with discovering and utilizing the meaning systems of a people group. To indicate a few resources: Khair-Ullah, 1976; Accad, 1976; Loewen, 1976; C. Kraft, 1977; Ahrens, 1977; Hwang, 1977; Taber, 1978; Corwin, 1978; Kelley, 1978; Hiebert, 1985.

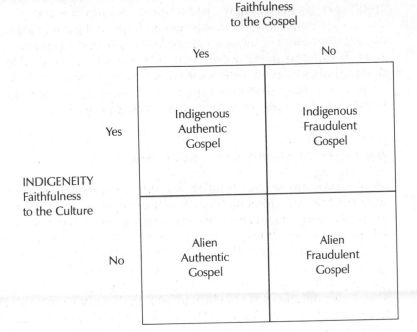

AUTHENTICITY
Faithfulness
to the Gospel

Yes   No

| | Yes | Indigenous Authentic Gospel | Indigenous Fraudulent Gospel |

INDIGENEITY
Faithfulness
to the Culture

| | No | Alien Authentic Gospel | Alien Fraudulent Gospel |

FIGURE 10.1   AN AUTHENTIC INDIGENOUS GOSPEL

gelist. What one mission agency or church may consider a confusion and compromise, another may see as a creative breakthrough.

This tension exists because we must communicate the authentic and unadulterated message of Christ, yet we must do it within meaning systems we don't well understand. We seek authenticity (faithfulness to the gospel) and indigeneity (faithfulness to the particular culture). There are four possible patterns we could follow. Figure 10.1 characterizes these possibilities.

We can offer a fraudulent gospel in foreign cultural terms. We can offer the true gospel in foreign terms. In both cases the gospel probably will not become deeply rooted among a people group. We can also offer a sham gospel in indigenous cultural terms or the true gospel in indigenous terms. This last is our goal. Without indigenization there is no meaningful encounter of religious systems. Nor is there an intelligent opportunity to say yes to Jesus Christ (Nida, 1960, pp. 184-88). Without the attempt at contextualization or indigenization, we risk confusion, offense, or even syncretism, a mixture of Christ and paganism often called Christo-paganism.

The Christian faith and practice that the cross-cultural missionary brings is itself questionable. Even we in the West have a mixture of authentic gospel and Western culture, and often are not sure of the boundaries between the two. Some observers speak of our own Christo-paganism (Christo-Americanism). Many Christians in the USA combine consumerism, patriotism (if not jingoism), the "American way of life," individualistic self-fulfillment, and the gospel of wealth and health with Christ.[6] This heady combination often results in the culture not being transformed. Rather, it tames Christ and makes him a mascot of the culture.

Nevertheless, we seek indigeneity or contextualization because we wish to follow the example of the New Testament. It took captive words and symbols of the culture of its day and put them into the service of communicating God's revelation. They used terms such as *resurrection, agape* (love), and *logos* (word, thing). This was not indiscriminate. Certain terminologies and approaches were rejected as incompatible (Bruce, 1977).

Careful study of the New Testament reveals how this process took place. The *Theological Dictionary of the New Testament* (Kittel and Friedrich, eds., 1964–1974) shows how Greek and Hebrew terms did not fully convey the sense of revelation. Nonetheless, God's people took them up, associated them with biblical narratives, and used them. By their use over time their meanings were transformed so that they increasingly came to convey the full weight of intended meaning.

New Testament study also reveals that the early church did not resort to "borrowed words," transliterated from another language and culture. Some resort to this practice on the theory that indigenous categories are impossible to convey key biblical ideas. But the early Christians entered the cultural worlds of their day as best they could. Then they boldly gave witness to Jesus Christ as Lord and Redeemer.

Several parts of the Willowbank Report on gospel and culture address this same issue:

> God's personal self-disclosure in the Bible was given in terms of the hearers' own culture. So we have asked ourselves what light it throws on our task of cross-cultural communication today.
>
> The biblical writers made critical use of whatever cultural mate-

6. Herberg, 1960; Berger, 1961; Sider, 1977; Quebedeaux, 1978; Dayton, 1984; Bellah, 1985.

rial was available to them for the expression of their message. For example, the Old Testament refers several times to the Babylonian sea monster named "Leviathan," while the form of God's "covenant" with his people resembles the ancient Hittite Suzerain's "treaty" with his vassals. The writers also made incidental use of the conceptual imagery of the "three-tiered" universe, though they did not thereby affirm a pre-Copernican cosmology. We do something similar when we talk about the sun "rising" and "setting."

Similarly, New Testament language and thought-forms are steeped in both Jewish and Hellenistic cultures, and Paul seems to have drawn from the vocabulary of Greek philosophy. But the process by which the biblical authors borrowed words and images from their cultural milieu, and used them creatively, was controlled by the Holy Spirit so that they purged them of false or evil implications and thus transformed them into vehicles of truth and goodness.

Sensitive cross-cultural witnesses will not arrive at their sphere of service with a pre-packaged gospel. They must have a clear grasp of the "given" truth of the gospel. But they will fail to communicate successfully if they try to impose this on people without reference to their own cultural situation and that of the people to whom they go. It is only by active, loving engagement with the local people, thinking in their thought patterns, understanding their world-view, listening to their questions, and feeling their burdens, that the whole believing community (of which the missionary is a part) will be able to respond to their need. By common prayer, thought and heart-searching, in dependence on the Holy Spirit, expatriate and local believers may learn together how to present Christ and contextualize the gospel with an equal degree of faithfulness and relevance. (Lausanne Committee, 1978, pp. 7-8, 14)

What a People Group Knows about the Gospel

Some people know absolutely nothing about Christianity, the church, or Jesus Christ. The number of these people has decreased dramatically in the twentieth century. David Barrett's measures of evangelization (focused on *exposure* to the gospel) suggest this conclusion. Many unreached peoples already have some information about Christ, even if it is incorrect or distorted. Knowing the depth and nature of a people's prior knowledge and attitude toward Christ and the church is important in devising a strategy.

People go through several changes of knowledge and attitude before they are ready to acknowledge Christ as Lord. The process of internalizing and evaluating the meaning of Christian faith continues even

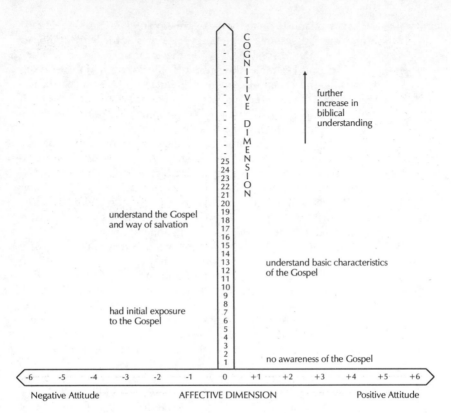

FIGURE 10.2   SØGAARD'S TWO-DIMENSIONAL STRATEGY MODEL

after such an acknowledgment. Sociologists and psychologists have dealt extensively with this idea. Studies on the diffusion of innovation have similar conclusions.[7]

There are a number of models of how knowledge of the Christian faith is part of a process of making a commitment to Christ.[8] The clearest and most useful model is a two-dimensional one suggested by Viggo Søgaard. The vertical axis is cognitive. As knowledge and understanding of Christian faith increases, a person or people group's location would move upward. The horizontal axis is affective with the negative feelings on the left, positive on the right. Figure 10.2 portrays Søgaard's model.

7. Rogers and Shoemaker, 1971; Engel et al., 1973; Janis and Mann, 1977.
8. Søgaard, 1975; Engel, 1979, pp. 182-83, 225; 1986, pp. 49, 65.

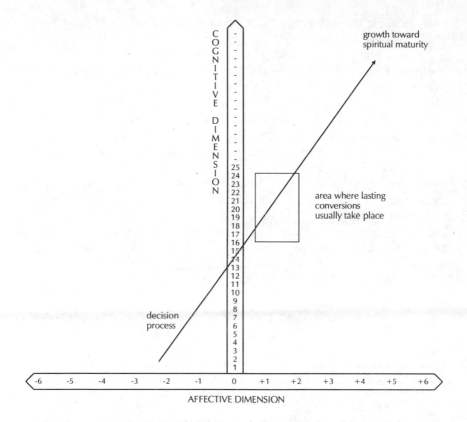

**FIGURE 10.3   SPIRITUAL PROGRESS AND THE ZONE
OF LASTING CONVERSION**

There is no fixed conversion point on the chart because it can take place at almost any point along the cognitive or affective axes. Some people know almost nothing about Christ, yet encounter and embrace him. They will need a heavy input of knowledge about him if they are to grow in grace. Others know many of the details as well as main outlines of biblical truth when they come to Christ. Their need is to express that knowledge in active obedience. The desired movement is toward the upper right hand corner. There we find people knowledgeable and positive in their relationship with Christ.

The point of decision most frequently occurs in a zone where knowledge is adequate and attitude has shifted to positive. There is no uniform process by which a decision for Christ takes place and the journey toward maturity continues. Changes within the person may fluctuate between cognitive and affective dimensions, or take place in both at the same time.

Søgaard argues that conversion is largely a matter of crossing the line from negative to positive. On the cognitive dimension, that crossing can take place almost anywhere. Nonetheless, Søgaard hypothesizes that for most it takes place somewhere beyond the point where the gospel and way of salvation are understood. Figure 10.3 characterizes the location where lasting conversions frequently happen.[9]

On the basis of research, we can locate individuals and even groups of people on this graph. Differences of awareness and attitude can then become the basis for selecting various sorts of methods and approaches. If the task is to raise the awareness of a people who know next to nothing about Christ and the gospel, then a method that stresses the conveying of gospel information is strategic. If the task is to change a negative or indifferent attitude among people who know the basics of the gospel, then a method that focuses on attitude change is strategic.

Søgaard illustrates various audience positions in Figure 10.4.

> On this example "A" may be a tribal group with next to no awareness of the Christian gospel, but they are not really opposed or negative towards the gospel. "B" may be a group of young people in a western country. They have been brought up in a Christian context, but they have been turned off by the church. . . . "C" is a field ripe for harvest. "D" is a new Christian, who has just accepted Christ as his Savior and Lord. "E" is a church which has been well taught in the Scriptures, but is pretty "cold" in their devotional life. "F" is a church which has had little teaching but excels in spiritual life and devotion. Each of these audiences will need a different approach, and different strategies will need to be worked out to facilitate true spiritual growth. (Søgaard, Ph.D. Diss., pp. 251-52)

UNDERSTANDING THE NEEDS OF PEOPLES AND PEOPLE GROUPS

Evangelization takes place in the context of human needs. A study of the ministry of Christ impresses us with how he constantly responded to obvious needs of individuals and groups. He healed the blind, the lame, and lepers. He blessed children and fed the hungry. He instructed those

9. Viggo Søgaard, "Applying Christian Communication," doctoral thesis, University Microfilms International, Ann Arbor, Michigan, 1986.

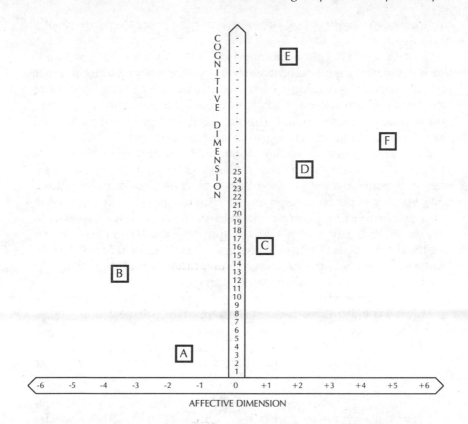

FIGURE 10.4   ILLUSTRATION OF VARIOUS AUDIENCE LOCATIONS

who sought the truth, forgave the guilty, accepted outcasts, and re-assured the fearful. He was sensitive to the deep needs of people and broke social conventions in order to help those in need.

The words that Christ shared about the kingdom of God were masterful expressions within the meaning systems of his day. But they also were masterfully in touch with the hurts and hopes of his people and the people groups of Palestine. He sensed the different needs and spoke differently to persons with different needs. To the woman at the well he spoke of the living water. Nicodemus heard about being born again. The rich young ruler, possessed by his possessions, heard the words, "Sell all. Give it to the poor. Come and follow me." To each Jesus particularized the meaning of the kingdom.

Needs Are Defined by Groups

What people feel deeply is profoundly affected by their culture. Needs are not abstract, disembodied realities. They are particular hurts or hopes that cause people joy or anguish. However, what an affluent American sees as an absolute necessity may seem an unimaginable luxury to a penniless and homeless person. Needs are relative to people in their social and cultural situations. They grow accustomed to certain life expectations that govern what they hope for and what makes them hurt.

Just as the gospel needs to be contexualized within the meaning systems of a people group, so also *it needs to be contextualized within the needs of a people or people group as they define them.* The meaning systems of a people group shape what they perceive to be their needs. No one would seriously suggest that a people learn our language so we can tell them the gospel of Christ. We accept a people's language as a given. We learn its vocabulary, grammar, structures, and meanings. We then particularize the gospel within that language.

We must also accept as a given the needs of a people *as they define them.* We must labor to learn the aspirations, drives, motivations, hopes, fears, and needs of a people group. The gospel must "scratch where they itch" or it will appear irrelevant to them.

We heartily affirm the spirit of the Willowbank Report where it says:

> There is the humility to begin our communication where people actually are and not where we would like them to be. This is what we see Jesus doing, and we desire to follow his example. Too often we have ignored people's fears and frustrations, their pains and preoccupations, and their hunger, poverty, deprivation or oppression, in fact their "felt needs," and have been too slow to rejoice or to weep with them. We acknowledge that these "felt needs" may sometimes be symptoms of deeper needs which are not immediately felt or recognized by the people. A doctor does not necessarily accept a patient's self-diagnosis. Nevertheless, we see the need to begin where people are, but not to stop there. We accept our responsibility gently and patiently to lead them on to see themselves, as we see ourselves, as rebels to whom the gospel directly speaks with a message of pardon and hope. To begin where people are not is to share an irrelevant message; to stay where people are and never lead them on to the fulness of God's good news, is to share a truncated gospel. The humble sensitivity of love will avoid both errors. (Lausanne Committee, 1978, p. 16)

Jesus Christ is Lord of all. His concern and control encompasses all that is human. The hungers of the body as well as the hungers of the spirit are deeply impressed upon the love of God. Clothing, housing, and health are all part of the concern of the church. "What God the Father considers to be pure and genuine religion is this: to take care of orphans and widows in their suffering and to keep oneself from being corrupted by the world" (Jas. 1:27).

Jesus touched all of these needs as he went about Palestine proclaiming God's kingdom. He dealt with more than subjectively felt needs. He was acutely aware of the objective discrepancy between what the world is and what the kingdom of God is. He not only met needs, he also challenged attitudes and structures that unnecessarily blocked people from entering the kingdom of God. Until Christ brings the fullness of the kingdom, we must proclaim and live out the good news in the context of the human hopes and hurts that surround us.

Culture Shapes Needs

Culture is an adaptive mechanism. It provides people with ideas and tools to meet the full range of their needs. Yet no culture is completely successful in meeting all the needs of its people. One of the results of sin is that cultures everywhere have demonic as well as admirable qualities.

Every society has unresolved tensions. Groups within society struggle with each other over scarce resources and use the culture against one another. Society brings people together in friendship and cooperation only to make them intimate enemies. Humans are sociable and antagonistic at the same time. The various valued aspects such as personality, physique, intelligence, and wealth are unevenly distributed. People have resentments, tensions, satisfactions, and fears of various sorts. These give daily life its emotional tone.

Knowledge of these needs is important to evangelism. People normally are reluctant to make new religious commitments. They are wary of new claims that differ from the traditions of their parents and people group. This is often coupled with a tendency to punish or reject those who do make a new commitment. People are unlikely to give serious consideration to the Christian faith unless they have experienced elements of strong dissatisfaction with their current tradition. Change happens where there is discontent with the way things are.

Normally discontent is as much unconscious as it is conscious. There is an interactive effect between agents who stimulate change and the target group that considers it. That is, appeals do not create needs into which the offered solution fits. They can bring that need into clearer focus among the target group.

119

STEP 2: THE PEOPLE TO BE REACHED

How can we discover the hopes and hurts of a people or a people group? It may seem simple, but the easiest way is to listen to them. Ask them about their life. Just be sure to ask six or ten people. Ask later respondents to react to what earlier respondents told you. There is no substitute for empathy and a sympathetic rapport that opens life to life.

A number of publicly available sources of information display the needs generated and felt in a culture.

1. Rituals and/or magic indicate areas of heavy emotional involvement. Anthropologists tell us that one of the primary functions of ritual and magic is to relieve anxiety (Malinowski, 1954; Howells, 1948). Various crisis or stress rituals focus on arenas technology cannot guarantee. Where the results of an endeavor are valued but not secure, ritual often appears. Lack of rain stimulates rain dances. Dangerous ventures often begin with divination or prayer. Sicknesses that are life threatening are treated with more ritual than simple headaches. The use of charms, astrological charts, and divination indicates areas of stress and anxiety about valued outcomes.

2. Ideals of a culture tell us much about needs. Observing the characteristics of people who have attained high status and respect in the culture gives clues to these ideals. In contemporary USA the corporate manager such as Lee Iacocca is such a model. Whatever hinders people in the struggle to live from achieving these ideals will be points of strong emotion.

3. Legal disputes point to felt needs. What are they about? How frequent are they? How many people get involved in them? How difficult are they to settle? Answers to these questions will map some of the felt needs.

4. Once there are Christians in a culture their attitudes and struggles will tell much about felt needs. Noticing the common "temptations" and questions of young Christians or older Christians opens the door to arenas where Christianity must provide help. Where there are continuing important needs not related vitally to Christ, there will be continuing failures.

An example of this is the failure of Western Christianity to come to terms with witchcraft and divination in much of Africa. Western medicine deals with the how of illness and misfortune, not with the why. African divination deals with the why. The very fact that African Christians continue to participate in native practices of healing (though often covertly for fear of missionary disapproval) reveals an unmet need. If Christ is Lord of all, then he must be shown to be Lord in the very areas a people feels most keenly.

Guilt and the Gospel

Every society has some standards of right and wrong. They are found in the ideals as well as in the behavior of a people. They are often very similar to the moral law of God (Lewis, 1947). Their application or importance, however, may be radically different from our own ethical ideals.

The guilt people feel will most frequently be related to their own ideals and standards for right and wrong. The gospel must be directed to pre-existing guilt. T. Wayne Dye has given a detailed example of how this worked among a people of New Guinea:

> Back before [the Bahinemo] had had Christian teaching, I tried to translate Jesus' list of sins in Mark 7. As each sin was described, they gave me the local term for it. They named other sins in their culture.
>
> "What did your ancestors tell you about these things?" I asked them.
>
> "Oh, they told us we shouldn't do any of those things."
>
> "Do you think these were good standards that your ancestors gave you?" They agreed unanimously that they were.
>
> "Well, do you keep all these rules?"
>
> "No," they responded sheepishly.
>
> One leader said, "Definitely not. Who could ever keep them all? We're people of the ground."
>
> I took this opportunity to explain that God expected them to keep their own standards for what is right, that He was angry because they hadn't. Then I pointed out that it was because they fell short of their own standards that God sent His Son to bear their punishment so they could be reunited with Him.
>
> This was a crucial step toward their conversion. For the first time the Scriptures were linked to what God was telling them through their consciences. Within a year most of the people in that village had committed themselves to Christ.
>
> Since that day in 1967, they have never lost the awareness that in the Bible God is concerned about their daily behavior and not just talking about strange taboos. Since then, they have changed their source of authority from inherited tradition to the Scriptures, and they have been learning how Christ through His Spirit can come inside them and give them power to attain the standards that they could not keep before. (1976, pp. 39-40)

The need for forgiveness is an objective one. We all stand before a holy God as guilty rebels who have sinned against his glory. No one is righteous in the presence of God. How God reveals our separation from him varies greatly. It is at the point of felt guilt that the gospel must offer repentance and comforting words of forgiveness.

STEP 2: THE PEOPLE TO BE REACHED

People who are without Christ are lost. They have wandered away from God and are separated from him. Like the lost sheep, the lost coin, and the lost son of Luke 15, they need to be found. As ambassadors of Christ and heralds of the King, it is our task to share the good news and give people the opportunity to respond and be found. It was this that motivated Jesus to spend time with the despised sinners of his day— he was finding those who were lost and reuniting them to their Creator and Redeemer.

Lostness, however, is expressed in a variety of ways. Just as there are skid row bums and crimes of poverty, so there are country club bums and crimes of the wealthy. Alcoholics, workaholics, respectable lawyers, and tyrants are all lost in their own ways and need to be found. They experience their alienation from God, from fellow humans, and from themselves in differing ways. One person may be carrying a burden of guilt because of some dark deed in the past. Another may have no deep sense of guilt—only a general sense of malaise and boredom with life. Whatever the reason for alienation, they all need the same Savior. They all need to become part of the same kingdom. Yet they sense that need in vastly different ways. The drug addict and the ulcer-ridden executive will seek God in different ways. They will need to see his love for them in such a way that it makes sense and is relevant to where their burning felt need drives them. The gospel must "scratch" where it "itches."

Another example of this can be seen among the BaHima of Uganda.

> It is a truism of the revival movement that the material of confession varies according to the social milieu. Those of the pagan BaHima pastoralists are mainly to do with infringements of tribal prohibitions—drunkenness leading to wife-beating; various dietary infringements; quarrelling at watering places; desertion of one's family; adultery as tribally defined—but also with breaking the Protectorate or codified Native Law—perjury in court, visiting diviners, hut-burning, and the like. (Stenning, 1964, pp. 271-72)

Such examples could be multiplied.[10] If we consider our own pilgrimage with the Lord, we see that he is always meeting us as and where we are. It is wrong to assume that God will encounter people with different experiences and culture in the same way he has encountered us or even the peoples of the New Testament.

10. Hile, 1977; C. Kraft, 1976; Loewen, 1976.

UNDERSTANDING THE BEHAVIOR OF PEOPLES AND PEOPLE GROUPS

A people's meanings and feelings are embodied in their patterns of interaction and relationship. Understanding observable actions and styles of getting things done is another important component in evangelism. These behavior patterns are the first sorts of things that we see, although we may be unsure of what they mean. Therefore, we need to learn a great deal before we can understand what is happening as Christianity is incarnated in a new cultural context. We discover that we don't need more education. We need a complete re-education (Hesselgrave, *Communicating*, p. 71).

Behavior patterns are the organized modes by which a people group goes about meeting its needs in institutions, roles, social structures, and customs. This element of culture puts the meanings, feelings, and actions together into the actual texture of life. To understand a people is to see the way in which their culture makes sense and has its own strengths.

Christianity and Culture

Culture is a mixture of good and evil. On the good side, Christians affirm the dignity and value of culture. God gave our ancestors commands that included the cultural activities of controlling nature, existing in families, and reproducing. Even in a fallen world, culture functions to limit the self-centeredness of individuals. It brings us together in small groups where love can grow and life can come to have purpose and meaning. Culture provides the means for achieving the good ends the Creator has decreed. Art, social organization, technology, music, agriculture, and science are all reflections of the Creator.

But culture also has evil dimensions. Selfishness appears in many social structures and cultural practices. Racial prejudice and sexism are not simply individual vices. They are ingrained into the fabric of cultures. Warfare, pride, greed, disputes, oppression of the weak and defenseless are found in all societies. No culture is perfect. Even religion is perverted and corrupt. In it people exchange the truth of God for a lie. They seek to create their own righteousness rather than accept a freely bestowed righteousness from God.

Because culture is an expression of the fallenness of humanity, it will change when impregnated with the gospel. Conversion changes the inner person, but it also changes the person's outward behavior and way of relating to other people. As Christians live out a new motivation and way of behaving, the culture changes. As the whole lump of dough is gradually leavened, so the kingdom of God will gradually affect every part of a culture. Yet it does so without creating a so-called Christian culture.

The gospel stands in dialectical tension with every particular culture. Revelation uses each culture to communicate God and his ways. At the same time revelation judges each culture. So the gospel is incarnate in a culture, yet continually breaking out of it to find new wineskins for its new dynamic. Consequently, the relationship between Christianity and every human culture is ambivalent and ambiguous. It has potential for great good or for a confusion that undermines the authenticity of the revelation of God.

> Sometimes people resist the gospel not because they think it false but because they perceive it as a threat to their culture, especially the fabric of their society, and their national or tribal solidarity. To some extent this cannot be avoided. Jesus Christ is a disturber as well as a peacemaker. He is Lord, and demands our total allegiance. Thus, some first-century Jews saw the gospel as undermining Judaism and accused Paul of "teaching men everywhere against the people, the law, and this place," i.e. the temple (Acts 21:28). Similarly, some first-century Romans feared for the stability of the state, since in their view the Christian missionaries, by saying that "there is another King, Jesus," were being disloyal to Caesar and advocating customs which it was not lawful for Romans to practice (Acts 16:21; 17:7). Still today Jesus challenges many of the cherished beliefs and customs of every culture and society.

> At the same time, there are features of every culture which are not incompatible with the lordship of Christ, and which therefore need not be threatened or discarded, but rather preserved and transformed. Messengers of the gospel need to develop a deep understanding of the local culture, and a genuine appreciation of it. Only then will they be able to perceive whether the resistance is to some unavoidable challenge of Jesus Christ or to some threat to the culture, which whether imaginary or real, is not necessary. (Lausanne Committee, *Willowbank Report*, p. 13)

Understanding the Facets of Behavior

Much is in print on this subject so we will mention only three of the many areas requiring understanding.

1. The "Silent Language"

A basic part of human behavior is "nonverbal" communication.[11] This includes the physical characteristics of people, body language (messages sent by gesture and motions of the body), spatial relationships, temporal relationships (such as punctuality, length of various events, seasons), paralanguage, body contact, and aesthetics.

The potential for miscommunication between people who have learned different systems of nonverbal communication is well known to those who have crossed cultural boundaries. When the verbal message is not reinforced by the nonverbal, one is quickly (and justifiably) seen as hypocritical, cold, uncaring, and strange. Much of the reeducation needed for the cross-cultural worker must take place in this area (Nida, "The Other Message").

2. Social Structure

The Church Growth movement emphasizes the importance of this aspect of human behavior. Humans create many kinds of social groups: kinship, tribal, communal, associational, and corporate. A mosaic of social classes, castes, ethnic units, status groups, and occupational sectors divides people from each other. Each has its degree of status, privilege, prestige, and life-style. Each provides its members with differing life opportunities. People relate to one another on the basis of their position in a social structure that includes all of these groups. Membership in the group is a prerequisite for intimacy with its members.

The church invariably grows in relationship to the known characteristics of the social structure. Leaders and "gate keepers" of social groups can facilitate or hinder the progress of the gospel. Each group has its own tolerance or intolerance for the stranger or outsider. How the missionary fits into the culture depends largely on the role the people group assign to this outsider (Loewen, 1975; Cohen, 1963).

Many of the debates about the ethics of mission strategy focus on questions of social roles and structure. What is Christian in family relations (polygamy vs. monogamy; male dominant vs. egalitarian; nuclear vs. extended; lineality)? What about caste (should we allow single caste churches?), social class, political institutions, and economic arrangements? Where does the Christian come down on issues of social stratification, single-party states, capitalism vs. socialism?

Because social structures influence human behavior, they must

11. Edward T. Hall's books have been particularly influential in developing this notion. Hesselgrave, *Communicating*, chap. 31, explores this topic in detail.

be considered when thinking through the implications of God's revelation. Christians have strong feelings about social structures—and so do the people groups who are being offered Christ. If we do not understand the how and why of social structures, we can easily confuse our own preferences with the gospel.[12]

3. Institutions

Institutions are formal and standard patterns for handling various affairs of life. They are a structured set of roles that people enact in customary fashion. Marriages, funerals, festivals, music concerts, and schools are all institutions. So are contracts, judicial proceedings, welfare arrangements, and fire-fighting. Institutions provide the pattern for much of public behavior. For that reason the individual does not have to dream up a way of behaving for most occasions.

A major part of understanding a people group involves understanding their institutions. This includes learning the expectations that go with customary roles—guest, friend, patron, religious leader, mediator, bargainer, and so on. It also means learning the social occasions where certain roles are appropriate. The way we play these roles opens or closes relationships that are fateful for the progress of the gospel.

We must also see a people's institutions within the larger national and international context. Many peoples have lost significant elements of control over their institutions. The power of the industrial order is such that it is transforming many institutions. As more and more people move to the large cities, more and more institutions are changing drastically. Customs and traditional patterns are changing realities and we need to be aware of their trajectory within the larger context.

Christianity will be incarnated within every people of the earth. That is both the command and the promise of the Great Commission. For it to happen with maximum benefit and authenticity, it must happen in a climate of understanding. The missionary is not the one in the end who bears responsibility for this incarnation. The Christians indigenous to their own people group must adopt and adapt the Christian faith. The missionary is responsible to help get that process off to a good start.

The meanings, feelings, and behavior patterns of a people together make up its distinct group identity. Through their meanings, in relationship to their needs, and by means of their behavior patterns

---

12. Further reading may be found in McGavran (1979), William Smalley (1979), Al Krass (1974), Nida (1960, chap. 5), Hesselgrave (*Communicating*, Part VII), Mayers (1974, pp. 81-191), Hiebert (1976, chaps. 7-17; 1985, chaps. 7, 10), and Tippett (1971).

Christianity will have a new beginning. There is little that is more rewarding than planting the seed that gradually grows up into the body of Christ. Christian leaders in reliance upon the Spirit and in constant study of the Scripture will grow in grace and truth. They will make the variety of decisions that will bring the kingdom of God near to the heart and soul of a social group.

Many Forms of Christianity

We assume that the message of God's kingdom is for all peoples. Parts of it will conflict with particular customs. Parts of it will fit wonderfully well. We are never sure ahead of time how well it will fit a new culture.

We know that some customs have been challenged by Christians: customs such as infanticide, suttee, foot-binding, human sacrifice, slavery, and head-hunting were confronted in the nineteenth century. Today we are embroiled in the issues of caste, international economic systems, global militarization, and totalitarian politics.

Westerners confront some issues with little sense of their importance. Polygamy and widow remarriage, extended family structures, and female initiation are examples of this. They are distant from Western culture and history for the most part but are crucial in African cultures.

Every culture has institutions and structures that appear on the surface to be incompatible with Christianity. At least they are incompatible with the Christianity we have developed in the West. The church eventually has to address these matters.

However, it is futile to try to get a people to feel guilt about some practice of which we disapprove, but they do not. Until God speaks to them about it, they will never respond to it from within their own conscience. Yet when and who should raise issues of incompatibility is difficult to determine. Who should settle the issue is an even knottier question.

On the one hand, there is an awareness that changing allegiance to Jesus Christ is a deeply significant event. It will revolutionize one's life and challenge some of the strongest commitments one has in a way of life. On the other hand, conversion to Christ should not de-culturize a person, removing one from social networks and cultural patterns that are appropriate. Least of all should the cross-cultural missionary force his or her own culture on new Christians. Every aspect of the cultural past will be scrutinized in the light of Christ's lordship. However, this does not mean the past will necessarily be rejected. In may well be that a new people group's culture has elements that are closer to biblical ideals than the missionary's culture. There may be patterns that are even better as channels of expressing God's love than our own cultural patterns. These are to be received with thanksgiving.

Yet we can expect to find in every culture some common practices clearly prohibited *by Scripture* (and not just a culturally biased understanding of it). We must ask: what are they? How important are they within the overall way of life of this people group? How deeply rooted are they in the meaning systems and group identity? How difficult might it be to see them changed? Are they matters for initial presentation of the gospel? Or are they matters for mention in later parts of the process of evangelization and Christian maturation?

Customs and institutions are intertwined with each other. The changing or elimination of one has potentially large effects on others. Often it takes years to sort out the meaning and ambiguities of an institution. Missionaries often have not thought deeply about the institutions of their own culture. Thinking deeply about the institutions of another culture is even more difficult.

Once the church believes a custom or institution is wrong it should make its position known, despite possible opposition from within the people group. The early church banned gladiatorial games and trade guild banquets with meat offered sacrificially to idols. It also took a stand against Christians acting as soldiers because of the religious dimensions involved. When a large number of pagans converted to Christianity in Ephesus (Acts 19:23-41), trade in the images of Diana declined so much that a riot broke out among the silversmiths. Yet the church must take a stand on many issues involved in everyday life in given cultures.

The result of the planting of a church in a new people group will be a new form of Christian life. As each people embraces Christ it learns to express the gospel message and gospel life in a new way. Already there is an astounding diversity of Christian practice among the twenty-three thousand Christian denominations. This ought to be as much a resource for evangelization strategies as a lament for the fragmentation of the Christian movement.

In assessing the fit between gospel and culture we can consider the particular biases and tastes of a people group. It may be that a charismatic, teetotaling, anti-polygamist, separatistic form of Christian faith may relate best to a given people group. Or a liturgical, drinking, polygamy-tolerating, ecumenical, noncharismatic Christian faith might do much better.

There is a legitimate diversity of commitment and style within authentic Christian groups. Pentecostals, Presbyterians, Baptists, Lutherans, Episcopalians, Methodists, Holiness groups, and Catholics are all part of the church universal. The potential fit between a given people and its culture and these various traditions is not equal. We ought to look for a maximal fit. There the message will be clearest, the relevance to felt needs and the utilization of customary ways will be the fullest. The diversity of the church should match the diversity of the peoples who are to be a part of it.

RECEPTIVITY AND RESISTANCE

Earlier we suggested that evangelization is an interactive event. The manner and the agents of evangelization can make major differences in the response of the target group. As evangelists, we all wish we could know the degree to which a people would respond or resist Christ. It would save a great deal of arduous and challenging culture learning.

At the least, we need to estimate the overall responsiveness and resistance of a people group. Figure 10.5 below is a scale to help us do so.

attitude toward the gospel

-5 -4	-3 -2	-1 0 +1	+2 +3	+4 +5
Strongly Opposed	Somewhat Opposed	Indifferent	Somewhat Favorable	Strongly Favorable

FIGURE 10.5   THE RESISTANCE / RECEPTIVITY SCALE

This tool asks only for an overall estimate. There may be particular individuals or subgroups within a people who differ substantially from the average of the group. Nicodemus' attitude toward Jesus was very different from that of the majority of the Sanhedrin. Still it is helpful to characterize the group as a whole.

We need to be both cautious and realistic in such an estimate. Studies warn us about the self-fulfilling nature of labeling a group "resistant" (Liao, 1972). If a group has a bad reputation, it is difficult to persuade Christians to expend the sacrifice and energy on them. Some have even argued that we discard the category of "resistant" since every people will resist evangelization when it is culturally insensitive.

The receptivity to Christian faith seems related to a number of variables:

1. *The degree to which a people is satisfied with its present fate in life.*

If their current customs and religion give satisfactory answers, they will be unlikely to listen for another way of life.

2. *The degree to which the rest of their life is changing.* Research shows that new immigrants or people who have recently moved to a new community are more open to new ideas and ways. So too are minorities who are away from their normal communities. They are no longer surrounded by friends who support their traditional identity.

3. *The cultural sensitivity of the gospel presentation.* Most people resist having their culture taken away from them. When Christianity appears to require leaving one's traditional culture, there often is strong resistance. If they are giving up their old culture, then Christianity must ride that trend as well and offer a new cultural identity.

4. *The agent of Christian faith.* Because of cultural biases and prejudices, some people receive a more respectful hearing than others. A young, Western educated missionary may not be as well received as evangelists with very different characteristics.

5. *The relative fit between the gospel and the cultural patterns that are presently dominant in a people group.* A deeply rooted religious system that stands in opposition to Christianity will create strong resistance to evangelization. This is true also of groups whose occupation puts them on the margins of society: drug traffickers, thugs, and pimps/prostitutes. They can be won to Christ. But their economic interests create a natural resistance that must be overcome.

The relationship between receptivity and strategy is not uniform. If the people group is extraordinarily receptive, then almost any strategy will work. They are waiting for something new and when it comes they sweep into the church. Mistakes are easily forgotten and rectified. On the other hand, the strongly resistant are difficult to win for Christ with even the best strategies and the greatest cultural sensitivity.

It is in the middle range of receptivity/resistance that strategy makes the most difference. With a good strategy sensitively enacted a large hearing of the gospel and a large harvest is possible. A poor or weak strategy combined with cultural insensitivity will not break through indifference or neutrality. In fact, it can create hostilities to Christian faith that previously did not exist. In this middle range a difference in approach, in the agent of the gospel, or in the tradition of Christian piety can produce either a large, virile church or a small, struggling body.

Understanding a people will help us make those decisions that can make dramatic differences in the resulting Christian movement.[13]

13. John Robb, *The Power of People Group Thinking* (MARC, 1989), gives further understanding of the importance of this approach.

Questions

1. How is a "people-centered" approach different from traditional methods of doing evangelism?

2. What role and meaning do the demonstrable differences in culture have on the task of evangelization? Should the church seek to maintain or preserve the cultural differences between peoples? Did New Testament evangelists utilize strategies conditioned by the cultures of the people they were attempting to evangelize?

3. When can we say that a people has "heard" the gospel? How many distinct or unique sendings of evangelists are necessary if the Great Commission is to be fulfilled?

4. What is a "people" and a "people group"? How are they different? What are the various sorts of human groups? Which ones are suitable for special targeting with tailor-made strategies?

5. Beyond the information we gather to *describe* a people, what do we need to know in order to *understand* them?

6. How do we go about "translating" and "transculturating" the meanings of the kingdom of God so they make sense in a new cultural context? How do we draw the line between what is genuinely indigenous and an authentic expression of God's message and way and what is a genuinely indigenous and yet inauthentic expression (what is usually called syncretistic or Christo-pagan)?

7. What kind of process do people go through in coming to faith in Jesus Christ? Can those who have an adequate and accurate grasp on who Jesus is and what the implications are for their lives reject him? Why are there billions of people not committed to Christ? Incorrect knowledge? Not enough knowledge? No indigenous expression of Christianity? The blinding effects of sin? The indifference of Christians to the evangelistic mandate?

8. What is the ultimate goal of evangelism? Increased awareness

of Christ, the church, and the gospel? "Decisions" for Christ? Increased numbers of worshiping Christians folded into Christian communities? Increased numbers of active propagators of the gospel? A cluster of worshiping Christian churches in every distinct people group? A just world order?

9. How did Jesus deal with human need in his ministry? What was the relationship between his preaching of the kingdom of God and his compassionate healing and casting out of demons?

10. Why is it important that evangelism deal with the felt needs of a people group *as it defines them* rather than *as we think it ought to define them?*

11. How are we to preach repentance? What types of things are we to connect to the call for repentance? What if a people does not feel guilty for some of the things that we know the Bible declares to be sinful?

12. To what extent does the larger contexts of politics and economics in which a people live help to define the mission? Are there times when the first thrust of evangelization must be to correct the social, political, and/or economic system in order to address the felt needs of a people?

STEP 3: THE FORCE FOR EVANGELIZATION

Considerations

1. The work of Christ flows out of a commitment to the body of Christ. Too often Western individualism bypasses this biblical principle.

2. The entire church is potentially available for the evangelization of any people.

3. There is a close relationship between the qualities of the people to be reached and the people whom God sets aside for reaching them.

4. Missionaries should view themselves and be viewed by the people being evangelized as a community, rather than as a group of individuals.

5. The "parachurch" agency or community is the basic vehicle through which the church communicates Christ to the world.

6. The structures of the mission community should be designed to fit the task at hand and the people to be reached. Structure should be a by-product and the means of a strategy that fits a unique people group.

7. Presently there are not enough cross-cultural missionaries to complete the task of reaching the unreached peoples of the world. The missionaries who are available are concentrated in the wrong areas. Some mission agencies should withdraw from the areas in which they are working.

8. God is just as interested in reaching peoples as in sending missionaries.

9. The missionary vocation is as complex and demanding as that of a medical doctor. Mission training should be thought of in a way analogous to the medical model.

10. The average view of missions is inadequate and must be changed. The average missionary is inadequate and must be changed. Change must begin with the local church.

11. The People Available

An initial understanding of the target people gives us a basis for the important consideration: whom to send to reach them. From the millions of men and women who are part of Christ's body, who is to make up the *force for evangelism?*[1] Who is God calling and sending? Who is best suited to *this* potential audience? Who has the qualifications, character, and motivation to carry out the mission of evangelization?

In one sense, every Christian in the world is potentially a member of the force for evangelism. Outwardly, we see thousands of denominations and dozens of traditions. Yet we know the Spirit is One and the body of Christ is one. All of us together are part of the force of people Christ mobilizes and sends. We can picture it as a large sun. At the core is the body of Christ, fired and empowered by the Holy Spirit. Radiating out are the particular beams of energy, special task forces from this body. Each goes to give light to a particular people. The source of their power rests within the total body; particular needs of the people group are supplied by the energy brought from the body. God does not call every Christian. Only some are capable of reaching hidden peoples. Many are called but only a few are chosen.

God is more interested in *reaching people groups* than in *sending missionaries.* Missionaries are sent to people groups to bridge the gulf so reconciliation happens with God. God uses those sent to bring a people to a saving knowledge of himself. To do so, the persons sent need to correspond to the profile of the people group to whom they are sent. We need to ask two questions: What is the need and the context in which God wants to meet the need? Whom has God called and equipped to

1. This apt phrase was first suggested by Frank Ineson. See Ineson and Read, *Brazil 1980* (MARC, 1973).

136

meet that need? Attempting to answer the second question will force us to clarify further the answer to the first question. Answering the question of means and methods will likewise drive us back to reconsider the force for evangelism.

Ultimately, the makeup of the force for evangelism is a matter to decide in the light of the whole strategy. A large support group prays for, gives to, trains, and communicates with the missionary. These people are an indispensable part of the force for evangelism. However, this chapter deals with selecting those who go and carry out the actual evangelistic strategy.

There are many questions to ask in discovering whom God has chosen for a particular task. Just as God gave Gideon a series of tests to trim down his force to those few with particular qualities (Jdgs. 7), we need to find the right people with the right qualities for each specific people group. For example, if there are no Christians among the target group, we must cross cultural barriers. From among the thousands of Christians who may desire to reach that group, we look for those able to cross those boundaries. There are other tests. Who will be acceptable to the target group? Who will be most likely to gain a hearing? Who is available? Who is called? Who qualifies? Who is able? Who is gifted in calling people to a new community? We will look at some of the most important questions that need answering.

WHAT IS THIS PEOPLE GROUP LIKE?

In Steps 1 and 2 we selected and described a people group. Given their characteristics as we know them, who might be ideal persons to communicate Christ to them?

The Søgaard Scale, with an accompanying rate of change scale, gives a compact overview of a people group. In Figure 11.1 on page 138 we portray three groups, A, B, and C. Before proceeding further, consider what force for evangelism might be most effective in each.

137

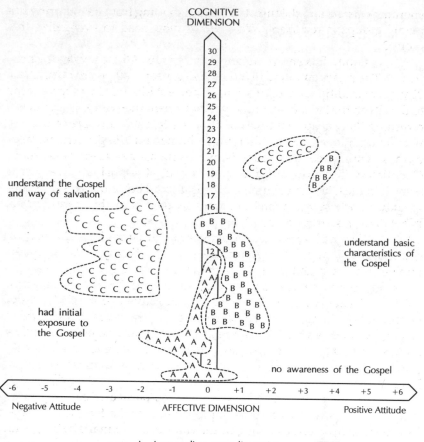

A. A nomadic, pastoralist society
B. An urbanizing society
C. A working-class stratum

FIGURE 11.1   GROUP LOCATIONS ON THE SØGAARD SCALE

Group A is a nomadic herding society. Cattle is the cultural focus and one's status depends upon the number owned. Half of the group are unaware of Christianity. That number is decreasing by two percent per year. Another 40 percent have some awareness, but their attitude is either unfavorable or neutral. A small number (about six percent) has some knowledge of Christian faith. They are neutral or somewhat favorable. Their number is relatively constant. There is no church. Of a total population of 50,000, less than 150 are literate. At present there is sporadic warfare and the threat of famine. Raiding from neighboring nomadic groups is recurrent. What would you need to evangelize this group?

Group B is an urbanizing tribal group. All are aware of Christianity. The major city in which they live is nearly 40 percent Christian, 25 percent traditional religions, and 35 percent Muslim. Most have come to the city in the last fifteen years, yet they retain their ties to the villages, returning there at special times of life. Nearly 2,400 now live in the city with an additional 15,000 still living in homeland villages. The number of those with some knowledge is increasing as they learn more about Christianity. The basic attitude of all is neutral to positive. Every year some join the Christian church. There is a small but growing set of congregations whose membership comes largely from this tribal group. What does this group require?

Group C is a working-class stratum in a traditionally Christian country. Everyone has some awareness of Christianity. Most belong to families that have had little contact with the church for several generations. The majority are negative to the church, feeling it has not cared for workers. A small number, however, remain active members of congregations. Their number is slowly declining over the years. None of them actively propagates the Christian faith. Every year one percent declare themselves to have no religion so as to avoid the state tax used to support the churches. Who might be able to reach this secularized and secularizing group?

In each case, the people group has particular characteristics that merit consideration in selecting a strategy and a force for evangelism. For example, one can imagine the value of a veterinarian along with a linguist and an evangelist on a team to people group A. Since group B already has the beginning of a church movement, assisting that movement and exporting it back to the villages might be imperative. Leadership enhancement and basic Bible training might be mandated. Group C is a secularized, relatively indifferent or hostile group in a nominally Christian context. Congregations not identified with the state-supported church are needed. Evangelists who understand the working-class perspective, ideally from such a background, might be commissioned.

As we have seen, understanding the cultural barriers of a people group is important. The cultural distance between a target group and a Christian group commissioning evangelization is a significant factor. We need to look at those available in terms of their cultural distance and acceptability within the target group.

First, are there *any* Christians already among the target group? How many? Where are they located? How acceptable are they to their own people? That there are Christians among a people does not mean they will automatically share Christ. Stagnant churches all over the world have no desire to trouble their waters by bringing in outsiders. Also, their own attitude toward evangelism is an important consideration if our goal is evangelization. Are they motivated—or could they be—so effective evangelization might happen through them?

Are the local Christians still culturally acceptable? Evangelistic methods can produce local churches that deculturize their members. This is especially true of the mission station approach. People are extracted from their culture (often employed by the mission) and set over against their native culture. Instead of being a sweet perfume of Christ to their own, the indigenous church is hostile to their own. It develops as a new subculture within the traditional society.

Sometimes the growth of the church reinforces prior social status barriers. This happened in India when tens of thousands of the untouchables became Christians. Though they speak the same language and live in the same village as the higher caste Hindus, they are unacceptable to them. Similarly, in Pakistan the majority of the Protestant church is from the Hindu minority. The Islamic majority views the Christians as a mixture: Hindu-Christians. Though the Islamic peoples and the Christians are geographically close and speak the same language, socially and culturally they are very distant. The so-called national church and the Islamic majority are indifferent if not hostile to each other. The West experiences this phenomenon along racial lines.

A people group is considered unreached until it has "adequate numbers and resources to evangelize the rest of its members without outside assistance." If there are no local Christians acceptable to the non-Christian sector of the target group, then outside assistance will have to happen. The first place to look for such help is among culturally similar peoples geographically distant. In most cases, E-1 or E-2 evangelism is preferable to E-3.

In the mid-1970s the New Zealand missionary Peter McNee noticed a pocket of Christian Garus in northern Bangladesh. Further west was a geographically separated group of Garus who were unreached. When they learned of this western group of their own people, the Christian Garus were quick to evangelize them.

The Ministry of International Students points out the strategic opportunity of foreign students at universities in countries heavily Christianized. When cared for sensitively, some of them become Christian and can return to evangelize in many contexts closed to Western missionaries. The tides of immigration pose possible opportunities to bridge back to larger unreached populations.

140

It does not follow, however, that those geographically closest to a target group are the most useful in evangelization. The issue is credibility. Those with the least cultural distance normally are our first choice for leading evangelization in a target group.

LOOKING FOR THE BEST FIT

Finding a match between a people group and the force for evangelism is a dialectical process. It involves assessing the crucial features of a people and those of particular evangelists. One place to begin is with those already experienced with the people group or with groups fairly similar. For example, the head of a denominational mission sought counsel from us as to how his mission might select an unreached people. There are so many that the issue is not a simple one. We asked him, "What groups are you now reaching?" Then we asked, "Are there other groups similar to the ones you are now reaching?" As it turned out, there were unreached groups within a country in which they were already working.

When looking for the best fit, the first thing we can do is identify the strengths that we already possess. God has taken us through a history and equipped us with experiences that can narrow our focus into the future. We need to claim the strengths we have and build on them. If we have capabilities and experience in urban evangelization, then we ought to seek to extend *that* strength. If we have had notable successes in dealing with small, illiterate tribes, *that* should help with our future endeavors.

If we are without significant experience, then we should seek churches or other missions already at work with the target people group. What is their experience? Are they effective in establishing growing churches? Are there individuals within their movement who have been effective? What can we learn from that experience? What does it tell us about the kinds of persons who are likely to be effective in evangelization?

Or we might seek Christians who have experience with similar people groups. We especially want to find both successful and relatively unsuccessful cases. Both are helpful in stimulating questions and conclusions about strategies and the agents of evangelization.

We have no doubt that God wants all peoples folded into his covenant people. That is why we want to discover where peoples are joining the church. We can build on the wisdom God is giving to other members of the body of Christ in evangelization. Sometimes we may conclude that the last thing needed are Christians of our sort!

STEP 3: THE FORCE FOR EVANGELIZATION

Nationalism and ethnic pride also set limits on a possible match. Certain members of the world church are unable to cross some national boundaries. The national and political differences between their two countries legally exclude them from entry. Even when entry is possible, strong political ideologies may make it an unlikely fit. The gospel has a marvelous ability to break down barriers and to transform ideologies. Yet we cannot be foolish or blind to the ways in which such barriers can hinder the initial hearing of the gospel. We seek to minimize the distance between the evangelist and the target group, not make it even greater than it need be.

Theological emphases and patterns of piety may also enter the picture. There is a wide diversity within the boundaries of the one body of Christ. Some stress the powerful presence of the Holy Spirit and visible gifts. Others emphasize the ordered ministry, priesthood, and traditional liturgy. The spiritual disciplines of study, giving, and corporate worship may be basic in one denomination. In another the disciplines of prayer, fasting, and the mystical quest for union with God may be central.

Research shows that differing theological emphases and piety styles affect gospel reception. The Pentecostals display powerful movements among the common people in Latin America and other parts of the world. Their focus on the spirit world and on *experiencing* God's power appeals to certain target groups. Others are better reached by a more reserved, quiet piety that has stronger intellectual components. Calvinism, though not teaching fatalism, is often more able to relate to a fatalistic outlook than is a strong free-will theology.

Ability to relate to and work with other Christian groups is another consideration. Churches exist in many countries, even if not among the hidden people which is the target group. Some may already be attempting to reach the hidden people. We cannot ignore the acceptability of new missionaries and agencies to the local groups. Can we relate to the groups already present? What effect will their presence have on our appearance and ministry?

Some argue that there is a "cross-cultural gift" just as there are gifts of preaching and healing. Some Christians, they say, have the supernatural capability to cross cultural barriers. When considering the force for evangelism, we need to consider each person's qualities and gifts for such ministry. Sometimes we discover such gifts and develop them only in the process of ministry. More and more people are engaging in short-term missionary experiences to test their capability for cross-cultural ministry. Clearly, some people thrive on such challenge and adapt well. If we have a choice, we certainly want such people on the missionary team.

142

Finally, who senses the leading of God's Spirit to the target group? God moves in mysterious ways. Individuals and organizations may say, "I believe this is what God wants me (us) to do." One way of testing that calling further is to discover whom else God is calling. Who has had a prayer burden for this people through the years? What research is being done on this people group? Does it match up to my understanding of what God is calling me to do?

THE GOING COMMUNITY

Biblical priorities demand commitment to Christ without reservation and without regret. That relationship leads to a commitment to fellow members of his body. Out of these two relationships issues the work that we do. Our ministry and tasks build on the foundation of our relationships. The force for evangelism is a "going church" that involves much more than individual missionaries.

The going church is to be a *community* of missionaries. The notion of missionary bands or teams goes back to the Apostle Paul, who always traveled with a band of fellow Christians. William Carey and his two partners considered themselves a church from the beginning of their mission. They formed a congregation as soon as they landed in India.

Such community needs to develop *before* moving into the people group. The day of jet travel has undercut this process. In the nineteenth century groups of missionaries developed deep relational ties during months of ship travel. In this day of individualized, Western Christianity, we need to rediscover the *missionary team* as a structure of the going church.

The going church is a *gifted community.* Ephesians 4 describes the body of Christ as made up of different members with diverse gifts. Through the balance and freedom of those various gifts, ministry occurs. When moving into a new culture, missionaries face diverse tasks from language and culture learning to mechanics and sanitation. Only a few unusual missionaries can be true generalists. Thus, there is wisdom to having the specialized missionary as part of a team of specialists.[2] Support and correction can enhance the quality of everyone's gifts within a team.

The going church is also a *self-understanding community.* We are aware of the need for self-understanding and acceptance of ourselves as

2. Hiebert (1985), pp. 281-83.

persons. We also need to understand our own culture of orientation with its biases and blindness. Often we do not see our own culture clearly until we learn an adopted culture. Then we realize how deeply we think and see the world by the culture that conditioned us as children. Then we face the crisis of self-understanding and self-acceptance at a cultural level.

Some people already are bicultural. A bicultural community is a localized society in which people from different cultures relate to each other. The bi-culture takes elements from at least two different cultures and uses them to expedite cross-cultural interactions. Bicultural people face different challenges in self-understanding. As cultural brokers, mediating one culture's resources to another, many feel alienated and marginal to both. The going church finds itself continually in between cultures. Yet that position gives it a unique vantage point from which to understand itself and the gospel as it enters new peoples.

The going church is a *hermeneutical community* (LCWE, 1978). The translation of the gospel into a new cultural context requires unusual sensitivity to both gospel and culture. The only human control we have in handling Scripture is the larger body of Christ. We continually cross-check what we think we are hearing from its texts with what other believers hear.

The hermeneutical community only begins with the missionary team. That team initiates the process of the translation of Scripture into the receptor language. In the bicultural stage a dialogue develops between missionary and indigenous Christians. Together they seek to hear how the gospel speaks in this new language and culture. Eventually the hermeneutical community must primarily be made up of Christians of the people group. The "fourth self" of self-theologizing can be done only by leaders of the people or the people group themselves.

The going church must be *a caring community*. In part this is a matter modeled by the missionary team itself. The division of labor within the team should maximize the ministry time. Too often missionaries spend the majority of their time in physically difficult settings simply staying alive. Caring for one another leads to mission accomplishment as well as modeling the meaning of the church.

This also means relating to the manifest needs of the people group. Missions is not for the benefit and glory of the going church. It is to be a part of what God is doing to keep Christ before the consciousness of every people on earth. This may well lead into community development, medical assistance, educational uplift. Caring for people means not dividing them up into falsely distinguished compartments.

The going church is a *witnessing community*. Caring that does not care enough to find out how to share Christ verbally is sub-Christian. Witnessing that does not witness in deeds as well as in words conveys a false message. In word *and* deed the going church seeks to bridge the gap between faith and lack of faith across cultural barriers.

People in other cultures may have difficulty grasping our expression of the gospel because of our differences in background. Yet they can sense and see our love. We have heard missionaries repeatedly testify how having children or parents with them opened new vistas of understanding. The target group could see that they too were people with family and relationship.

Finally, the going church is a *researching and understanding community.* Experience is always a short commodity in a new setting. Research and careful listening supplies that lack. As brokers of the gospel of Christ, we may well have to learn how to broker him by the target group members themselves. Every relationship and event is an occasion to learn. Finding and being mentored and tutored by an older member of the people group can bridge years of inexperience and misunderstanding.

All of these characteristics can be acquired in the missionary setting. What we are advocating is that missionary teams begin learning them *before* deployment. Once such a community is established in the field situation, it can in turn accept new members into its midst. As a caring community it will have experiences helpful in forming a bi-culture and in receiving additional missionary workers.

A number of missionary agencies already use elements of this approach. The Agape Program in Campus Crusade for Christ trains people as teams. Overseas Crusades is establishing teams as these move into new areas. One agency sending teachers of English as a second language into China orients all candidates in team settings.

Different peoples require different forms of communication to understand the gospel. The missionary of the 1800s usually came from a large, extended family. Many of them were from farms and small communities where relationships were much less individualistic than they are today. Community and relational teams have become a newly attractive form of life for Western individualists. Rather than export our own sense of loneliness and isolation, why not re-establish community at the center of our missionary structures?

RECRUITING

There are still thousands of people groups reachable only by new initiatives. Many of them are reachable only by Western churches. The demand to make disciples of all the world has not been withdrawn. No segment of the church is immune from response to this command of Christ.

Since World War II, the number of countries closing their doors to the vocational missionary has been increasing. This is not to say "tent-maker" missionaries cannot minister in creative ways.[3] There are still ways in which Christians can get behind political barriers. Yet even if mission agencies focus only on countries open to them, the number of unreached peoples within *those* countries far exceeds current capacities and plans to reach them.

The day of Western missions is hardly over. However, we need creative new ways of thinking about the task. Some say that two hundred thousand missionaries from the United States and Canada could effectively be put to work by the year 2000. They would, of course, have to be the right sort of missionary.

What would it take to have that many effective North American Protestant cross-cultural missionaries by the year 2000? Really not much. In 1988 there were about three thousand new career personnel entering North American mission agencies. We may assume that a similar number continues to enter at the present. That number needs to be about 15,000 a year.

In 1988 the amount given to missions from the United States was $1.721 billion. By the year 2000 that would have to increase to about $6 billion to support the increase in missionary personnel.

The overall number of agencies would not have to increase at all. Of the 814 agencies listed in the fourteenth edition of *Mission Handbook* (Roberts and Siewert, 1989), only twenty listed 500 or more overseas personnel. That number would have to increase to 175 agencies of that size. Some mission agencies are growing at relatively rapid rates. The five largest agencies in 1988 grew from 7,384 in 1973 to 12,138 full-time, career missionaries. Had all missions experienced the same rate of growth, there would have been 64,617 career missionaries instead of 43,648. Yet even at that rate there would only be about 80,000 career missionaries in the year 2000. Obviously the rate of growth must increase dramatically to reach a goal of 200,000.

The number of short-term missionaries has been skyrocketing (more so in the United States than in Canada). In 1988 nearly 43 percent of the 70,969 overseas missionaries from the United States were short termers. If a significant minority or even half of them decide for the career path of missionary service, then the shortfall might be overcome.

3. Yamamori (1987).

Comparisons don't always tell the whole story. Nevertheless it is significant that in 1975, with 2.9 million members, the Mormons fielded twenty thousand short-term missionaries. At their present rate of growth they will be fielding nearly one hundred thousand by the year 2000. The Mormons *expect* every Mormon young man to serve a two-year mission assignment, self-supported or supported by his family. This happens *before* he begins a career vocation.

The Southern Baptist convention numbers among its members nearly fourteen million. If it mustered an equal percentage of its young people into short-term experience, almost one hundred thousand people from among their ranks would be in cross-cultural ministry. If only 10 percent of them continued into career missionary work, there would be five thousand new missionaries every year between now and 2000! Our vision and our performance simply are not what they need to be. What looks impossible is impossible only if we accept the anemic status quo.

Robert Coote's comments in the thirteenth edition of the *Mission Handbook* are well worth pondering here as well:

> The sending ratio for the U.S. in the mid-1970s was one missionary for every 4,800 people. Canada and Switzerland did twice as well as that; the Netherlands and Spain did nearly four times as well; Belgium did nearly five times as well. Even Sweden, where only 5 percent or 6 percent of the population attends church weekly, sent more missionaries per capita than did the U.S. If the U.S. were to do today as well as Spain did in the mid-1970s, it would be sending out 188,000 missionaries. If it were to do as well as Lutheran Norway, it would be sending out 85,000. Instead it does half as well as Norway. (Wilson and Siewert, 1986, p. 43)

One of the major dilemmas in mission enterprise is the tendency to support missionaries rather than missions. The majority of the sixty-seven thousand total Protestant missionaries receive support as individuals or couples. Most of their agencies have worked out formulas for the funds they will need in their country of service. Local churches and individuals participate in supplying funds for this support. Often it is raised directly by the missionary in the process of deputation.

Yet it is a historical fact that there are thousands of missionaries with only minimal support. They are able to get to the mission field, but then do not have the ministry dollars necessary to carry out the task they came to do. Another by-product of this practice is the difficulty agencies sometimes have funding the overall management functions. Dollars spent on the home office or management means less dollars for "ministry." The ministry of administration is not viewed as intrinsic to goal accomplishment.

Equating mission with the missionary conveys a subtle message: God is more interested in missionaries than he is in missions. We contend that God is as interested in reaching people as he is in sending missionaries.

The *total costs* of the strategy are costs to be covered by the supporting constituency. The type of planning advocated in this book will provide a very comprehensive picture of those costs. Sharing them as a whole aids realism and generates more funds than hiding them. We should not fool ourselves into thinking we can sell only part of the costs and still be able to carry out a complete strategy.

Some mission executives have argued that the local churches are already having difficulty supporting the individual missionary. They wonder how any church can possibly increase its support to cover project funds. Yet the experience of recent years makes clear that Christians will give generously when they understand the full picture. World Vision International, a Christian service agency, was the first to exceed an annual budget of $200 million a year. It raised funds for overseas work through existing churches by presenting needs and projects. Funding does not focus on the support of individual missionaries.

Clear purposes and sharply focused goals motivate people to take a part in the mission task. They also stimulate people to provide the prayer and financial support necessary to carry out the task.

THOUSANDS OF YOUNG PEOPLE ARE WILLING TO BE TRAINED

Unfortunately, mission agencies are not well equipped to train them. In recent years the InterVarsity Urbana Conferences filled the auditorium with over nineteen thousand attendees. In Urbana 1987 more than eight thousand indicated a willingness to serve overseas if God opened the door. In 1976 nearly nine thousand made the same commitment. Yet we know from experience that only a small percentage of these will ever attempt to become involved in overseas service. Why is this so? The calling of "missionary" is not at present accompanied by a well-defined career path. Those who show an interest and willingness often have little idea of how to get from willingness to career effectiveness. The steps from here to there are not clear.

This lack of a clear career path is the result of many things.

Some Christians believe that little more than a "definite call" is required. Others suppose that the responsibility is God's; those of us in the profession or mission enterprise need only sit back and the candidates will file through our doors.

One of the serious obstacles to training is a lack of commitment by those involved in the missionary vocation to prepare well-equipped men and women. Mission agencies seldom have personnel set aside and qualified to train others and design career paths. Fortunately, a few agencies do have such programs. Wycliffe Bible Translators' Summer Institute of Linguistics trains personnel in the technical aspects of language acquisition and reduction. It also has a jungle training camp to test and train people under situations of extreme environmental stress.

But providing a cross-cultural experience is difficult for agencies in North America, despite the fact that most cities are now multicultural. It is too easy for the candidate to step back into his or her own primary culture. The burgeoning short-term mission opportunities have opened up new contexts for such training.

High requirements do not seem to discourage many dedicated young people. The Christian and Missionary Alliance traditionally requires two years of pastoral experience before mission field service. Many young adults continue working for years past the B.A., as nearly forty thousand young adults reach the Ph.D. level every year in the United States. Most of these do it on their own, with some help from scholarships. Evidently they are highly motivated; those entering the mission field are, too.

Yet where do all the young college students go after Urbana? Why are they not channeled into a program and sequence of training designed to equip them for the missionary vocation? Part of the problem is that churches, agencies, and schools do not agree on the need or method of certification. One missionary professor wrote:

> There's still a prevailing notion that one can major in any subject in college or seminary and be a good missionary. No special courses are necessary! Most leading missions have a minimum requirement— one year of Bible—nothing is said of missions! I think this is a great mistake. To go overseas without missionary anthropology, cross-cultural communication, area studies, missionary life at work—to say nothing of the history of missions and non-Christian religions, is an act of consummate folly![4]

What kinds of training are essential? Imagine this situation. A young person decides she wants to be an engineer. She wisely starts by

4. J. Herbert Kane in a letter to Edward R. Dayton, dated April 4, 1979.

talking to various companies who employ engineers to find out what they look for when hiring an engineer. Yet to her distress the answers are of little help. One company says all they want is a person with a one-year course in history. The second says they look for a full seven-year course in the engineering sciences. The third responds that all one needs is a strong desire and sense of vocation for engineering. So she turns to the training programs. Here she finds 250 graduate and undergraduate schools offering engineering somewhere in their curriculum. Only 4 teach engineering exclusively at the graduate level and 25 teach it exclusively at the undergraduate level. There is a large discrepancy both in the courses offered and in the standards set for an engineering program. Further discouraged, she turns to friends and members of her local congregation. "What is engineering all about?" she asks. Some say engineering is a very exotic profession with lots of excitement. Others say that it is hard work. Still others reply that as far as they can see, being an engineer means giving up a lot.

The analogy should be clear by now. What people say is necessary for the vocation of missionary in terms of training and qualifications is rather chaotic. Part of the chaos relates to the lack of clarity on the missionary role.

We would suggest that acquiring the missionary role is a difficult process. Probably no profession requires greater commitment and flexibility. It requires equally high levels of spiritual insight and education. Yet probably no profession has paid less attention to its potential members and how they are recruited, and to what standards govern excellence.

The difficulty is not that there are no graduates who desire an overseas Christian career, and very few graduate schools interested in training missionaries. The difficulty is that the profession is not geared for on-the-job training. The result is too many poorly trained missionaries, too many talented men and women who are challenged but never make it overseas, too many complaints from national churches that missions and missionaries are insensitive to their situations. How can this be rectified? Is there a good model to follow?[5]

As a point of departure, let us consider the training required to become a medical doctor. After completing undergraduate work in "premed" the student enters a three-year medical school associated with a teaching hospital. The daily mixture includes classroom and laboratory

---

5. For further analysis of the problem and a helpful workbook guide for those attempting to respond to the missionary call, see *You Can So Get There from Here* by Edward R. Dayton (MARC, 1980).

work and direct experience with patients. As the student advances, he or she is given more and more opportunity to diagnose and develop the treatment for patients. After this, the person graduates with an M.D. degree. The next step is internship, actually working in medical practice under the supervision of more senior physicians. This normally takes from a year to several years, depending upon the specialization being developed. Still the education is incomplete. Before the doctor moves out into full and independent practice, he or she will serve a residency in a hospital. Here another year or two is spent in practice, this time supervising interns as well.

It is our contention that the "doctor of souls" in cross-cultural settings probably requires a similar level of preparation. We use a number of terms to label the stage a medical doctor has achieved: pre-med, medical student, intern, resident, practicing doctor. We do not expect the medical student to perform major operations. In like fashion we need to understand the different levels at which missionaries exist. The missionary title masks the vast differences in training and experience. It would be helpful to have terms to designate the candidate, the missionary student, the apprentice missionary, the assistant, the associate, and the senior missionary. Somehow the stages of skill and experience acquisition need dramatization. That way we have some sense of the different levels between "missionaries" that reflect the differences in ministry capability. With these six designations, we could imagine a much clearer, more rational career path.

Such a set of stages would signal the need for continuing education. If we recognized the various components necessary to produce the full-orbed senior missionary, we could then channel those who want to be missionaries but don't know how to do so. Further, we could enhance the missionary vocation. Such stages would signal the interdependence of missionaries, with senior and associate missionaries being involved in the apprenticing of younger missionaries. It would also provide relief from the guilt that entry-level missionaries often feel when they cannot reach effectiveness immediately. The "teaching hospital" for the missionary candidate would be the cross-cultural setting. On-the-field training means settings where such ministry is already happening. Mission agencies need to accept such training as part of their job. Some of this is happening with short-term missionaries, but it needs to be more systematic and integral to the missionary career.

This approach to the missionary task opens up an entirely new world for recruiting and missionary education and training. By recognizing that it is impossible to make the leap from layperson to professional missionary in the span of a year, missions would give their potential recruits a clear path to follow. Local churches would under-stand the long-run process and could support their own people in all of the phases through which a missionary passes. Let's look at how this might happen.

Those who seek a missionary vocation would begin with the "pre-mission" apprentice program. They could enter the program any-time after their junior year of college. They would be taken under the care of a mission agency in the same way that churches often take can-didates for ministry under care. At the same time these apprentices would come under care of their church. The agency would agree to give them spiritual, financial, and educational guidance. The apprentice would agree to abide by the regulations of the agency.

The agency would provide career path planning for the ap-prentice. It would design a program that would take the apprentice about eight years to move through the various stages to full missionary status. During this time the apprentice would receive additional educa-tion, on-the-job training, and exposure to cross-cultural experience.

When a candidate is accepted into such a program, the church would undertake his or her support in the same way it does a person overseas. Donors would see their responsibility as extending to the prep-aration phases of mission, not just the sending phase.

What might happen in such a program? In January or Febru-ary a candidate would be accepted into the on-going apprenticeship. During the summer following the junior year, the pre-missioner would be sent for a short-term mission experience under the guidance of field staff. At the end of the summer the apprentice would attend a two- to three-week debriefing and training event. This would process the sum-mer's experiences as well as lay plans for the senior year and following year.

During the senior year the pre-missioner would receive a reg-ular newsletter describing the activities and goals of the agency, news of what mission interns were doing, and prayer needs. The January inter-term would be spent in an intensive course such as those given at the Overseas Ministries Study Center in New Haven or the Fuller School of World Mission in Pasadena.

The status of the pre-missioner would be changed to intern upon completion of college. If he or she had little biblical training or sem-inary study, plans would be made for an additional two or three years in such subjects. This would be combined with on-going on-the-job training. The assumption would be that the mission intern would be en-gaged in a twelve-month job with two weeks of vacation.

At the end of formal education, the intern would go overseas for the "first term." This is equivalent to the medical profession's residency. During the language learning phase (which would mean in many cases a trade language and a primary language), there would be several intensive courses in cross-cultural communication, the cultural history of the area being served, the religion of the people, and the Christian religion. This would involve from two to four years of work.

At the end of this time the intern would receive the first regular short furlough, during which a thorough evaluation would be made of the progress made. A decision would be made at that point as to whether the intern would return to the field and even continue the career with the mission agency.

Returning to the field, the missioner would now be upgraded to a "missionary associate." He or she would have full status in the field council and would be placed in a full position of missionary work. Missionary associates would be responsible for the writing of a self-development program as well as ministry plans and goals. These would be up-dated annually through an evaluation of progress made in terms of the set goals. Missionary plans would also be integrated with the overall agency and field goals.

Promotion to full missionary and finally senior missionary status would happen according to standards set by the agency and field. Each promotion would represent the passing of a minimum set of years (perhaps six years or two terms with short furloughs). It would also represent the achievement of personally set and publicly shared goals for achievement in mission.

In this way every mission agency would have pre-missioners, interns, missionary associates, missionaries, and senior missionaries in its ranks. The general expectations at each level would be clear. Each missionary would be modifying and applying common standards to his or her own progress toward missionary excellence. To be complete we would have to add a category of retired or emeritus status for missionaries who complete the full career.

At first glance this proposal may seem almost impossible, particularly financially. However, if the funding required for each candidate is clearly spelled out and if churches and individuals set aside a portion of this funding, say 10 percent, there is no reason it cannot be managed. There *is* an obvious minimum size to such a program—at least ten apprentices would be required to make such a program viable.

Figure 11.2 illustrates this proposal. Not every mission agency will accept it. However, when one considers that there are more than 25 mission agencies with over 315 career overseas missionaries, the possibility for such an approach is very real. The hundreds of smaller agen-

TRAINING AND EXPERIENCE LEVELS	TYPE OF PREPARATION		
	CLASSROOM	FIELD TRAINING	EXPERIENCE
LEVEL I — Pre-Mission: Four to five years of undergraduate work	College undergraduate: Bible, sociology, anthropology & theory of language, French or Spanish	One year formal education in another culture and language	Four summers or interterms with two different agencies and fields
LEVEL II — Mission Training: Three to four years of graduate work	University graduate study: theology, biblical studies, Greek, missionary anthropology and sociology, communication theory and practice	One to two years of field work in area near expected service	Field work done in cooperation with and under supervision of selected mission agency
LEVEL III — Intern: Two years of language acquisition and people study	None	Coaching by senior missionary and former professors via correspondence. Language study.	Assignment to specific people group. Language study among group.
LEVEL IV — Associate Missionary: Two to six years of work on field	Nine months of field work at School of World Mission at end of field work. Review, evaluate.	Supervision by senior missionary	Work with mission team attempting to evangelize assigned group
LEVEL V — Missionary: Two to six years of work on field	None	Supervision of associate missionaries	Decision on assignment to new field or continuance in present field
LEVEL VI — Senior Missionary: Four to eight years of field work and teaching	Two years of graduate study leading to PhD or equivalent	Teaching of trainees and interns. Field evaluation assignments.	Decision to return to a people or to a field teaching situation

FIGURE 11.2   A MODEL FOR MISSIONARY TRAINING

cies should be challenged to join together on some major rethinking of present candidate and educational programs.

THE CHALLENGE OF TRAINING

The missions community increasingly recognizes that cross-cultural training in communicating the gospel and planting the church is essential. The founding of the School of World Mission at Fuller Theological Seminary in 1965 began a dramatic strengthening of mission training in the USA. One thinks of the excellent programs now at Asbury in Kentucky, Trinity Evangelical Divinity School in Illinois, and Columbia Bible College and Seminary in South Carolina. William Carey International University, Dallas Seminary, and many other schools have instituted significant programs in missions.

The need for training centers *within* other cultures, however, remains. Some programs are in place and being strengthened. Daystar University College in Nairobi, Kenya, offers an excellent curriculum in association with Wheaton and Messiah colleges. It attracts students from all over the world. What is needed are regional schools that have direct access to and oversight of existing attempts at cross-cultural ministry.

The task of on-site training of missionaries needs to be viewed as the *highest* missionary calling, not an interruption of the real task. This need is as real and crucial for the new Two-Thirds World missionaries as for the Westerner. The mistakes made and obstacles faced in cross-cultural ministry are similar regardless of the culture of origin. A large agency or a consortium of smaller ones needs to inaugurate such a training center. The Wycliffe Bible Translators have given us a model. Others need to follow.

THE LOCAL CHURCH CAN CHANGE THE WORLD

Some years ago we were involved in designing a training seminar for local churches. It was entitled "The Local Church Can Change the World." The local church provides the missionary vision that its members absorb, leading them to volunteer for service. The local church provides the great bulk of finances and prayer support.

One of the positive signs of the times is the tremendous growth of the Association of Church Missions Committees. Under the banner of "Churches Helping Churches in Mission," it has equipped many local

155

congregations to become more effective support bases. It bridges the gap that often exists between the local church and mission agencies.

In recent years a second Association of International Mission Services (AIMS) has encompassed both local churches and nearly emerging charismatic agencies. The genius of ACMC is that it is completely ecumenical or trans-denominational. It accepts membership from any local church. It desires to push no particular doctrinal emphasis other than finding a firm biblical foundation. Hundreds of local churches are discovering new financial resources that previously have not been tapped. They are also discovering a new interest in the world that lies outside their own country. AIMS's focus on charismatic churches is touching another major segment of churches.

A close look at denominations reveals the difference a church can make when it desires to do so. At one time over half of the overseas missionaries serving under the United Presbyterian Church came from only *six* Presbyterian churches throughout the United States. Concerned and effective Christians are found throughout local congregations. Relationships within the body are what inspire new passion and vigor. Ultimately, the local church will change the world.[6]

Yet it will have to change the people who sit in its own pews first. Many mission executives and a number of thinking missionaries know there is a need for radical changes in the way missions happens. Yet most of them seem to think, "You can't beat the system." They act as though those in the local churches will support only a certain style and philosophy of missions. We believe they are fooling themselves.

What is the average layperson's view of missions?

- Mission is carried out by individual missionaries—men and women of exceptional faith and dedication. It is carried out through individual programs.
- Mission is carried out on a shoestring budget. One of the major indications of the dedication and spirituality of the missionary is his or her willingness to "make do" on an impossibly small income.
- Most missionaries work in areas where there are few, if any, other mission agencies.

6. For more information about the ACMC, write them at 327 Gundersen Drive, Carol Stream, IL 60188. AIMS (Association of International Mission Services, P.O. Box 64534, Virginia Beach, VA 23464) is similar to ACMC except that it includes not only local churches but mission agencies and Training Schools. It is a rapidly growing, primarily charismatic group.

- The basic qualification for a missionary is spiritual dedication, rather than training and education. The latter may be necessary for "specialized" ministries, but for the evangelist a knowledge of Scripture and some knowledge of the language are all that is needed.
- The churches begun by missionaries are, of course, very grateful to them. They need the continuing presence of the missionary to help them mature spiritually.
- Peoples of other lands, particularly non-Western peoples, are like children who need the guidance of the more sophisticated Westerners. They cannot be trusted to adapt the gospel to their own culture.
- The younger, and usually poorer, churches are not to be trusted with no-strings-attached funds.
- The number of missionaries supported by a church or recruited by a mission is a direct indication of the success or effectiveness of the church or mission.

This admitted caricature is the result of a self-reinforcing system of recruiting and fundraising. Young people who feel called by God to serve in a foreign land must believe some, if not all, of these things. In order to present themselves and their work as worthy of financial and prayer support by their lay constituency, they usually must espouse these views.

The local church *can* change the world. It *will* change the world as it gains a more realistic and adequate understanding of the task God is calling us to and gets involved in the excitement of reaching the unreached.

12. The Organizations Available

The Lord must love diversity! There are over twenty-three thousand Christian denominations. In addition there are thousands of local congregations not denominationally affiliated. Added to these are the so-called parachurch agencies. *Parachurch* means "alongside the church." An organization working for the Lord outside the direct control of the local church or denomination, such as the Gideons who distribute Scripture, is a parachurch agency.

Christians often feel uncomfortable about this diversity. Part of the multiplication of denominations and Christian organizations is the outgrowth of sinful factionalism. Christ prayed that his people be one. Yet we are thousands! There are even thirty different Catholic denominations in the United States. Can this be God's will? The ecumenical movement has focused on bringing Christian bodies together in physical, organizational unity.

Even more controversial are the parachurch agencies. Some Christians argue that there should be no separation between the local church/denomination and those set aside for special ministries. Whatever ministry happens in the world should come directly from local congregations/denominations and be accountable to them. Any other structure is a purely human creation hindering God's work. Nevertheless, even denominational practice makes a distinction between the home base and those "set apart" for specific tasks. The New Testament also contains such a distinction (Acts 13:2).

To understand how the parachurch differs from the local church, we need to understand how the latter operates. The local church is a comprehensive organization. It must nurture all those who name Christ as their Lord. It deals with the "walking wounded" whose growth and healing are prerequisite to effective service. Its energies and resources turn inward to deal with the needs and upbuilding of the local body. This goal often becomes so predominant that the church becomes what Frank Tillapaugh calls the "fortress church." "Church work" becomes the work of the church and Christians see their major task as keeping the local congregation humming.

The local church has an additional goal that often conflicts with this inner orientation. It must proclaim Jesus Christ in word and deed to all the world. To do this it must send people forth into the world. Energy, gifts, and resources turn outward. Only those with motivation and adequate maturity to reach beyond their own needs can go. Here the potential for ministry is unleashed into a hoping and hurting world. Rather than waiting for the world to come to the church, the church goes to the world.

Often these conflicting goals are irreconcilable—at least within the local church.[1] That is why the parachurch structure is so effective. It is a second-level commitment structure. To belong to it one must have made the first commitment to Christ as Lord; one must also take the sort of step pastors make in churches: a commitment to specialized, usually professional ministry. Since the parachurch agency exists for a specific ministry task, its goals are less conflicting. Its constituents are adult Christians. Unlike the local church, it does not seek to meet all the needs of its personnel. The local church carries out five or six functions (worship services, choirs, fellowship groups, Christian education, youth groups) and considers its job done.

In the last forty years the parachurch agency has become *the* place of choice for ministry in the USA. Teen ministry is the specialty of Campus Life (Youth for Christ), Young Life, and other paraministries. College campuses are the province of Campus Crusade, InterVarsity Christian Fellowship, the Navigators, International Students, and others. The major problems of alcoholism, drug addiction, homelessness, crisis pregnancy, health care for the poor—even evangelism—are the concern of hundreds of parastructures.

The criteria of the parachurch are training for and effectiveness in specialized ministry. In contrast, the criteria of the churches have been nurturing and fellowship functions. Ask the average church member to go and minister to an apartment complex. The request will frighten many of them. Most will have no idea where to start or what to do. Ask the average parachurch member to do the same thing and they will go and begin ministry.

---

1. In *Strategy for Leadership* (1979) Ed Dayton and Ted Engstrom point this out as a reason why leadership and management of the local church is so difficult. Part of the reason the local church is one of the most complex organizations is because of its conflict of goals.

Parachurch structures have been the primary carriers of the experience of target group ministries. Even denominations have specialized ministry agencies. Most local churches no longer have significant people-group ministry beyond the walls of the church building. But this is slowly changing. The "Unleashed Church" philosophy of ministry is being put into practice in more and more local churches.[2]

Nevertheless, Christian organizations formed for a specific purpose of ministry must select Christians from local fellowships who are gifted for that task. In so doing they must seek those sufficiently healed that their major energies can flow into ministry. Mission agencies cannot take the "walking wounded" with them. Certainly missions must care for those wounded in the midst of the task. Ultimately, though, if they do not recover, they have to return to the nurturing environment of the local fellowship.

ORGANIZATIONAL STRUCTURES

If the force for evangelism is a going church, a community of Christians in relationship to each other, then it will need some formal structure. Every formal organization has a variety of relationships, and a variety of models exist for describing those relationships. Christian executives spend significant time considering the type of organization best suited to their distinctive task. At times the impression is given that the *right* organizational structure would solve all of our difficulties.

One useful model focuses upon the purpose and goals of an organization. This model is particularly helpful for thinking about reaching another people with the gospel because it focuses on why an organization exists (Dayton and Engstrom, 1979). The purposes and goals establish the *boundaries* of the organization (Figure 12.1). Purposes are why we attempt to do something. Goals are the specific, measurable events we hope will come about through that attempt. This model does not stress the *activity* of the organization but what it wants to *accomplish* by its activity.

Within this boundary *motivated and skilled people* who have *adequate resources*, a good *communication network*, and an *appropriate structure* are needed. Together they form the basic elements of organization struc-

2. Frank Tillapaugh, *Unleashing the Church: Getting People out of the Fortress and into Ministry* (Regal Books, 1982); *Unleasing Your Potential: Discovering Your God-Given Opportunities for Ministry* (Regal Books, 1988).

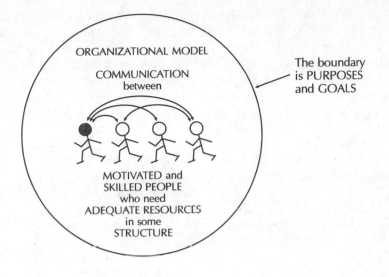

FIGURE 12.1 AN ORGANIZATIONAL MODEL

ture by which evangelization can happen. Let's look at the key elements more closely.

Boundaries: Once we have a clearly stated purpose, we have taken the first major step. This purpose allows us to challenge others to join us if they sense God calling them to fulfill that purpose. Our mission definition contains the purpose for which we exist. We purpose to proclaim salvation in Jesus Christ and call people to fellowship with him.

However, purposes need to be further defined so others know specifically what we intend to do. We mentioned earlier the mission executive who stated the goal of his mission as "To lay Japan at the feet of Christ." This is a high and noble ideal. Its expression, however, is in such broad terms that it is meaningless. We need to know what that would look like: how would we know it has happened? The clearer we are in stating goals and purposes, the more likely we are to attract motivated and skilled people.

Skilled and motivated people: It is much easier to attract people who already are motivated than to motivate people to a new undertaking (Maslow, 1972). We attract motivated people in part by clearly stating our purposes and goals. We do this by defining the people we seek to reach and by stating the means and methods we are to use. We will attract those who also want to reach them through this particular approach.

161

STEP THREE: THE FORCE FOR EVANGELIZATION

Wycliffe Bible Translators is a prime example of an organization that has grown tremendously by using clearly stated purposes and goals. Their general purpose is to make the Scriptures available in all languages. They concentrate on the minority peoples of the world and seek to reduce spoken languages to written form. There are many more oral cultures than they can now serve. So their purpose becomes highly focused on a limited number of particular peoples. The goal becomes very clear: "To reduce the language of the _____ people into writing and to translate the New Testament into it by _____." Wycliffe was the third largest agency in 1988 with 2,585 personnel. That fact reflects the power of clear goals in recruiting people.

People must not only be motivated; they must also be gifted and skilled. Natural abilities, learned skills, and spiritual gifts are all important components in those who are active in an organization. People also need adequate training and experience. It does little good to have people who are willing if they are unable to carry out what needs to be done. A strong desire to drive an automobile does not insure that an inexperienced driver will be able to start the car or keep it on the road safely.

Adequate Resources: Motivated and gifted people need adequate resources. These include finances, materials, prayer support, and a variety of physical necessities. By mobilizing resources, people can make an impact on the world and accomplish their goals.

Communication: Communication between human beings is much more difficult than most of us recognize. There are a variety of ways to communicate: speech, writing, body language, symbols, appearance, actions, and so on. These have different roles in the communication network. People have differing levels of ability to utilize them, and differing needs for the various kinds of communication. However, all organizational actors need communication informing them of their progress toward their goals. They also need to know the relationships they are to have with fellow organizational members.

If there is a group of motivated, gifted people who have adequate resources to carry out the task, a good communication system between them, a commonly shared purpose, and specifically identified goals, then there is a high probability of reaching the goals.

Organizational Structure: The relationships and communication network of an organization require some form of structure. People, resources, and relationships are *formally organized.* There is a wide variety of models of such explicitly stated arrangements (E. Dale, 1967). Of course, the formal organization never functions with complete efficiency. Thus, informal organizational patterns develop alongside the formal to accomplish some tasks better. Together the formal and the informal are the structured patterns of interaction and activity that direct energy toward goal accomplishment. (Admittedly, at some levels they may also direct energy in very different directions.)

Attributes of an effective structure include: a clear picture of the lines of authority, responsibility, and communication; a division of labor defining each individual's activity in terms of the organization's goals; a system of evaluating and reporting progress toward the goals; a way of handling problems and resolving conflicts within the task groups.

In selecting the force for evangelism, we need to consider more than individual gifts and roles: we need to describe some form of structure. Specifically, we need to consider possible structures in relation to the culture of our target people group. They have their own patterns of decision making and resource mobilization. We must never forget the power of building indigenous churches by using indigenous methods. Nor must we forget the power of imitation. The resulting church often models itself after the community from which it heard the good news. Frequently the structures developed by the evangelizing agency become an essential heritage. In the devolution from mission to church the organizational structures that do not fit indigenous life have a deadening effect. It is like David trying to wear Saul's armor when facing Goliath (1 Sam. 17:38-39). The armor was cumbersome and David knew he could fight more effectively without it. There was nothing essentially wrong with the armor. However, in a life-and-death situation the question becomes what is efficient and effective. Just so the vital goals and purposes of evangelization may be lost in the struggle to keep cumbersome Western organizations going.

The *ideal* organizational structure would be one that is similar to structures already present in the culture. Or alternatively it may be a structure that members of the culture are already adopting because *they* see it as workable and effective. The principles of such an organizational structure may be very different from those the missionary understands.

PRIORITIES FOR THE CHRISTIAN ORGANIZATION

We believe there are three levels of Christian priority that should order our lives individually and organizationally. Foremost is our commitment and loyalty to God in Jesus Christ. Nothing should have higher value than our obedience and focus on who God is and what he wants us to be.

A close second in importance is our commitment to the body of Christ. The great commandment requires us to love God and to love our neighbor. Within the horizontal relationship we are to show particular loyalty and love to those who are fellow members of the household of faith. This includes our own family: husband, wife, children, and near kin.

Third in order is our commitment to the work of Christ. What we do flows out of a life properly rooted in relationship with God and with his people. The temptation of the activist West is to give first priority to work and career achievement. Family, church, and God end up sacrificed to the imperative of task achievement. Unfortunately, this results in shattered lives and relationships. Christian workers become overwhelmed by the demands of their work, and their relationships weaken.

The forces working within an organization normally come from the force of one's position and the power belonging to the individual. But there is a "third force" operative in the Christian organization: the power of the Holy Spirit. In a way unlike that in any other organization the Holy Spirit guides each person within the Christian organization. There is a common allegiance to something higher than the organization itself. Secular organizations have an allegiance to professions, which transcends the organization or to the trade sector of which it is a part. This modifies the allegiance to the particular organization. The Christian's allegiance is ultimate.

Any profound allegiance is subject to manipulation. People then are put in the position of being tools rather than integral members of a body of Christ. Christian organizations have a clear model for testing the adequacy of their organizational life: "Those parts of the body that seem to be weaker are indispensable, and the parts we think are less honorable we treat with special honor" (1 Cor. 12:22-23). There is no room here for structures that assume that leaders give directions and followers carry out tasks regardless of their relationships to each other.[3]

3. Recent publications parallel what Christians should have known all along. Harry Levinson (1968) indicates that the effectiveness of people in work depends heavily upon how they feel about each other. Organizations more and more are being viewed as like organisms. The machinelike model that underlies much of Taylor's Scientific Management model is rapidly being discarded, especially in organizations noted for their excellence. See also Thomas J. Peters and Robert Waterman, Jr., *In Search of Excellence: Lessons from America's Best-Run Companies* (Harper & Row, 1982) and Peters and Austin, *A Passion for Excellence: The Leadership Difference* (Random House, 1985). Gareth Morgan, *Images of Organization* (Sage Publications, 1986) portrays eight ways of modelling organizations with the strengths and limitations of each.

AN ORGANIZATIONAL CHECKLIST

An organization can ask itself a number of questions in deciding if it is qualified to evangelize a particular people.

1. Do we have enough information about this people to make this decision? Do we have adequate research and information?
2. Are we already working in this country? If not, do we understand the complexities of working within this particular national boundary?
3. Have we ever worked with a similar people group? What have we learned from that experience? Were we effective? If not, why do we think we might be effective with this new group?
4. Do we have skilled and motivated people available to serve as the force for evangelism? Will we have to provide further training?
5. Do we have adequate mature leadership to move into the field?
6. How many people should be on the team sent to reach the people group?
7. How long do we think it will take before a church or cluster of congregations comes into being?
8. How long before we anticipate that it will be capable to evangelize its own people by E-1 evangelism?
9. Are we able to expand the current organization to carry this additional responsibility? Will we need to move from the place(s) in which we are now working? Is this an opportunity for withdrawal from previous work?
10. Can we expect a wide base of support from those who give us financial support? Will we be able to communicate what we are doing in such a way as to build the necessary prayer support?
11. Will our present structure fit this need or will we have to change our structure? Will any organizational changes meet strong resistance? Are we able to change?
12. Will we be able to work with others who are working in the country or among this people? Will we be a welcome addition to the local church that may be there or others working with the people group?
13. Is there another organization that might do as good a job as we can? Why are we the ones to do it? Have we really sought

the mind of the Holy Spirit? Is there a general consensus among our group based on prayer and meditation?

MISSIONS IN PARTNERSHIP

As we consider available organizations we cannot overlook the tremendous growth in "Third World" missions. Demographically there are more evangelicals in the Two-Thirds World nations than in the traditional centers of Western Christianity. The future axis of world evangelization may well be shifting. The center always coincides with the most vivid and vital sectors of the World Christian movement.

In his study of Third World mission agencies (1989), Larry Pate calculated at least 1,094 cross-cultural mission agencies with about 35,924 missionaries. We cannot ignore this dynamic growth and reality when considering the appropriate organizational arm for evangelization.

Western mission organizations have two sorts of possibilities for involvement with Third World missions. One involves the internationalizing of traditional Western agencies. This can happen in part by bringing Christian leaders from the younger churches of Asia, Africa, and Latin America into positions of power and advice on boards. It can also happen by bringing such Christians into the body of frontline missionary church planters and into administrative positions. The Western agency need not confine itself simply to its traditional force for evangelism.

The other possibility is partnership in missions. A Western agency need not assume it must be pioneer and patron. It can be partner and servant to organizations indigenous to the context in which church planting is to happen. Many unique problems for Two-Thirds' World mission agencies (such as currency restrictions) find solutions in partnership with Western structures.

At the least we should assume we cannot go it alone. One of our organizational goals should be to bring together the force for evangelism already present in a country. One of the most significant roles we can play is to bridge some of the gulfs between existing groups. Then we need to get out of their way as the dynamic of the unity of the body begins to work. Our money and expertise are not always what is needed most. Nor are our organizational structures the only means for facilitating evangelization.

For example, the Missionary Prayer Band in India originally emerged to pray for non-Christians. This praying resulted in people being led to go to those for whom they were praying. There was little formal structure and no need for outside assistance. The itinerant evangelists were integral to the culture, used its transportation, lived at its standard. It was indigenous in every way. Far more appropriate evangelization occurred because of the nature of its structure.

As we face the decade of the 1990s, we are aware of a continuing dissatisfaction among young people with existing mission organizations. Becoming a missionary is a difficult and daunting undertaking. The policies and procedures that govern agencies, the concern about raising necessary support, and the burdens of debt, family, and education create challenging difficulties.

One of the realities of late twentieth-century cross-cultural missions is the skyrocketing cost of supporting the average Western missionary. Best estimates indicate that current expenditures for overseas ministry are more than $33,100 per person/year unit (as of 1988).[4] What implications this has for developing new and changing old organizations for maximum effectiveness in *world* evangelization is worth pondering.

A number of churches send missionaries directly from the local congregation (Elkins, 1974). The strength of such a structure is the warm and supportive home base that usually is well informed about the ministry. The weakness of such a structure is the lack of knowledge and experience. Too often a fervent heart replaces a fertile mind. Without the larger network of people and relationships, it is difficult to capitalize on insight and experience for maximum effectiveness. How often we reinvent the wheel!

It is possible to begin new mission agencies. The number of mission agencies founded in North America has actually *increased* each decade in the twentieth century.[5] Entrepreneurship in cross-cultural missions is alive and well. Some new agencies begin as parachurch structures. Our advice when considering this direction is to look before you leap. This involves a great deal of homework and learning from others. We would suggest that a person or group considering entrepreneurship here go through the ten steps described in this book.

Before launching something new, read a survey of what others are already doing. Fortunately, there are a number of good publications surveying Protestant mission agencies. *Mission Handbook: North American Protestant Ministries Overseas* comes out every two or three years. The 1989 edition of that reference is a gold mine. There are also handbooks for Great Britain and Europe. Many new agencies have begun in the decade of the

4. *Mission Handbook*, 14th ed., p. 51.
5. *Mission Handbook*, 14th ed., p. 53; 13th ed., pp. 593-94.

1980s. Many more will begin in this coming decade. Yet it is hard to avoid the impression that many also will fail for lack of careful forethought.

It is also our experience that established mission agencies are open to well-organized programs proposed by those outside the agency. Often these agencies have incorporated such programs into their overall structure and activities.

In all of this we need "just enough" information to help us move forward in planning and acting. Planning strategies for evangelization is a *process*. We cannot accurately predict the future. Our organizations will have to be responsive to unanticipated changes as well as pro-active in seeking to control its own activities in goal fulfillment. We never have as much information as we want. Yet we can increase our effectiveness and efficiency as we become more aware of organizational possibilities and partnerships that will further world evangelization.

Questions

1. How would you describe the faith and vision necessary for the missionary?

2. How does Western individualism affect the whole concept of mission?

3. What is the role of the "call" in deciding the force for evangelism?

4. What sorts of considerations are crucial in selecting the best people for evangelizing cross-culturally?

5. Are there Christian churches and mission agencies already present in this country? What is their attitude and relationship to the people group you have targeted? What is their attitude likely to be if you go ahead in evangelizing that people group?

6. What kind of experience should a missionary team have? What gifts will be needed? What training? What resources will need to be brought? What steps will be taken to insure that they go as part of a missionary *community*?

7. Is there any group successfully evangelizing this people group? What sorts of methods and approaches are they using? What sorts of methods and structures will most likely be able to be used by the indigenous church, once it is in existence?

8. Why do you think there are not enough missionaries to match the needs of world evangelization? Why do you think the majority of the current missionary force is not focused on the unreached peoples?

9. What do you believe are the steps needed to prepare adequately a cross-cultural missionary able to reach a specific people group? Are our current training programs and structures adequate to this job?

10. How can we help the average person see the mission task as

it really is? What are some of the common myths and illusions that hinder clear vision?

11. Why is it important that the local church sees that it needs to be involved in missions?

STEP 4: MEANS AND METHODS

Considerations

1. The right use of the right means is not the key to success in evangelism. Nor is leaving the results in God's hands alone.

2. More and more we are inserting technology between us and those we seek to evangelize. Our contacts are increasingly more impersonal and fleeting. Yet all our studies indicate that the nature and length of contact is the single most important element in evangelism.

3. The multiplicity of peoples requires a multiplicity of methods. Every method excludes some types of people from authentic witness and must be complemented by other methods that include them.

4. We cannot protect the vital role of the Holy Spirit in evangelism by denying the means of the Holy Spirit. Methods play a causal role in producing the effects we seek.

5. Methodology that is ill conceived and poorly applied without regard to cultural differences leaves us with no humanly justifiable reasons for thinking evangelization is being forwarded.

6. We must continually be modifying a method as we evaluate its results.

7. Wherever we look for methods for ministry, we ultimately will have to incarnate them in terms that make sense for the particular context and people among whom we are evangelizing.

8. The very people we seek to evangelize may be able to teach us the best methods by which they can be most effectively evangelized.

9. There is something contradictory about trying to create an indigenous church by using nonindigenous methods.

13. Selecting Means and Methods

Up-to-date equipment in perfect working order never guarantees a bumper crop in farming or a full hold in a fishing boat. Tools and techniques are only a part of any human endeavor. The skill and experience of the person using them make a significant difference. Weather, unusual plant diseases, or pests also affect results.

Right methods and tools do not guarantee a large harvest. But the wrong methods and tools can be a quick road to failure. When the seed is misplanted or an apple orchard harvested with a tomato picker, the results are disastrous.

When Jesus told the disciples to let the net down, they caught more fish than ever before (John 21:1-14). They had caught nothing all night. Yet had the net not been in good working order, they would have caught nothing even at his command.

Means and methods in evangelism are important even if they are not sufficient to guarantee desired results. Any strategy that takes the gospel seriously must take the means and methods of communicating it seriously. In this section we will look at the place of tools and techniques in the overall strategy for evangelism. Tools are simply the instruments we use to achieve our goals. Techniques are the way in which the tools, labor, and skill are put together to reach goals effectively and efficiently.

There is nothing magical about means and methods. They are the links between our expenditure of time, energy, and resources and our desired goals. A method is a regular or orderly way of doing something. It is a standardized procedure for producing a given result. Experience or research tells us a method or procedure produces the results we seek. Methods discipline our action and thought by providing a pre-thought pattern for what we do and how we approach a task.

Defining our mission tells us what we are to do and why.

Selecting a people group tells us those we take as our target audience. The force for evangelism outlines the personnel available for mission accomplishment. Means and methods answers the question *how*.

METHODS AND THE HOLY SPIRIT

Some years ago John Nevius wrote: "Let us bear in mind that the best methods cannot do away with the difficulties of our work which come from the world, the flesh and the devil, but bad methods may multiply and intensify them" (1958, p. 10). A concern for methods, their effects, their relationship to the Holy Spirit, their justifiability, and their integrity is not new in Christian circles.

Wherever new tools and methods appear in evangelism, there is bound to be controversy. We grow comfortable with the patterns of doing things accepted by prior Christian generations. The dramatically new, often aimed at people groups never reached or no longer being reached by those old patterns, disturbs the status quo.

Some methods, however, contradict the nature of the message and life being communicated. The cult group, Children of God, used "sexual fishing" as a method for winning converts. Sleeping with potential converts was considered "witnessing." So a concern about means and methods is legitimate.

Some missiologists fear a focus on methods may well subvert our dependence upon Christ. *He* should tell us where and when to lower our nets. Dr. H. Kraemer once said: "I never did agree with you Americans. You seem to have the idea that by getting together and using the proper methods you can do anything. You leave out of consideration the operation of the Holy Spirit" (in Douglas, 1973, p. 243).

One famous event in the history of Protestant missions turned on this same sentiment. William Carey felt the urge of the Spirit to evangelize in pagan countries. The older leaders said, "Sit down young man. When God wants to convert the heathen, he will do it without your help." In 1792 Carey responded with the powerful *An Enquiry into the Obligation of Christians to use Means for the Conversion of Heathen*. He even argued that the mariner's compass was a key invention for reaching the lost of the world. He then went to Serampore, India, and demonstrated how God could win the lost *with* his help.

Again the problem is the extremes of pride or sloth. Pride makes too much of the human factor, believing everything turns on the effectiveness of our methods. Sloth estimates human means too lightly,

175

believing nothing turns on our methods. The one leads to burn-out and constant guilt. The other leads to sloppiness and irresponsibility. Both are forms of self-deception.

It is a false theology that tries to protect the work of the Holy Spirit by denying the means of the Spirit. God does use means, and not all means are equally good instruments for carrying out his will. Different strategies using different means and methods do have different results.

If we were Christian farmers, we would not ignore the laws of nature and simply hope for a good harvest. We would not think the more ignorant and backward we are the more room God has to bring in the harvest.

When we translate the Bible into a new language, we do not refuse to use modern linguistic techniques. We do not suppose we can bypass years of language learning and careful study. We compile dictionaries and analyze sentence structures. Is this really *less* spiritual than were we to sit and hope the Holy Spirit would give us the words directly? Dare we tempt God in that fashion?

Means and methods are not enemies of God's activity in our efforts. God works *through* us. That means we can trust him to use our imperfect efforts channeled by imperfect means to accomplish his perfect ends. God does through us and our methods what we can never do alone: work the miracle of new birth. John R. W. Stott has some sound words:

> Some say rather piously that the Holy Spirit is himself the complete and satisfactory solution to the problem of communication, and indeed that when he is present and active, then communication ceases to be a problem. What on earth does such a statement mean? Do we now have liberty to be as obscure, confused and irrelevant as we like, and the Holy Spirit will make all things plain? To use the Holy Spirit to rationalize our laziness is nearer to blasphemy than piety. Of course *without* the Holy Spirit all our explanations [or methods] are futile. But this is not to say that *with* the Holy Spirit they are also futile. For the Holy Spirit chooses to work through them. (1975, p. 127)

WHAT DIFFERENCE DO METHODS MAKE?

Methods are not abstract things. They are related to the skill of the people who use them and the context of their application. A skilled surgeon using a particular surgical procedure might save a life while an average surgeon could not. Yet some patients are so ill that even the best surgeon with the best equipment and team could not help.

What difference does the presence or absence of love make

when people communicate Christ? Or the undergirding of prayer? Or cultural sensitivity? Or the nationality or race of the communicator? Methods and means have an impact because of who uses them and how they are used. Effects produced are more than matters of a correct ordering of tools and sequence of procedure.

We cannot fairly say that differences in the quality and depth of spirituality are at the root of differences in results. We all know that prayer is crucial to the work of the kingdom. We also know that even the purest and clearest version of the good news can fall infertile when sown on hearts not yet ready (Matt. 13:1-23). We can point out two Christian groups with what we perceive to be roughly equal levels of prayer, purity, piety, and passion for the lost. Yet one experiences a significant harvest and the other does not, even in the same context with the same target group. All things being equal, the means chosen to achieve the goals can make significant differences in the results. Consider the following example:

> *Case Study 1:* Two gifted and dedicated lady missionaries were sent by their missionary society to Northwest China. Their mandate was to evangelize and plant congregations in a cluster of villages. They spoke fluent Chinese; they labored faithfully and fervently. After a decade, a small congregation emerged. However, most of its members were women. Their children attended the Sunday School regularly. The visitor to this small congregation would easily detect the absence of men.
>
> In their reports and newsletters, both missionaries referred to the "hardness of hearts" that was prevalent among the men. References were also made to promising teenagers who were opposed by their parents when they sought permission for baptism.
>
> *Case Study 2:* In 1930 a spiritual awakening swept through the Little Flock Assembly in Shantung. Many members sold their entire possessions in order to send seventy *families* to the Northwest as "instant" congregations. Another thirty *families* migrated to the Northeast. By 1944 forty new assemblies had been established and all these were vitally involved in evangelism. (Chua, 1975, p. 968)

In both cases the goals and the people group were the same. Orthodoxy and dedication marked both groups evangelizing. What caused the differences in results? The most obvious answer is the difference in the force for evangelism and evangelistic approach and method. Chua Wee Hian analyses the differences in this fashion:

> Consider the case of the two single lady missionaries. Day by day, the Chinese villagers saw them establishing contacts and building the bridges of friendships with the women, usually when their husbands

or fathers were out working in the fields or trading in nearby towns. Their foreignness (dubbed "red hair devils") was enough to incite cultural and racial prejudices in the minds of the villagers. But their single status was something that was socially questionable. It was a well-known fact in all Chinese society that the families constitute basic social units. These units insure security. In Confucian teaching, three of the five basic relationships have to do with family ties—father and son, brother and younger brother, husband and wife. The fact that these ladies were making contacts with individual women and not having dialogues with the elders would make them appear to be foreign agents seeking to destroy the fabric of the village community. A question that would constantly crop up in the gossip and discussion of the villagers would be the fact of the missionaries' single state. Why aren't they married? Why aren't they visibly related to their parents, brothers and sisters, uncles and aunts and other relatives? So when they persuaded the women or the youth to leave the religion of their forefathers, they were regarded as "family-breakers."

By contrast, the Little Flock Assembly in sending out Chinese Christian families sent out agents that were recognizable socio-cultural entities. Thus the seventy families became an effective missionary task force. It is not difficult to imagine the heads of these families sharing their faith with the elders of the villagers. The grandmothers could informally transmit the joy of following Christ and of their deliverance from demonic powers to the older women in pagan villages. The housewives in the markets could invite their counterparts to attend the services that were held each Sunday by the "instant congregations." No wonder forty new assemblies were established as a result of this approach to church-planting and evangelism. (1975, pp. 968-69)

Methods make a difference, but only as part of a wider set of things. In this case the agents of evangelism, the cultural expectations of the target group, and the focus of evangelistic communication were all significant. The effective strategy was that which aimed at evangelizing whole families by whole families.

We noted earlier that the effectiveness of methods relates to the resistancy/receptivity of a people group. Where the gospel is strongly opposed or forbidden, not even superior methodology in the hands of compassionate and sensitive evangelists will win many. Where a people group is coming into the church faster than it can assimilate them, almost any method will reap the harvest. We say *almost* any method because experience shows that a particularly bad methodology can stop a people movement in its early phases.

Methods make the most difference in the middle range of receptivity. Where there is moderate interest or resistance, the selection of a proper method can make enormous differences in the final results.

The actual cultural patterns, institutions, and social structure of a people group will affect the way a method functions. Major differences in the applicability of a method can be the result of slight differences in outlook, values, and social structure. For example, suppose our goal was to evangelize the barrios of the Philippines. A careful study of methods concludes that winning families, whole networks of relatives, is the most effective approach. Friendship evangelism seems the preferred method. So we make contacts with the male heads of families, not realizing that the cultural head of the family there is the woman. The same method focused on the woman or the man will produce very different results.

David Hesselgrave describes a similar experience:

> Missionaries working out of Manila have found that the house-to-house survey method of making contacts for evangelistic campaigns which has been relatively successful in Manila meets considerable resistance in outlying villages. City-dwellers are more used to doorbell-ringers and their rather prying questions. Village-dwellers are suspicious of the motives of strangers who invade their quiet communities asking personal questions and inviting them to meetings sponsored by outsiders. On the other hand, missionaries have found that the villagers are often responsive when local friendships are established and utilized, identity and purposes are clarified, and the message is given by precept upon precept over a period of time. (*Communicating,* p. 371)

We must admit in all of this that we do not have as much control over results as we would like. Our real concern is to give people a culturally sensitive, spiritually authentic opportunity to discover Jesus Christ and decide whether to submit to him. Methodology is important in creating that opportunity. Where it is ill-considered and poorly applied, there is no human justification for believing any such opportunity is happening.

Working with human beings is an endlessly exciting and frustrating experience. We are continually learning and revising our ideas about how things work in a given group and social setting. What we think will work at times produces the very opposite effect we seek. So the Holy Spirit must open our hearts and eyes to new ways of doing things more in line with his goals for evangelization. We may not be able to control the effects we seek as completely as we can. Yet we can accept responsibility to grow in grace and wisdom. We can become more knowledgeable and skillful in sharing Christ among a given people group.

179

Finally, there is no "one best method" for a given context. This notion comes from the scientific management movement begun by Frederick W. Taylor. Applied to industrial production techniques, it studied the work process and worker movements to find the one best way of organizing and implementing the task at hand. It led to tremendous increases in productivity in the twentieth century. But it is not entirely applicable outside the highly controlled, repetitively ordered production line of a factory.

Several methods may be highly effective in moving a people toward encounter with Christ and incorporation into a church. Allen J. Swanson points out the striking contrasts between two rapidly growing independent church movements in Taiwan:

> The point is that there is no one set pattern to church growth. One group has large, ostentatious churches, and the other does not. Church polity and organization are almost opposite one another. One pays the leaders from the national headquarters and the other is completely anonymous and by faith. One uses tongues and faith healing, the other only secondarily. One appears to have money, the other does not. One uses a seminary and the other does not. One uses Mandarin and the other Taiwanese . . . yet both use translators. One relies heavily upon spiritual revival meetings, the other stresses intensive lay training. One has three sacraments and a fairly worked-out theology. And yet both grow. They grow because they practice the doctrine of the priesthood of all believers. They grow because they are churches of the soil belonging to the Chinese and served entirely by the Chinese. They grow because all are vitally concerned with their walk in Christ and in sharing this life with others. They grow because the Spirit blesses their churches also. (1971, p. 218)

With this awareness we cannot fall into the trap of the method-mania of Western culture. In every area of life—education, politics, personal adjustment, athletics, oil exploration, electronics, organizational administration, counseling—a frenetic drive for the most effective and efficient techniques is dominant. Some critics of Western culture say means and methods are so important that the West no longer knows what ends it should seek.

Much of popular Christian culture in the USA is dominated by a technical or method orientation to the Christian life. Countless "how to" books line the shelves in Christian bookstores. Louis Schneider and Sanford Dornbush's *Popular Religion: Inspirational Books in America* (1958) documents the roots of this in popular piety. Faith itself is instrumentalized. We are offered a toolbox of spiritual techniques guaranteed to deliver the Holy Spirit, health, wealth, and power.

Christians have rightly been uncomfortable with this line of thinking, especially when applied to evangelization. Charles Finney (1792–1875), for example, argued that a "revival" (what we today call a successful evangelistic campaign) "is a purely philosophical result of the right use of the constitutional means." By *philosophical* Finney meant an inevitable success:

> The connection between the right use of means for a revival and a revival is as philosophically sure as between the right use of means to raise grain and a crop of wheat. I believe, in fact, it is more certain and that there are fewer instances of failure. (McLoughlin, 1959, p. 85)

Read contemporary literature from some of the large ministries in North America. It is surprising to see how many claim their methods to be heaven-sent answers to the challenges of world evangelization. Their proponents are as messianic (and naive) about them as Finney was about his methods. Methods are important and make significant differences given all the other factors. Yet in the midst of it all we must not lose sight of who we are in relationship to God and his gospel. Pope Paul VI has well said:

> The first means of evangelization is the witness of an authentically Christian life, given over to God in a communion that nothing should destroy and at the same time given to one's neighbor with limitless zeal. . . . St. Peter expressed this well when he held up the example of a reverent and chaste life that wins over even without a word those who refuse to obey the word. It is therefore primarily by her conduct and by her life that the Church will evangelize the world, in other words, by her living witness of fidelity to the Lord Jesus—the witness of poverty and detachment, of freedom in the face of the powers of this world, in short, the witness of sanctity. (1976, p. 28)

WHAT ARE MEANS AND METHODS?

We define *means* or *methods* as humanly devised tools and procedures with an associated pattern of action and organization aimed at producing given results and changes in the world. Because they are humanly devised, they are subject to change and improvement. Even "biblically based" methods are based on our limited human understandings of the Scripture. Thus they are relative, not absolute. Their legitimacy comes from the degree to which they serve the will of God in the evangelization of a specific people or people group.

Methods are a grouping of tools and procedures. A visitation evangelism method might include letters, printed literature, the phone, certain transportation facilities, and a training program to equip staff for the actual evangelistic presentation.

Methods also imply some type of standardized or regularized behavior on the part of people. It specifies how the tools and procedures are to be used, in what sequence, and by whom. It coordinates the activities and relationships between people in order to maximize effectiveness. "New Life for All" in Africa is a saturation evangelism method that coordinates various activities of many Christians from all churches. The "Four Spiritual Laws" booklet attempts to standardize the verbal presentation of the gospel to individuals.

Methods are goal-oriented. The question of method is a "how" question, the best *means* to an end. Methods are developed and used to achieve some results and not others. Each has a limited ability to change our world. An evaluation of a method always relates to the end it is to achieve. For example, a screwdriver can do many things besides tighten or loosen screws: it can poke holes in paper, pry open a tight window, or even stab a person in the back. But it cannot turn a rusted bolt or cut a piece of glass. A method or tool must be evaluated by the goal it is intended to accomplish.

Methods are *patterns,* sets of principles or prescriptions that inform us how to act to achieve given results. Manuals for training in *Evangelism Explosion* (Kennedy, 1983) or In-Depth Evangelism supply that kind of information. James Montgomery's DAWN (Discipling a Whole Nation) is a pattern by which evangelization can reach out to all peoples in a country. All three describe the methodology used by the way it is supposed to work, the plan, and procedures for action.

Methods are also *actual performances,* the events that attempt to carry out the principles of an evangelism methodology. To see a method as practice we observe the people who gather to train or to evangelize. We watch to see the procedures and techniques of the pattern they have adopted. Methodologies can be well or poorly performed: the results will differ. Evangelism in Depth in Guatemala was an implementation of In-Depth Evangelism principles. When Rose Hill Quaker Church called fifty thousand homes to invite the unchurched to their worship, they put the principles of the telemarketing method, "The Phone's for You," into the real world.

Methods can become *philosophies.* This is especially true of the more comprehensive methodologies. They often develop elaborate rationales and explanations for their legitimacy and effectiveness. They may even have critiques of alternative methodologies, seeking to gain the allegiance of Christians. As philosophies of ministry they attempt to provide more than just means and methods. They offer a theory and theology of method.

These distinctions are important when we discuss or evaluate the usefulness of methods in different contexts. Here is a list of some commonly characterized methods that are used in the evangelization process:

Ashrams or retreat centers	Film strips
Tract distribution	Gospel records
Cassettes	Mass crusades
Telemarketing	Video recordings
Door-to-door visitation	Personal witnessing
Mail campaigns	Bus ministry
Drama presentations	Crisis centers
Television programs	Literacy classes
Newspaper advertising	Healing services
Medical evangelism	Counseling
Industrial evangelism	Evangelism survey
Open-air preaching	Movies
Camping programs	Billboards
Christian schools	Revival meetings
Athletic contests	Social service
Correspondence courses	Prayer breakfasts
Recreation centers	Christian books
Bible translation	Dialogues
Home Bible studies	Church services
Christian magazines	Tentmakers

These examples are actually *classes* of similar methods, of similar "grammars" or patterns for achieving evangelistic goals. All camps and camping programs have some common elements—they are away from home, most stress activity in the out-of-doors, and so on. Yet each actual camp has its own schedule, organization, age, and social class groups. One might stress basketball, baseball, and archery. It might be rather expensive and last for a three-week period. Another might be inexpensive, rugged in facilities, focused on water sports and horseback riding. Some are explicitly aimed at evangelism; others stress enhancing the understanding and leadership qualities of Christians.

Visitation methods are all similar in that they seek to meet people at their home. Some, however, make unannounced calls, as in a canvassing of a residential area. Others call only on people who have come to visit the church. Some give out literature as part of the visit. The purpose of the contact may be only to get to know the family. Or it may be to make a gospel presentation and seek an immediate decision. For some groups visitation is a way of fulfilling a church requirement (such as the Jehovah's Witnesses). Each program of visitation has a different training component and utilizes a different "pitch" (verbal presentation).

In-Depth Evangelism, a saturation evangelism method developed in Central America by Kenneth Strachan, illustrates all three levels on which methods can exist. Orlando Costas writes:

> The generic term *In-Depth Evangelism* stands for a worldwide evangelistic movement which had its *formal* inception in an experiment carried out in the Republic of Nicaragua in 1960. It can be succinctly described as an effort to *mobilize the church of Jesus Christ with all of her resources for a comprehensive witness in the world.* It represents, at once, a dynamic evangelistic concept, a comprehensive strategic methodology and a coordinated, functional program. (Costas, 1975, p. 675)

As a "concept" (what we call *philosophy*), In-Depth Evangelism offers a comprehensive view of the world, the church, and the message of Christ. This is what gives it theological rationale and depth. As a "comprehensive strategic methodology," it rests on the principle that "the successful expansion of any movement is in direct proportion to its success in mobilizing and occupying its total membership in constant propagation of its beliefs."[1]

As a set of principles to *pattern* activity, it seeks to mobilize Christians to witness through consciousness raising, analysis of needs and resources, planning for action, coordination of the efforts of many churches, and evaluation. The most common elements at this level are the formation of prayer cells, the training of laity, a visitation program to contact every home, and special evangelistic campaigns.

Seen as *practice,* the method "can take many different programmatic forms" (Costas, 1975, p. 687). Costas offers examples from a nationwide effort in Cameroon, a denominational thrust in Vietnam, a program strategy for a local congregation in North America, and a citywide interdenominational effort in Santiago, Chile. In each case the pattern or principles were modified to suit the scope and culture of its application. Costas argues, "In-Depth evangelistic programs are relative to the needs, cultural characteristics, historical circumstances, and resources of the church everywhere. *There are no fixed program patterns*" (1975, p. 693).

Keeping these three levels in mind helps us analyze and eval-

---

1. Roberts, 1971, p. 86; also Roberts, 1967; Peters, 1970.

uate methods. At times the philosophy of the method is so dominant it masks the lack of goal achievement of the method as practiced. When we seek to evaluate or criticize a method we must be clear what it is we are doing. Are we evaluating the pattern on which it is based or the philosophy of ministry that justifies it? Or are we concerned with the actual implementation and results of the method in action?

When we consider carrying a method into a new cultural context these different levels may not translate equally well. We may continue to believe strongly in the philosophy of ministry while radically altering the pattern and practice because of cultural considerations. Many of the problems associated with Western evangelism techniques in cross-cultural settings come from the confusion of these three levels. The attempt to sustain them as a single package is usually misguided.

In sum, we define means and methods as humanly devised tools and procedures with an associated pattern of action and organization aimed at achieving a given result in the world. Methods exist at three levels: as ideal patterns of action, as philosophies of ministry, and as actual performed implementations with measurable results.

CLASSIFYING METHODS

Methods as pattern and practice possess certain key qualities that help us understand them. Classifying methods is one way to analyze those qualities. As yet there is no accepted set of questions to use in qualifying methods. How methods are classified depends on the reasons for their use. Here are some ways in which methods for evangelization might be classified.

- The degree to which a method is biblically justified
- Technological sophistication required by the method
- Implementation by laity or by experts
- Length of time for the method to complete one cycle of its implementation
- Relative financial cost
- "Church" vs "parachurch" methodology
- Relevance of a method to a given evangelistic goal

Each of these ways of looking at a methodology helps us understand it. We will look at only a few areas of particular relevance for selecting and evaluating a method for evangelistic strategy.

STEP 4: MEANS AND METHODS

1. Contact between the Evangelist and the Target Group

Many studies show that the personal relationship between evangelizer and evangelized is of chief importance. John Nevius wrote that the greatest number of conversions in China one hundred years ago was "to be referred to private social intercourse" (1958, p. 84). Marion Cowan described the growth of a Christian movement among the Huixtan Tzotzil of Mexico, which he attributed almost entirely to family ties. Half of the eighty cases studied came to Christ through the influence of "blood" (consanguineal) relatives. The others came through the influence of relatives by marriage (affinal). Only three were without kinship ties (1962).

Studies of the growth of the church in Japan show how important the nature of the contact can be. The early missionaries began schools for training college-level students in Christianity and in Western science. Those flooding into the schools were top-level samurai thrown out of power by the Meiji restoration. They felt they had no future in the new Japan except as experts in the powerful techniques and knowledge of the West. Many of them came to Christ. Consequently, the origin of the Protestant movement in Japan was among educated, urban people. To this day such a social class location is still characteristic of the Protestant church there. The method chosen (setting up colleges) formed in-depth relationships with the samurai class.[2] Samurai became church leaders and attracted more urban, educated Japanese into their denominations.

By contrast, the schools developed in Africa as a means of evangelization were very different. Few Africans were literate; therefore, mission schools opened at the elementary level. As a result the church became identified with education and children. The older men of the tribes did not convert or attend the churches. That was for children and those who read (Shoemaker, 1970). Traditional, rural, and older people were bypassed in favor of the younger who were willing to be educated.

Methods may be long-term or short-term. Evangelism through schools is a long-term method—the contact is extensive, personal, lasting for years. Handing out tracts to strangers on a street corner is brief, usually impersonal. Itinerant evangelism can be either short-term (preaching only once in a village and then moving on) or long-term (visiting the same village once a week for a full year). Al Krass described a program in which the evangelist preaches the gospel each week at an agreed-upon time to as many as are curious.

2. Yamamori, 1974; K. Dale, 1975; Thomas, 1959.

> The Evangelical Presbyterian Church has a rule that inquirers shall receive regular Christian teaching for a period of at least one year before baptism. Therefore, we did not have to raise the question of acceptance or rejection, or of baptism, the sign of acceptance, until at least one year had passed. (1969, p. 245)

Some methods create a face-to-face relationship, while others are indirect and rather impersonal. Direct methods mean personal contact. Bible distribution, radio broadcasts, advertising, and correspondence courses do not necessarily bring Christian and non-Christian into such contact. Technological advances have made more of our methods impersonal and fleeting than those of one hundred years ago.

Methods play on different sorts of relationship as means for evangelistic approach. Some visitation programs contact people never previously met (this, in American slang, is a "cold turkey" approach). Others contact only those who have visited a worship service or other event of the congregation. Or visitation can deliberately focus only on near relatives and friends of those who have already become Christians.

2. Types of People Reachable by the Method

We often do not think about the scope of a method. Yet every method excludes some people in the general population. Printed literature excludes those who are illiterate, who cannot read the particular language it is in, or who are blind. Every piece of literature also assumes a certain level of education and age. Radio broadcasting excludes those without access to radios or interest in Christian programming, or who are unable to listen at the times of broadcast. Crusade evangelism requires people to come to a central location at a given time. It excludes those whose work hours conflict, those too sick to come, and often the handicapped. Furthermore, most crusades advertise in the mass media, excluding those who gain their information from other sources.

We may wonder how anyone could not know about Christ when so many evangelistic efforts are going on. Part of the answer is that most of our methods are standard solutions, based on the assumption that everyone is reachable by one method or by just a few. In reality, we often overlook certain sorts of target audiences (that is why we call many of the unreached "hidden peoples").

One example is the nomadic peoples of the earth, who live in a strip stretching from Morocco through Africa, into the Middle East and up into Central Asia. Not a single paper was devoted to their evangelization at the Lausanne Conference in 1974. The number of missionaries devoted to evangelizing them *as nomadic peoples* is minuscule. Most missionaries are sedentary and seek to turn nomads into settled farmers, setting up sedentary churches and schools. What is needed instead are modern-day Abrahams, living off cattle and sheep, living in tents, moving with the nomads, worshiping God around campfires. Our normal methods, which assume a sedentary people, will not reach these hidden peoples. We will have to develop "caravan churches" such as those of the Assemblies of God for the nomadic gypsies of Europe.

Rural evangelization is also distant from the methods most Western missionaries find congenial. Nearly 2.8 billion people live in rural conditions. In Asia about 65 percent of the population are farmers. Many current methodologies do not evangelize the rural lost. Consider the 1971 survey in a rural farming area (seven hundred households surveyed) within two hours travel of Tokyo:

> We were very surprised to discover that 97 percent of those farmers had never heard the Gospel. The other three percent had heard through radio or by receiving a tract when they had been to the city. The nearest church to that village was about a one-hour walk, and it was a weak church of about twenty members. (Cho, 1975, p. 625)

Farmers can be reached, but only by very different strategies than those for cities and urban areas. Dr. Cho relates the extraordinary tale of a Japanese evangelist's vision for rural evangelism. His approach was to learn the technique of growing strawberries and then to settle in a very poor village.

> At first he did not say he was an evangelist or even that he was a Christian. But silently he made a new strawberry patch, and grew his berries. The farm people noticed this particular stranger and watched him curiously. At Christmas he harvested many fine strawberries, and made a greater profit than any of the farmers could have imagined. They gathered at his house and begged him to teach them how to grow strawberries in this way. For the first time he told them that he was a Christian. He arranged that if they would come to his house every Sunday and hear what he had to say, he would teach them how to grow strawberries. Now the entire village is Christian, and he is not only the pastor of the church, but head of the village. Not only has evangelism had good results, but that village has become famous for strawberry production. (1975, pp. 628-29)

3. The Major Results of the Method

Every method has its primary effectiveness. It can produce some changes far better than other methods. For example, radio as a tool of evangelism is effective for some tasks. Research in communication shows it works best when used to create awareness of Christ. It is not as effective when used to stimulate a specific commitment to Christ. Radio is also highly effective at discipleship training. When mixed with other methods, such as correspondence courses, face-to-face gatherings of radio audiences with evangelists, and audio cassette programs, it can begin to fulfill its peculiar competence for evangelism.

The Summer Institute of Linguistics/Wycliffe Bible Translators has created a superb methodology. It reduces a language to writing and introduces a translated New Testament into minority languages. It produces an orthography for them and helps in literacy programs. It has had good success in stimulating the birth of Christian churches among such peoples. What it doesn't do well is give those churches a sense of church identity. The infant churches at times fumble along with little guidance in what name to give their church, how to relate to other Christian denominations, or what forms to use in Christian life (Tuggy and Toliver, 1972, pp. 123-24).

The same type of analysis is valid for the many other methods: medical and health methodologies, education as a part of evangelism, newspaper advertising, telemarketing. These are all legitimate methods. Yet we must ask: What can they do best? What do they leave undone in the overall scheme of sharing Christ with a target group? So long as we are aware of the limited capabilities of our methods, we will be aware of what else must be included in our strategy.

4. Complexity of the Method

By *complexity* we mean the number of people involved in carrying out the method, the level of training, skill, and education required to perform to minimum standards, the length of time the method will be in use, the resources needed, and possibly the number of people who will be evangelized in a direct and sustained fashion. Think of it as a continuum with at least three distinguishable points:

(a) *Tools* are the simplest element. These include such things as printed literature, an advertising brochure, a telephone.

(b) *Programs* combine several tools in an evangelistic effort. A number of people are involved and several weeks or months are required to complete the program. A Vacation Bible School for two weeks or a weekly visitation program are two examples.

(c) *"Grand Plans"* are the most complex. These aim at mobilizing many churches and Christians in a process that may take several years. These usually come with training programs and philosophies of ministry. New Life for All and Evangelism in Depth, New Life 2000, Target 2000, and Evangelism Explosion are examples of this. The YMCA movement in its early years was an elaborate plan for evangelizing young men. Its organizational structure is an indication of the complexity of the method.

Why do we seek to understand methods by their different qualities? This helps us fit methods to the goal desired and the people group being evangelized. The methods chosen must correspond with the characteristics of the target people. Bible distribution to a people 99 percent illiterate or a residential school for nomadic peoples are examples of contradictions between methods and people. We must choose methods *because they have real promise of furthering evangelization among a given people group.* Too often we choose them because we know how they work even if they are unsuited to the target group.

SELECTING METHODS FOR EVANGELIZATION

If we see our methods and means through the needs and eyes of our target group, we will be able to make more adequate choices for our strategy. Already we have a number of clues about the viability of a method for evangelization. Three final questions needing answers will help us select the methods to use: Is it biblical and ethical? Does it fit the other components of our plan? Does it fit the profile of our target group?

1. Biblical and Ethical Concerns

We cannot simply adopt a method because it is effective. Church history shows how many times Christians resorted to highly questionable methods. The desire to see Muslims yield allegiance to Christ is commendable. To seek to do it by brute force in Crusades was deplorable. As Augustine said, the only force to be used in convincing non-Christians is the force of love.

We cannot use deception to further the progress of truth. Propaganda or psychological manipulation to produce a "decision for Christ" should be anathema. We cannot use methods that change the nature of the gospel. When does entertainment become the end and the religious message no more than a decoration? When does advertising make Christ a slogan instead of a Savior? How many of the "hidden persuaders" (Vance Packard, 1951) can we package into a gospel presentation before proclamation becomes manipulation?

These are not easy questions, especially in cross-cultural settings. The biblical and ethical criteria are not all equally clear in their application. Nor can we be fully confident that our strong feelings or judgments are based on the Bible. Some "biblical" criteria are based on mono-cultural biases not well debated and justified. The culturally provincial consciences of Christians can become roadblocks to adoption of effective methods.

It is here that Paul's discussion of the differences between weak and strong Christians is important (Rom. 14). At times it is difficult to gain consensus among Christians. It is then that the love and freedom we allow other Christians is tested to its utmost. Here the tension is between grieving and quenching the Spirit. If we are entangled with sub-biblical and unethical practices we grieve the Spirit. If we are rigidly unyielding as the Spirit tries to move into new, unfamiliar arenas, we quench the Spirit.

One of the dividing lines in evangelistic methods in the West centers around music. Some see rock music as demonic and evil, associated with drugs and loose sexual ethics. Others see it as like the bar songs of Luther's day, music to be redeemed for Christ. The spread of "contemporary Christian music," much of which uses contemporary genres of popular music, also has been controversial.

Not too many decades ago Western Christians divided over the use of movies and television for Christian purposes. These debates show the difficulty at times in gaining clarity as to what is biblical and thus legitimate and what is not. It is more difficult when multiple cultures are interacting (e.g., Western mission attitudes about drums in Christian services compared with African evaluations).

2. Strategic Criteria

We already mentioned the importance of selecting a method to fit the various other elements of our strategy.

- Will it achieve the goals for evangelization?
- Does it fit the culture of the target people? When missionaries

leave, can the Christians of the target group use the method as they continue evangelization? Does the method create unhealthy dependency between the missionary and the indigenous Christians?

- Can the methods chosen be implemented by the force for evangelism? Or is it too complex, requiring too high a level of education or technical skill?
- What sort of relationship will the method create between the evangelizer and the evangelized?
- Are the resources required to carry the plan to completion available? Does the method require resources not available after the missionaries leave?

We could elaborate on each of these points. This list at least suggests the sorts of considerations that go into a well thought-through strategy. The parts must fit and should encourage continuing evangelization after the missionaries depart.

3. Methods and the People Profile

Søgaard's model suggests that peoples go through a process as they move toward Christ. It is important to ask about the effect of methods on that process.

If we subdivide our target group, we can see roles for different methods. One method might be most effective at moving people from no or little awareness to minimal awareness of Christ and Christian faith. Radio does an excellent job at that. Another method might relate to that part of the people group who know about Christ but are not yet positive in their attitude. Another will seek to enhance the skills of the Christians in the group in sharing their faith.

In any case, the questions that arise at this point include: Does the method move the people group closer to a decision for Christ? Does it attempt to challenge them for commitment too soon? Does it respect the common patterns by which they deliberate about major decisions such as this? Does it work with the social structure and those who are gate-keepers (influence leaders)? Do the methods complement one another? Or might a method having a positive effect on one part of the process have a negative effect on another?

PERSPECTIVE ON THE SELECTION PROCESS

Not all of the considerations and questions posed about methods are of equal importance. Methods are justified finally by their capability to reach the ultimate goal. We are in the business of bringing about churches that have the numbers and resources to complete evangelization among their own people. If a method passes most tests for selection but does not harvest ripe fields and produce new congregations, it is not suitable. We cannot be indifferent to the results of our labors as co-partners with God.

Our calling is not to create a large splash in the Christian pond. It is to catch the fish Jesus sends us to catch. No method, however honored and well worn, can continue to be sustained once it loses its potency to produce the results sought. Nor can we discard a good method in the lust to make a name for ourselves by innovating a dazzling method.

The selection process is no more than a series of points in time. We never select a method forever. We continually evaluate what is happening as we move forward. Any means or method has the potential in a fallen world to subvert our goals. We find it all too easy, having invested time and effort, resources and emotions into our methods, to identify with them. Then we see any objective evaluation as a threat to our identity.

Means and methods are to be no more than paths to the accomplishment of the kingdom goals. When they become more than that, they become ends and we are out of the evangelization business.

14. Developing Means and Methods

Finding means and methods for our mission is a critical part of our planning. Because people groups differ, the methods to approach them will differ. Every situation has its specific logic, which we must respect. When we do, we meet a people at the point of need, in their meaning systems, and through their cultural forms.

Methods not responsive to the target group are at best irrelevant and at worst confusing and offensive. Wherever we look for models for ministry, we want to incarnate them in a way that makes sense to the target group.

There are no universals in methodology. By working in the logic of a situation as we understand it, we discover hidden resources of creativity. God will give us insight and new patterns. Seeking unique strategies is a longer and more demanding process, less secure than imposing standard solutions on unstandard situations. Yet it is far more fruitful in the end.

Our basic philosophy affects the search for means and methods. We believe there are no sinful tools, only sinful people who can misuse them. We are free in Christ by his liberating Spirit to cast our net of research and creativity wide and far for ideas. At the same time we are aware of the real possibility of self-deception and corruption. We return again and again to biblical materials to test ourselves and our methods.

We cannot take the proud attitude that we have all the answers. Our education, history, and civilization may have rich resources. Yet they may be inadequate to the challenge of the future evangelization of the peoples of the world.

The very people group we evangelize may teach us the methods by which they can most effectively be evangelized. Or we may

194

have to devise completely novel approaches not found in any archive or written in any missiological journal. We need to be ready to do just that.

NEW TESTAMENT EXAMPLES

When the Old Testament people of God wanted strength and guidance they often remembered what God did in the past. We also need to remember how God acted through his people in past ages.

Some missiologists argue that our best resource in finding appropriate methods is the Bible (Coleman, 1963). For them the real issue is, as the title of Roland Allen's book puts it, *Missionary Methods: St. Paul's or Ours?* They say we fail in missions because we try to do *God's* work with *our* methods. If we rediscover the biblical pattern and methods, we will experience a new surge of success.

This view raises the pertinent question: To what extent is the New Testament pattern of evangelism normative for us today? Does it make any difference that our culture and social setting differ? Does the New Testament provide a pattern that all evangelism ought to follow?

This is a delicate subject. There is a normative evangelistic *message* that is our pattern. We have seen that it has various ways of expression. It is not as clear there is a normative evangelistic *method*. The life of Jesus as well as the early church exhibits principles of good communication, organization, and cultural sensitivity. These are worthy of imitation in all evangelistic settings. Ethical and normative criteria also are important for evaluating methods.

Yet these principles suggest the freedom to vary the forms and methods of communication. The early church responded with sensitivity to its own context. It used methods and approaches suited to the target groups in its environment. It is not our duty to mimic the methods of the New Testament church but to follow the same principles that guided it. As Michael Harper writes:

> We need to distinguish in the Bible between what is a fixed and unalterable truth—which does not change either in the course of time or in the context of cultural variety—and where the passage is describing how the Holy Spirit inspired people in an *ad hoc* situation. In this latter instance, we are not to follow slavishly how people were led *then*, but to learn from the example of their response to the guidance of the Spirit, and expect ourselves to be led by the same Spirit, though perhaps in a quite different manner.

195

> In other words we have to distinguish between what is exemplary in scripture and what is mandatory. (1978, p. 24; see also Peters, 1975)

What we need is the sensible dividing of forms and functions, of patterns and principles. The New Testament is not a handbook of evangelistic methods. It does not set forth any single model of ministry as a pattern for our methods. It does present principles by which to test our methods. The forms the early church used differ from our forms. The functions they fulfill should be dynamically equivalent.

The New Testament provides broad principles that should shape our philosophies of ministry. Using them, we can undergird a wide range of methods. When he created "The Phone's for You" program, Norm Whan was challenged by many who questioned whether it was biblical to use telemarketing. Since there were no phones in Jesus' day, we cannot appeal directly to the Bible for support. Yet Jesus did use all the means at his disposal to relate the message of the kingdom of God to his target group. It is reasonable, were Jesus here in the flesh, to think he would use all the facilities now available to reach the lost. Tens of thousands have come to know Christ as Savior as a result of this new strategy. Norm Whan's answer is, "We don't know if he would have used the phones in his day. We do know he is using them now!"

Michael Green made a very comprehensive study of evangelism in the New Testament. Here is his conclusion about methodology:

> There does not seem to have been anything very remarkable in the strategy and tactics of the early Christian mission. Indeed, it is doubtful if they had one. I do not believe they set out with any blueprint. They had an unquenchable conviction that Jesus was the key to life and death, happiness and purpose, and they simply could not keep quiet about him. The Spirit of Jesus within them drove them into mission. . . .
>
> Their methods on the whole, while varied, were unremarkable. There is no key to instant success to be found by ransacking the methods used by the early church. . . .
>
> Perhaps [the priority of personal conversation] is the greatest lesson we can learn from the early church in the very changed situation of our own day. The most effective method of evangelism and the most widespread, in the long run, in its results, is conversation evangelism, where one who has found Jesus shares his discovery, his problems, his joys and his sorrows with one who is still groping in the dark. There is no joy like introducing a friend to Christ in this way. . . . If all Christians set about doing this, they would not need much other methodology from the early church. (1975, pp. 165-66, 168, 171-72; see also Green, 1970, chap. 8)

Green suggests that the New Testament's pattern is to use whatever creates vital, direct contact between Christian and non-Christian. The apostolic church engaged in personal conversations, open-air preaching, lectures, the writing of literary works (the Gospels), and house-to-house visitation. Personal contact was crucial in the spread of the gospel then and now.

We would be foolish to think we needed to preach in the synagogues of our day in order to be truly New Testament in our pattern. It is not the specific form of early church methods that instructs us. It is the example they leave of spiritually empowered, faithfully motivated, continuous communication of the good news.

When we evaluate evangelism and church growth in the contemporary scene this conclusion is just as clear. Churches and missions with wide ranges of methods are effective in bringing men and women to Christ and forming vital congregations. Some show striking similarity to the forms of the New Testament. This occurs where evangelization takes place in societies with conditions and cultures similar to the New Testament. Where there are large differences in context and culture from the New Testament, there are large variations in methodology.

God makes available to each generation those tools necessary to carry out his will. We study the Bible to discover the type of dynamic and motivation that is to lie behind our contemporary community and evangelism. We can view our own day through the lenses given us by the Bible. What we learn is that we need to discover strategies *for our day* that are compatible with the kingdom of God. We can see that we need not make the anachronistic attempt to force all time and all situations into the forms used by the New Testament.

THE EXPERIENCES OF OTHER CHRISTIANS

A second source of methods is successful evangelism models.[1] We observe what others are doing and adopt those that seem appropriate for our context.

---

1. The literature in this area is extensive, although much of it is relatively unsystematic. Part of the problem is the sort of records kept by churches around the world. A great deal of research still needs to be done utilizing much more sophisticated research methods. Some of the better studies include: Neil Braun, *Laity Mobilized: Reflections on Church Growth in Japan and Other Lands* (1971); Lyle L. Vander Werff, *Christian Missions to Muslims: The Record* (1977); Phil Parshall, *Beyond the Mosque: Christians within Muslim Com-*

STEP 4: MEANS AND METHODS

This is a strong theme in the Church Growth literature: look for the places where the church is growing rapidly and find out why. Adopt the methods and approaches that work. Seek methods that produce growth from new converts (not from proselytes or transfers). The Church Growth movement seeks to clear away all confusion and unsystematic thinking about methodologies. It wants the church to examine fairly and fully whether or not what is being done now leads to real church growth. The results of their research can be characterized by a few simplified principles.

(1) Evangelization happens when churches make it a priority goal. Something is a priority when it has money and people concentrated on it. A low budget and few people seeking to disciple the lost indicates little priority for evangelism. Evangelism does not just happen automatically. It is the result of concern and commitment.

> Churches which are not growing are usually churches in which the responsibility for growth is all loaded onto one person, usually the minister. On the other hand, a church where everybody is working for growth, where everybody is concerned that the Gospel be known, that is a church which grows. Where everybody works at getting obstacles out of the way, where everybody learns as much as possible about the growth of the church, where the church board or session spends half its time planning for church growth, there church growth occurs. (McGavran and Arn, 1973, pp. 12-13)

(2) Large church growth comes when evangelism respects the sociocultural boundaries and decision-making mechanisms of a people group. Methods that allow and encourage people movements are more fruitful than those that minimize the sociological factors. Individuals enter the church in people movements because of multi-individual, mutually interdependent decisions to become Christians.[2]

Where a particular people's needs have been met and their meaning systems used, where the cultural forms harmonized with their own, it has been much easier for a people to decide for Christ. Where this has not been the case, allegiance to Christianity has seemed disloyalty to one's own people.

> It is evident that people receive the gospel most readily when it is presented to them in a manner which is appropriate—and not

---

munity (1985); Darrell Whiteman, *Melanesians and Missionaries* (1983). There are a great many articles in the various Church Growth Bulletins.

2. Tippett, 1971; Cook, 1971; Read, 1965; Pickett et al.,1973; McGavran, 1955; Gibbs, 1985; Wagner, 1987.

alien—to their culture, and when they can respond to it with and among their own people. Different societies have different procedures for making group decisions, e.g., by consensus, by the head of the family, or by a group of elders. We recognize the validity of the corporate dimension of conversion as part of the total process, as well as the necessity for each member of the group ultimately to share in it personally. (Lausanne Committee, *Willowbank Report*, p. 22)

(3) A wide variety of methods has been effective in bringing about church growth. While some of these are objectionable to our own current standards, we can only admit that God was able to use them at the time.

How would we feel about Christianity being made the "law of the land" in a pagan country? The Icelanders became Christian when the pagan seer, Thorgeir, uttered a startling decree at Iceland's governing body, the All-thing. He said that from thence "all men shall be Christians and believe in one God . . . but leave all idol worship, not expose children to perish, and not eat horseflesh" (McGavran, 1970, p. 25). It took many years for the law to work itself out, but it turned the tide in the evangelization of Iceland.

Witness bands, mass crusades, small secret house churches, systems of education, retreat centers, celibate missionary orders, selling oneself into voluntary slavery—a wide variety of methods have produced successful evangelization. We agree with Melvin Hodges' conclusion, "There is no single method for raising up churches" (1973, p. 32). We need methods that produce the greatest harvest. McGavran's comments about methods among responsive peoples is to the point.

> Among such populations the choice of method is a minor matter. The Nevius method, the Chandra Singh method, the tent-teams, the unpaid witness, the paid leader—all will multiply congregations. But some methods will multiply more than others and some better than others. Some will lead more rapidly to self-support and others will delay it. Some methods appear foreign, generate resistance, or create non-productive churches. Others appear indigenous, generate goodwill, and stamp in patterns possible of indefinite reproduction. (1959, p. 129)

THE EXPERIENCE OF PSEUDO-CHRISTIAN AND OTHER RELIGIOUS MOVEMENTS

A third source of methods are models suggested by the study of pseudo-Christian and non-Christian religious movements (e.g., Hesselgrave,

1978a). The Christian movement is not alone in seeking to win the allegiance of the peoples of the earth. Many other religious movements have taken up the task of winning people to their cause. Some of them are within the boundaries of the Christian tradition. Others are not.

We can learn much about means and methods from the independent church movements around the world. Allen Swanson (1971) sought to do just that from a study of these movements in Taiwan. The African Independent Church movements are enormously diversified and vital.[3] Because many broke off from Western missionary–generated churches, they offer clear contrasts in theology, cultural adjustment, and evangelistic approaches. The church stimulated by the preaching of Simon Kimbangu is the largest non-Catholic, non-Protestant, Christian body in Zaire. It has as many as three million members in Africa.

One may also point to marginally Christian movements such as the Mormons in the USA or the Iglesia ni Christo (a unitarian movement in the Philippines with nearly one million members). What is the secret of their successful recruiting? Part of it has to do with the struggle afoot because of the invasion of this age by the kingdom of God. There is a conflict of kingdoms going on. The religious movements that oppose God's way have a seductive power. Yet we must also say that these counterfeit movements are doing some things right. We need to learn from their positives.

Some growing movements are not Christian at all. In Japan the Sokka Gakkai and Rissho Koseikai are two powerful and successful lay Buddhist movements.[4] Missions to Japan should observe them carefully for the elements that make them attractive to the Japanese. The Islamic brotherhoods and Muslim religious forms may suggest new avenues for Christian adaptation. Phil Parshall's *New Paths in Muslim Evangelization* (Baker, 1980) is an example of adapting Muslim patterns to facilitate sharing Christ more effectively.

Whole new vistas open up when we compare these movements with one another and with Christian movements. The dramatic differences between dynamic, growing movements and stagnant, struggling ones stimulates a great deal of creative thought. Those differences show how traditional methodologies are unresponsive to the characteristics and needs of the people being evangelized. They show the unnecessarily Westernized character of many of our approaches.

Some missiologists believe that this avenue of developing new

---

3. Barrett, 1968; Turner, 1967; Daneel, 1971; Murphree, 1969; Sundkler, 1961; Loewen, 1976.

4. K. Dale, 1975; Braun, 1971; McFarland, 1967; Hesselgrave, *Dynamic Religious Movements.*

methods is dangerous to the Christian mission. What can the Marxists, Mormons, Moonies, or Muslims teach us?[5] We should not think that borrowing a methodology is an illegitimate or shameful affair. Is this pride whispering in our ear again? We learn most of what we do by example. Perhaps the most honest answer is to say we are often creatively bankrupt. We need the stimulus even of "our enemies" to become creative and fresh again.

A careful study of the backgrounds of the New Testament reveals that a number of facets were adopted from other groups. For example, the early church's organization as a community and its style of worship is patterned on the Jewish synagogue. They recognized there were many good and true, right and honorable elements in their society (Phil. 4:8). These they accepted. Some they modified and brought into the center of a new Christian life-style. Without compromise of message or ethics there is much we can learn from the dynamic movements afoot in our day.

These pseudo-Christian or non-Christian movements are often making skillful and judicious use of social and cultural mechanisms. The Mormons are growing at a rate of more than two hundred thousand a year. How much of that growth is due to their wise use of good communication methods? Jesus told us to be as wise as serpents and as harmless as doves (Matt. 10:16). One implication is that we ought to learn from the good examples of bad people without adopting their false values or ideas.

THE MEANS AND METHODS OF THE PEOPLE GROUP BEING EVANGELIZED

Every people group that the Christian missionary enters already has many means and methods. A communication network and its roles is already in place. Important news and ideas move from person to person. It may be as simple as word of mouth or as sophisticated as satellite borne television. There are traditional means for communicating religious information that lead to changes in religious allegiance.

To the extent that we become culturally sensitive, we will enter a new situation looking for *the people group's own means and methods.* We may no more need to invent or import new methods than we need to in-

5. Hyde, 1966; O'Dea, 1957; Arrington and Bitton, 1979; Lofland, 1977; Edwards, 1979; Barker, 1986.

vent a new language. Our ingrained habit is to think of new situations in terms of our prior solutions. We see them in the light of our predetermined methodologies asking not "How can I fit into their patterns?" but "How can I fit my methods into their life?"

Such a bias can blind us to some of the most effective, indigenous patterns for evangelization. Because we normally use written materials, we may think we must make a people literate in order to reach them. We will overlook the many ways in which they already communicate and store significant information without writing and reading. If we use their methods, we may penetrate their consciousness rapidly and deeply. Then the process of developing literacy will take its place when it becomes motivated by their own sense of need.

Several illustrations of the use of indigenous patterns for communication make this point. In early Meiji Japan (1868–1912), Western ideas and life-style became popular. The works of such key Western writers as Rousseau, Robert Louis Stevenson, and Jules Verne were translated. Shakespeare's plays were also translated but were not understood or appreciated. The Western dramatic mode did not fit the traditional Japanese dramatic mode. Only after Shakespeare was retranslated into the Nō play form did his works gain popularity in Meiji Japan.

The Baliem Dani of Irian Jaya's highlands have a traditional way for making important announcements or conveying significant news. A powerful man will send an invitation to neighboring clans and hamlets. All are invited to assemble on a given day for a feast. The most valued and prestigious source of meat, the pig, is butchered and cooked. Everyone feasts on the meat and the fat is smeared on important guests. As the people finish eating, the person who called the meeting stands. He makes his announcement in a traditionally stylized manner. Everyone knows the message is extremely important and gives keen attention to it. For weeks the message will be discussed as people cultivate their yams and exchange goods. If the missionary has an important message to share, the Dani have a method for announcing just such messages!

Chuck Kraft attempted to devise a method for evangelizing villages among the Higi of Nigeria:

> I once asked a group of Nigerian church leaders how they would present the Christian message to the village council. They replied, "We would choose the oldest, most respected man in the group and ask him a question. He would discourse at length and then become silent, whereupon we would ask another question. As he talked others would comment as well. But eventually the discussion would lessen and the leader would talk more. In this way we would develop our message so it would become the topic for discussion of the whole vil-

lage." I asked them why they didn't employ this approach in the church. "Why, we've been taught that monologue is the Christian way," they replied. "Can this be why no old men come to church?" I asked. "Of course—we have alienated them by not showing them due respect in public meetings," was their reply. (1973, p. 50)

DEVELOPMENT AS EVANGELISM

Development is an authentic expression of Christian love. It has the potential when well done to touch immediate needs and lift people to new levels of socioeconomic well-being. Can it also serve as a method in the process of evangelization?

Some argue that it cannot. On one side are those who say that development is sub-Christian, aiming at lesser needs than the eternal welfare of human beings. It detracts from the true mission of the church and entangles resources and personnel in the good to the detriment of the best. They say we ought to stick to evangelism (meaning verbal proclamation). On the other side are those who say development is an important act of Christian compassion. We must clothe the naked and feed the hungry and care for the orphan and widow. But this act of compassion is sullied and tainted when turned into a *means* of evangelism. Sharing Christ while helping physically is unfair, unauthentic, or coercive. It smacks of "I'll feed you *if* you become a Christian."

We do not agree with either extreme. Development *can* detract from Christian mission *and* it *can* be a form of coercive evangelism. Neither danger warrants stopping development or divorcing development from evangelization.

Those who love invariably become entangled in the real needs of the people group they seek to evangelize. Those who evangelize invariably make their verbal witness to Christ a part of their compassionate service. Those who serve in hospitals and health care services or education and agricultural development see people commit their lives to Christ (Seaton, 1976). A good example of this is the "Faith and Farm" project in Nigeria.

> It is geared primarily for the farmer and his household who make up 95 percent of the population of Nigeria. The aim of the highly successful project is to train African Christians to teach other farmers and their families to recognize that Jesus Christ is Lord of every part of their lives. As a result, starchy, low-yielding crops have been replaced by nutritional foods with reinforced proteins. Inefficient hand-

tools have been replaced by more practical instruments. Harvested crops have been properly stored and protected from the ravages of white ants and other termites. But more. Children sick and dying from disease and malnutrition have been given a new lease of life by a regular reinforced diet, and thousands of unemployed school-leavers have been given not only useful occupations but a new-found dignity and a fulfilment in a rewarding enterprise. . . .

In the northeast area of Nigeria, where the work has been extended, one incident took place which is not in isolation, and serves to illustrate the evangelistic by-product of this kind of program. One of the Faith and Farm agents saved the grain store of a Muslim and his family and protected his valuable millet and guinea corn against destruction by white ants. This was all the family had for the year. Quietly the African Christian farmer shared his skill and knowledge as he worked alongside the Muslim farmer in preserving his crops. Later the Muslim inquired, "What makes you give up your time and come to help me?" The farmer replied, "Because we want to be like our Master, Jesus Christ, who fed the people when they were hungry." And that day the Muslim farmer listened with a sympathy to the Gospel message for the first time, and he began to understand it. (Hoffman, 1975, pp. 703-4)

The 1982 Consultation on the Relationship Between Evangelism and Social Concern sought to find the relationship between the two. The following year a three-part consultation, "I Will Build My Church," was held at Wheaton, Illinois. One of the three consultations was entitled "A Christian Response to Human Need" and dealt with the practical implications of what had been said at the earlier consultation. The results have been what one may hope is a new wholism, a refusal to put priority over one or the other. The road to Jericho sets its own agenda!

The stark fact that the vast majority of unreached peoples are *poor* faces us with a challenge greater than any we have faced to date.

FINAL CONSIDERATIONS

Much of what we have said will require new research. The effectiveness of many methods is simply not well known. Much evaluation is unscientific in its approach. It seeks *to confirm* the value of the method rather than determine *if* the method is valuable and effective. In many cases it measures the wrong items. If we are in the business of making disciples, then we must measure the number of disciples made. Too often we measure how many meetings are held, how many pieces of literature distributed, how many visits made, how many people attended. All of these are measures of *activity* but not of *results*. It is like a company measuring how many widgets it produces rather than how many it sells.

Indigenous means and methods warrant much more research. If we desire an indigenous or contextualized church to grow in each people group, we must begin to use more indigenous methods. Much of the difficulty in transition from mission to church is due to the Western methods insisted upon.

Along with research we need to conduct more pilot experiments. In them we can deliberately try out methods on a small scale with careful evaluation. Without such experiments we can theorize, counter-theorize, object, and counterobject to all sorts of ideas. We must discover more effective and efficient ways of doing the old task of evangelism. Otherwise we will not have the means we need to carry evangelization forward in the next half-century.[6]

---

6. For further insight on how to carry out research among people groups, see John Robb, *The Power of People Group Thinking* (MARC, 1989).

Questions

1. What role do methods play in producing the evangelistic results we seek? What criteria are important in evaluating the usefulness and limitations of a method?

2. How do we relate the Holy Spirit to the means and methods we use?

3. What criteria are important in deciding which methods to select or develop in order to evangelize a particular people group?

4. Are there biblical or ethical norms that rule out certain means for achieving our goals? What are they?

5. What indigenous means and methods for communication and organization can be used for evangelism? Have we considered them *before* resorting to nonindigenous methods we bring with us?

6. Have we checked the experience of other Christian groups who have attempted to evangelize this people group or similar groups? Which of their methods can we use?

7. How can evangelism be an integral part of our other activities, such as development, health care, education, and so forth?

8. What pilot projects need to be undertaken in order to test or develop new methods for evangelization? Are we engaged in such experiments? Does our agency spend any funds on research and development? Why not?

STEP 5: DEFINING AN APPROACH

Considerations

1. It is God's desire that every people be given the message of the gospel. Our task is to uncover his will and become an active partner in a strategy to reach these people.

2. Strategies are always dynamic. They are always time-bound.

3. The strategy's ultimate outcome should always involve the formation of a dynamic church.

4. Church growth is seldom linear. The diffusion of innovation normally is shaped like an S-curve.

5. The major problem with many planning efforts is the failure to discuss the assumptions on which they are based.

6. The most difficult assumptions to uncover are assumptions about ourselves.

15. Planning the Strategy

The planning model we are following is organized in a linear and rational fashion. We begin first by defining our basic task, our mission. Then we consider in sequence the target group we intend to evangelize, the force for evangelism, and the means and methods to be used. Now we come to Step 5: "Defining an Approach."

Although this model is organized in a linear fashion, the actual process of following it is an iterative, that is, repetitive, process. It is impossible to think about the target group without also thinking about how to reach them. Nor can we isolate means and methods from what we know of the target group. The decisions we make at each step modify the decisions made at the other steps. Yet through the process of reflection and of answering a series of questions, we accumulate enough information to set forth an initial strategy. With what we know as a result of going through the first four steps we make a preliminary statement as to *the overall approach* to reach our target group.

As we indicated in Chapter 5, a strategy is both inclusive and exclusive. By defining what we *will* do we often define what we will *not* do. Making and refining a strategy statement is a very useful process. Initially, we have very few ideas of how to reach a particular people group. We gather information. We try to understand what God wants to happen in the evangelization of this group. Eventually we hope to complete a plan and then act.

Figure 15.1, "Degree of Planning Uncertainty," pictures this process. To the left is the point in time when we start planning. Within the confines of the cone on the left, the degree of uncertainty about what to do decreases as we move toward a point of action. Somewhere along this planning stage we have to make an initial statement about our strategy. This will eventually lead us to the completion of our planning.

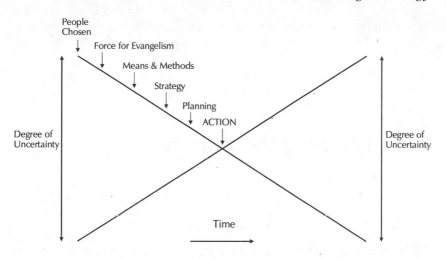

FIGURE 15.1   DEGREE OF PLANNING UNCERTAINTY

Note that from the point of action onward the degree of present uncertainty about the future increases. In other words, the further away things are from the point where we put a decision into action, the more uncertain we are about the future. One implication of this is that we must continually rethink our plans and strategies.

Another way of thinking about this diagram is to think of the cone on the left as a decreasing spiral. As we go through the planning process, asking questions about the target group, the force for evangelism, and the methods to be used, we gain a better understanding about how to evangelize a people.

LEVELS OF STRATEGY

Strategies, like plans, come in all sizes. The levels of strategy are related to the ultimate goal of our mission. In the case of first evangelization among unreached people groups our primary goal is to see a cluster of churches established, churches with the people and resources to complete evangelization through E-1 evangelism.

For this overall endeavor we need a *grand strategy*. This would be a statement about how we hope with God's help to bring into being the first cluster of such churches. An *intermediate strategy* might be a statement about how we expect to see the initial founding congregation

211

brought into being. A *short-range strategy* might deal with our procedure to move into the people group and engage in culture and language learning.

An example of this is found in the use of Søgaard's two-dimensional model for an "All Media Penetration" project in Bangkok, Thailand. The project aims to confront every person with Jesus Christ as a living option. It also seeks to penetrate the culture in such a way that Christ is a culturally acceptable option. All available media are to be utilized in a comprehensive program. Søgaard describes the objectives as:

> (1) Climatizing the City. That is building awareness and positive attitudes towards Christianity. This part would be based on mass media strategy: television, radio, newspapers, and news events.
>
> (2) Confronting the Interested. That is creating responsiveness by public presentations of the Gospel. This part will also be mass media strategy, but using such media as films, concerts, and drama.
>
> (3) Contacting the Responsive. That is calling for commitment by those who are responsive. Here the strategy would be totally decentralized, based on outreach by local churches. They will use a wide variety of media.
>
> (4) Churching the Committed. That is incorporating new converts into churches, discipling them etc. This is also a decentralized strategy, and the churches will use relevant media, including cassettes, print, correspondence courses, seminaries, etc.
>
> (5) Catalyzing the Church. In order to carry out such a campaign of comprehensive church planting, it is of crucial importance that the church members be trained to play their significant roles in this strategy. So, this fifth point becomes, chronologically speaking, point one. (Søgaard, p. 258)

Figure 15.2 is a diagram of these various points along the Søgaard scale.

It is very helpful to break the evangelism task down into its various phases. In Søgaard's example of Bangkok we imagine people at different points in their awareness and attitude toward Jesus Christ. The various media are aimed at communicating to people where they currently are found informationally and attitudinally.

Another way of thinking about the process is to focus on a single people group. This makes the task a little more manageable than a city of four million. What we want to know are the phases by which a group, initially located almost completely in the bottom left quadrant of the Søgaard scale, is brought to the condition of goal fulfillment.

In Phase One very few in the people group are aware of the

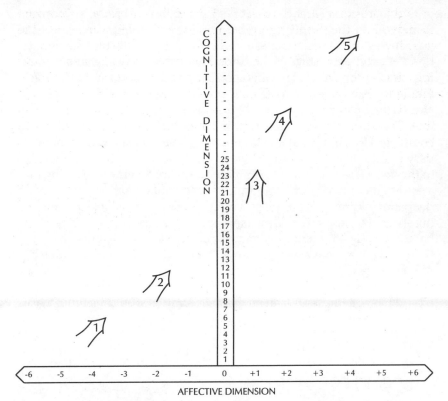

5. Catalyzing the church.
4. Churching the committed.
3. Contacting the responsive.
2. Confronting the interested.
1. Climatizing the city.

FIGURE 15.2 BANGKOK ALL MEDIA PENETRATION PROJECT

gospel, although a small number have had an initial exposure to it. During this phase the evangelizing force locates itself, engages in language and culture learning, and begins communicating the gospel.

In Phase Two the techniques of communication are well in hand. The force for evangelism has tried and discarded methods that are unproductive. The task in Phase Two is greatly to expand the numbers who have awareness and to move at least a small number through the steps to commitment to Christ.

STEP 5: DEFINING AN APPROACH

In Phase Three the task of E-3 evangelism is basically complete. A majority of the people group has at least an initial awareness of the gospel. The important thing is that there are now a cluster of congregations. A good percentage of the Christians are actively engaged in sharing their faith with fellow members of the people group. The overwhelming majority of new Christians are now being brought into the church by E-1 evangelism.

Phase Four is the task of the indigenous congregations to complete. Here the people group is evangelized to the fringes. There are very few adults in the culture who have not at some time been exposed to the gospel. Mechanisms are in place to ensure that those growing into adulthood have the same opportunity. Movements of renewal and the deepening of spiritual life are occurring. Some of the leaders are actively involved in contexts with Christian leaders of other people groups. Some have gone for graduate theological education. The awareness of the world Christian movement is growing among the Christian leadership of the indigenous church.

In terms of our levels of strategy, the *grand missionary strategy* would include Phases 1-3; an *intermediate strategy* would include Phases 1 and 2; and our *short-range strategy* would include only Phase 1.

THE EXAMPLE OF THE TURKANA

Two examples of grand strategies for reaching the same people illustrates this process. The Turkana are a nomadic people living in a northern desert region of Kenya to the west of Lake Turkana (formerly Lake Rudolf).[1] Most of the two-hundred thousand Turkana subsist off cattle, goats, and camels, though some are subsistence farmers along the Turkwel and Kerio rivers. Others settled on the shores of Lake Turkana because of a great drought in the 1960s and learned to fish. The majority of the Turkana remain nomadic, struggling to survive in average temperatures of 95 degrees Fahrenheit and rainfall of less than ten inches a year. They move from place to place, building new manyattas (dhom palm leaf huts). Their diet consists in large measure of milk and blood— a high protein diet that produces tall, handsome people. They are polyg-

---

1. Initial studies on the Turkana were done by Gulliver (1951). More recent studies include Raymond H. Davis (1978), a World Vision funded study by Bedan Mbugua (1977), and a research project of the Christian Missionary Fellowship completed by Eddie Elliston (reported in Schreck and Barrett, 1987).

amists and each new boy is celebrated as an additional hand to herd cattle. They have an old and well-developed culture.

Events conspired against the traditional way of life in the 1960s. National borders were closed to the north and west. A growing population and extended drought left many of them starving. A number of feeding camps were opened by the Kenyan government along the shores of Lake Turkana. Missionaries were allowed in for the first time. The Kenyan government encouraged development projects aimed at settling the Turkana into farming, fishing, and town settings.

Over the years a sedentary community of fishermen (perhaps four to five thousand) came into being. The Africa Inland Mission established a station next to a small gulf on the 150-mile-long lake. Through the preaching of the missionaries and one Turkana pastor, a small but steadily growing congregation formed among the fisher population. Surveys indicated continuing movement between the sedentary Turkana and their nomadic relatives.

The grand strategy of the Africa Inland Mission (AIM) is to establish a church along the lakeshore that will become strong enough to evangelize the nomadic sector of the Turkana. Part of the underlying assumption is that modernization will continue to move very rapidly through Kenya. Eventually the Turkana will move from primarily nomadic to primarily sedentary patterns. Then a strong church will be multiplied throughout the population.

The intermediate strategy is to establish a strong congregation in the lakeshore community and to train and develop Turkana evangelists. These evangelists will serve as the primary workers to reach the nomads.

The short-range strategy is essentially survival. The environment is extremely harsh and difficult for Western missionaries. Rain is scarce and dust storms are violent. Physical survival as well as learning the language and culture of the Turkana have been the short-term goals.

The overall AIM strategy was predicated on the assumption that the nomadic Turkana were unresponsive. This led to a strategy focused on the Turkana who were changing to a sedentary life-style.

The Christian Missionary Fellowship (CMF) entered the Turkana some years after the AIM. Research the CMF commissioned concluded that the evangelical churches already present followed urban or Western forms in their programs. They were not using many of the indigenous communication patterns. In fact, the majority of the Protestant missionaries could not speak Turkana fluently (unlike the Catholic missioners). The lack of responsiveness noted among the nomadic Turkana was felt to be the result of not adequately contextualizing the methods and message of the gospel presentation.

215

This led to a very different strategy. The grand strategy of the CMF is to plant numbers of congregations in the semi-nomadic villages. The leadership is to be indigenous, unpaid by outside sources, utilizing Turkana models. The assumption is that the church will first be semi-nomadic in form and will be able to penetrate not only the nomadic but the sedentary sector as well. It will also mean that the congregations will reflect the age/sex population profile rather than be made up principally of women and children as is true of most Turkana Protestant churches.

The intermediate strategy is to contextualize the church in ways that are sustainable and reproducible among the Turkana. The natural lines of communication and prestige are to be followed. Men rather than women would be approached first. Key leaders are to be sought out since their conversion will have repercussions through many villages and clan networks. Special friendship lines and initiation-set ties would be emphasized. Nonformal methods of training are used since literacy is low. This will mean the establishment of a church among one clan which will be able to bridge to other Turkana clans.

The short-range strategy is survival along with language and culture learning. The establishment of special friendships with traditional leaders of repute will serve as the bridge to the widespread network of clan and initiation ties.

It is too early to tell what the long-term impact of these two strategies might be. They are complementary in that one focuses on the sedentary Turkana and uses urban/Western models while the other focuses on the nomadic villages (manyattas) and clans of the Turkana and stresses contextualization. Both the AIM and the CMF have on-going movements and congregations. It is true that the CMF has shown the assumptions about resistance among the nomadic to be false. They do respond when a very different evangelistic approach is taken than that followed by the AIM in the past.

THE DIFFUSION OF INNOVATION

New ideas are seldom accepted at a uniform rate (Rogers, 1962). In almost all human endeavor output is rarely directly proportional to input. When illustrated in diagram form (Fig. 15.3), it almost always looks like an "S"-shaped curve with two axes, output and input. Input might be time, energy, resources, or a combination of all three. Output could be the spreading acceptance of an idea, church growth, or numbers of people folded into congregations.

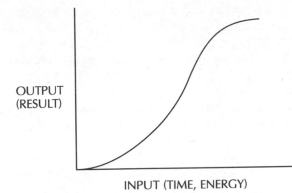

FIGURE 15.3   INPUT vs. OUTPUT

The bottom of the curve is flat because in most settings innovations are rarely accepted immediately. It takes time to gain acceptance, to build trust, and to be understood. Once acceptance happens, the rate of acceptance accelerates. People within the culture become the advocates and are much more effective.

Near the end of the curve—the top of the "S"—the acceptance rate flattens. Those who resist or are uninterested become much more evident. Those who will be persuaded have been persuaded and the remaining population is the most difficult to reach.

This curve is useful in understanding what happens as people move up along the Søgaard scale. In one sense, as we attempt to move people up the scale, this type of curve repeats itself. Understanding this will help us think through the strategy.

This diagram also is useful in understanding how churches grow. Vergil Gerber's book *A Manual for Evangelism and Church Growth* offers an excellent discussion of this. Church growth theory usually deals with growth in terms of a decade. This smooths out the small spurts or declines. What is important is the long-term pattern of growth.

In our evangelistic zeal, we keep planning new strategies to win people to Christ. Yet we often fail to make plans to incorporate them in the community as mature members. For fifty years large numbers of people have professed Christ and become church members through the ministry of the East African Revival. Yet their lives do not seem markedly changed. A close examination of what is happening reveals a primary need for teachers. A strategy that calls for evangelism and does not call for adequate teaching will eventually fail. If our strategy brings people

217

into relationship with Christ but does not help them to grow so they become propagators, we have failed.

A good approach is to plan for an intense evangelistic effort for a period of time, say a year, followed by intensive on-the-job training. This is working well in some of the rapidly growing Pentecostal churches in Brazil. The new convert is immediately put to work as a witness within his or her community. In his book, *Dedication and Leadership*, Douglas Hyde describes how well the Communists have used this in their training.

STATING OUR APPROACH

Having said all of this, we are now ready to state our strategy. The following is a sample form of such a statement:

> We intend to evangelize _____ *(name of a people group)*.
> We will begin with _____ *(a specific part of the group)* who are located attitudinally and informationally at _____ on the Søgaard scale.
> We will do this by utilizing the following methods: _____
> _____ .
> This will be carried out by the following people: _____
> _____ .
> It is our intention that _____ percent of this group will _____
> _____ *(goal)* by _____ *(date)*.

Using the above form, we might have a strategy statement for the Turkana that looks like this:

> We intend to evangelize the nomadic Turkana of northwestern Kenya. Our approach will be to begin with one clan of whom 98 percent have no awareness of the gospel. A single missionary will attempt to establish a relationship with the clan chief and/or diviner. Once this is established, the single missionary will be joined by a missionary couple with children. They will live adjacent to the particular clan for a period of a year. During this time their chief task will be language and culture learning as well as building trust. When and where appropriate they will share the power of Jesus Christ to meet everyday needs. At the end of the first year we will expect 95 percent of the clan to feel positive about Christianity. At the end of the second year almost all of the adults will have some understanding of Christianity. The headman will have been confronted with the claims of Christ. As people accept Christ, we will build a temporary shelter similar to the

palm thatch temporary housing of the Turkana and have this designated as a worship center.

We will share our strategy with other missions in the area, especially the Africa Inland Mission. We will ask that the missionaries living with this particular clan remain basically isolated for the first year and during the second year have only minimal contacts with other missionaries.

In the process of reviewing our strategy we will put all the elements of our previous steps together to see how they reinforce and build on one another. We may need to discard some of them. We are not going to attempt to reach all the clans. Nor will we seek to evangelize the sedentary farming or fishing Turkana. There are no plans to build a permanent church building (as the AIM has done). Nor will various development, health, or educational projects to be brought into the area. Those who become Christians will not be brought into the AIM congregation with its more urban, settled church traditions. In addition, the life-style of the missionary and the outside contacts will be such that they will be in as complete dependence on the traditional Turkana as possible. They will not bring in a lot of Western trappings or build a Western house.

This does not mean that these sorts of decisions are the correct ones. It may become clear quickly on site that the local diet is not suitable for someone with a Western background. Food may have to be brought in regularly. Yet it is helpful to make these going-in statements. The important thing about these strategies is that they are *statements of intent*. They help us narrow down what we will and will not do so we can get on with the business of acting and learning to become effective accomplishers of our primary goals.

After making a strategy statement, it is a good idea to go back and review the whole process preceding it. Planning is a thinking process and part of it is the rethinking that must be done as we get more and more specific.

Here we ask if our proposed strategy is compatible with our original understanding of our mission. Does it fit our own capabilities as we understand them? Is our organizational structure such that we can manage to carry on evangelism of this sort? To the extent that they do not hang together in a natural way, we will have to modify various elements.

Stating an initial approach is comparable to a stopping-off place on the way to anticipating the results we seek from our expenditure of energy and action. It is an attempt to organize, in a clear and communicable way, what it is we want to accomplish.

16. *Assumptions*

U p to this point in our analysis we have assumed that we need answers to a series of key questions. If we secure the information necessary to answer these questions, we can assume that a strategy in line
with God's plan to reach all peoples will emerge. However, the difficulty
with this approach is that every situation is different and every people
and people group is unique. No matter how lengthy our list of questions,
there will always be some that need to be added or modified for a particular people and time.

Another way to expose the nuances of the situation and our relationship to it is to discover our *underlying assumptions*. Everyone works
and thinks with certain taken-for-granted notions. These are our "of
courses." They seem so self-evident to us that it often seems silly even to
state or question them. In the same way that few of us are aware of our
own culture, few of us are aware of the presuppositions and assumptions
we make about life. When we question such assumptions or try to justify
why we take a given approach, we become self-conscious of our unex-
amined biases. Yet making a list of our assumptions has many benefits.

Listing our assumptions often uncovers *hidden agendas*. Our
own personal biases often reappear in our own agendas, those things we
want to see happen. At times we are unaware of what they are. One person may be seeking to reach the unreached so as to further the overall
goals of the organization. The hidden agenda may be a sterling success
story that will lead to a position teaching evangelism in a school of mission. Another person's hidden agenda may be to create positions for his
or her children who seek significant jobs within a Christian organization.

Hidden agendas are not bad in themselves. We all have mixed
motives as we are involved in the organizational life of the church.
Several needs may be met in the process of devising and carrying out

plans for evangelism and church planting. However, it is important to recognize these hidden agendas or they can displace the more basic and public reasons for what we are doing.

Listing our assumptions helps us discover *missing steps or needs*. We may realize that we have been assuming that someone else will be responsible for a particular role when in fact no one else is planning to take that step.

Listing our assumptions helps us clear up any *misconceptions* we might have about ourselves and our situation. We may have entirely different conceptions of the future than do others. We may be assuming that the political situation will remain relatively stable and open. We may see the economy heading into steady expansion. Others may assume that the future will be chaotic and the economy declining. Disagreement about plans will follow. If the political and economic factors are seen as deteriorating, then the plan may really need to be different than what we are proposing. Different assumptions can lead to different plans.

Listing our assumptions helps us *communicate more effectively*. We are able to let our co-workers know what we are expecting to happen and what we hope to gain from it all. When we recognize that our assumptions are different, we can state those differences and seek common ground.

There are very different assumptions about why evangelization is important and even what it means, that is, what kinds of activity are considered *evangelistic* activities. One person thinks evangelization means verbal proclamation of the name of Christ and a call for a decision. Another says it means a whole process whereby people are made aware of the name and power of Christ. Rather than look for a single decision point, evangelization seeks to initiate a process.

There are very different assumptions about the nature of the individual and the relationship of the individual to his or her groups. In the West we normally assume that people are free *as individuals* to make religious commitments and decisions. We assume that it does not matter whether children or women make such decisions before parents or men. When we plan to bring people to conversion, we assume they will come one-by-one to register their decision. We may even assume that a heroic decision of an individual made against the opposition of friends and family is the most authentic type of decision. Others from more communally-oriented cultures may assume that people only make religious commitments *in consultation with kin and clan*. The only authentic decisions are those validated and agreed to by the majority of one's primary social group. Thus, assumptions about decision making will influence how we plan for conversion and decision making.

STEP 5: DEFINING AN APPROACH

We need to know our assumptions about ourselves, our organization, our church or mission, and the country within which we will be living. All of these will be nested in basic assumptions we make about the world and time in which we live.

ASSUMPTIONS ABOUT YOURSELF

What is your understanding of the problem? What is the *why* in your life? Why do you seek to evangelize? Why evangelize the unreached people? What problem do they have that you seek to solve? How do you know about this problem? How accurate is your information? Is this the common understanding of others? Do the others seek to evangelize because they see the problem in the same way you do? Why do you believe you are capable of understanding the problem? Do you see only part of it? We are reminded of the large sign over a doorway of a major aerospace firm: "If you can smile in the face of the situation, you just don't understand the situation."

What are your gifts and capabilities? Are they the gifts needed to reach the target group? Are your gifts in the arena of planning and managing but not in the area of carrying out frontline ministry? Where do the gifts of understanding, planning, solving, acting, evaluating fit?

What is your role? We will discuss this at some length in a later chapter. What do you see as your role? Why do you believe you are the one to carry out that role? Do others in your group see you as the logical person for that role?

What ability do you have to bring about change? After all, this is our ultimate goal—to change people from ignorance and indifference to knowledge of and allegiance to Christ. We must convince people of the claims of Christ on their lives. What are you assuming about your ability to bring about change?

How are you perceived as a person? Who do *you* say you are? Who do *others* say you are? What is your role as perceived by others in the situation, for instance, by others in the organization?

What is your perception about what your organization will allow you to do? Have they allowed others to do this same kind of thing? What do they forbid? Why? What evidence do you have that the answers to these questions are so? What is your experience with this organization?

Do you have the courage to carry out this task? Leadership can be lonely. Do you have the courage to be misunderstood? To be wrong? To fail? To sacrifice? It does not take a lot of courage to face a known situation. Courage is most needed when we recognize that there is a high possibility that we will not succeed.

Do you have the right to move forward with this task? What are your other commitments—to your family, friends, the organization? Many people love a new challenge primarily because it relieves them of the responsibility of dealing with an old and difficult challenge.

Why do you want this to happen? What needs do you have that will be met by this program? What are your present personal goals? Where do you picture yourself ten or fifteen years from now? What is it you really enjoy doing?

ASSUMPTIONS ABOUT THE ORGANIZATION

What are the organization's purposes? Why does it exist? Is it doing the same thing today it was doing originally? Does it demonstrate that it really believes in its purpose? Does the organization assume it is carrying out its purpose when, in actuality, it is not?

What are the organization's goals? A goal is a measurable future event that the organization plans to make a past event. Are the goals of the organization clearly stated? Have the goals been communicated and understood? Are these goals owned by particular people within the organization? Are they the generally accepted goals? Are they actually process rather than accomplishment goals? For example, an organization may have a process goal of publishing one hundred thousand gospel tracts. Its goal of accomplishment would be what it expected those tracts to do for the kingdom.

Is the organization willing to change? Is there any evidence of this from its past history? Is the organization in the process of changing now? How rapidly is it changing? What ability do you perceive it has to change? Has the organization settled down to a point where it is more interested in efficiency (how well things are done) rather than effectiveness (what it gets done)?

What is the organization's mode of operation? How does it go about doing things? What is it that it can or cannot do as related to this particular project?

Does the organization have the ability to carry out the plan and support it? Does it have people, resources, spiritual strength, and community spirit?

What are the relationships within the organization? Who is in charge? Is there a strong and formal organization that has a great deal to say about the operation of the organization? Are the relationships within the organization apparent to the organization? Is the organization chart at least 75 percent accurate?

ASSUMPTIONS ABOUT OTHER CHURCHES AND MISSIONS

There will normally be other churches and mission agencies as well as other individual Christians with whom you will and should relate in order to reach a people group.

How much cooperation can you expect? What do these other organizations think about you and your organization? How do they perceive your motives? Do they have the ability to do the things that they have committed themselves to?

Are other organizations willing to allow this to happen? Will they oppose it, stay neutral, or cooperate?

Do other organizations or churches desire to see change? What evidence is there that they are content with the present situation? Is there discontent?

What is your view of these other Christian organizations? For example, do you see them as "separated brethren" or sub-Christian? Do they have traits that make them unacceptable to your group?

Does your organization have common goals with other organizations? Are the organizations moving toward opposite goals?

What is the other organization or church's self-understanding? Do they consider themselves the *national* church? Do they see themselves as part of a larger body or as separated from a larger body?

What is the other organization's view of mission? Is mission something that results in the planting of a church? Do they believe that the church should grow and can grow? Is this view of mission held by all of the people in this organization?

ASSUMPTIONS ABOUT THE COUNTRY IN WHICH YOU WORK

What is the national stance toward religion? What laws exist about religious organizations? What freedom will you have to preach? What freedom does the church have to reach out to others?

Does the government have active plans regarding the people you are trying to reach? Do they see them as a people or people group in the same

224

way you do? Do they have plans for helping or hindering this particular people?

What is the role of modernization in this country? Is the government planning to see the country developed? If so, how rapidly and in what direction? Do they plan to nationalize any of the industries? Do they plan to nationalize the church? How successful do you think they are going to be?

What legal restrictions will the government put on the type of approach you are planning to use?

What is the political situation inside the country? Is it stable? Will it change? Are there factions in the country? Rebellious groups?

What is the status of justice and liberty within the country? Is this an authoritarian regime? Will you ethically be able to operate within this type of political structure?

What is the future of the economy in the country? What impact will this have on your ability to support yourself or your organization? Are there any restrictions on financial exchange? Are the material resources needed to carry out your task available in the country?

ASSUMPTIONS ABOUT THE WORLD

It may seem rather grandiose to try to state our assumptions about the world, but because we do it so seldom, it can sometimes be quite surprising to see what our view of the world is, particularly our view of the future.

What will be the future of the world's economy? Will it be such that it will be able to support our type of endeavor?

How does the world in general perceive our ministry? For example, some believe it is wrong for religions to seek to change the religion of others. Others believe that Christianity downplays this-worldly affairs so that evangelism ignores the physical conditions of people.

WHAT NOW?

We are always in tension between the amount of time we should spend in thinking compared to the amount of time spent in carrying out our plans. After you have reviewed the questions dealing with assumptions, you will need to add your own. You will discover that some are very appropriate, while others have no bearing on what you are setting out to do.

What you need to do is to consider the answers to those appropriate questions. What impact do they have on the general approach you defined? Do you still feel comfortable about your proposal? Do you still think it is realistic to aim at the movement along the Søgaard scale? Are the people whom you are suggesting as the force for evangelism the most appropriate?

As a result of looking at what is assumed in your strategy, restate it. Then you are ready to move on to step six: anticipating the results.

Questions

1. What will be your grand strategy to reach a particular people group? Your intermediate strategy? Your short-range strategy?

2. What will your strategy exclude? What will it not seek to do?

3. Does your strategy modify your ideas about the makeup of your force for evangelism?

4. Does it suggest changes in the methods and means you tentatively chose?

5. Why is it important that you state your assumptions about the task? About yourself? About your organization? About the country in which you will be working?

6. Which assumptions are so critical that if they turn out not to be true your whole strategy will be in jeopardy?

STEP 6: ANTICIPATED OUTCOMES

Considerations

1. We expect great things to happen when the gospel is proclaimed because it has done great things in transforming our lives.

2. Conversion is more properly thought of as a process than as a single event. We experience conversion throughout our life as we continually put off the old and put on the new.

3. When we anticipate outcomes, we are not limited to the threshold events of decision, baptism, and membership.

4. Our control of the future is much less than we think. We can state what we think would please God if it were to happen in the future and then make new statements of faith as the future actually unfolds.

5. We cannot project a detailed blueprint for the resulting church. But we can use methods that give local Christians the freedom to decide what the blueprint looks like when it can be developed.

6. Authenticity is twofold: an authentic church is one rooted deeply in its own culture and recognizably shaped and invigorated by the Bible.

7. The ultimate goal of evangelization is the creation of new communities engaged in evangelization.

8. The easiest way to avoid accountability for results is to confuse means with ends.

9. Most churches and missions report their results in terms of how much has been done instead of how much has been accomplished. Activity is not accomplishment.

10. One of the major changes that takes place when a new people group is evangelized is the change that takes place within the evangelist.

11. Questions are universal, while the answers are always unique to the situation.

17. Movement toward Christ

See how patient a farmer is as he waits for his land to produce precious crops. He waits patiently for the autumn and spring rains.

James 5:7

The farmer who has done the hard work should have the first share in the harvest.

2 Timothy 2:6

Every farmer has a crop in mind when the seed is sown. This anticipation includes what will happen to the crop. Is it to be sold? Who might buy it? What will be done if the rains are late or pests infest the growing crop? The farmer keeps an eye on the weather, the market, and the labor force. He responds to the various events as they unfold—all with an eye on the harvest.

Like the farmer, the evangelist must anticipate the results of his work in faith and hope. If we believe God will accomplish his work, we must prepare to do something with the results of our labor. If we do not anticipate the outcomes our approach will produce, we will not be ready to form churches, train Christians, or endure persecution. Forewarned is forearmed! We must stretch into the future and imagine, "This is what I believe will happen. . . ."

We know the power of God can transform human lives. He transformed our own. Large numbers of people are becoming Christian. In Africa more than four thousand will convert to Christianity each day of 1990. In Latin America some seven thousand new churches will begin their existence this year.

232

As we proclaim the message of Christ and his kingdom, we must believe God can bring the increase. Little faith will see little results. With William Carey we must "attempt great things for God; expect great things from God" (Neill, 1964, p. 262). We agree with the Willowbank Report:

> Messengers of the gospel who have proved in their own experience that it is "the power of God for salvation" (Rom. 1:16) rightly expect it to be so in the experience of others also. We confess that sometimes, just as a Gentile centurion's faith put to shame the unbelief of Israel in Jesus' day (Matt. 8:10), so today the believing expectancy of Christians in other cultures sometimes shows up the missionary's lack of faith. So we remind ourselves of God's promises through Abraham's posterity to bless all the families of the earth and through the gospel to save those who believe (Gen. 12:1-4; I Cor. 1:21). It is on the basis of these and many other promises that we remind all messengers of the gospel, including ourselves, to look to God to save people and to build his church.
>
> At the same time, we do not forget our Lord's warnings of opposition and suffering. Human hearts are hard. People do not always embrace the gospel, even when the communication is blameless in technique and the communicator in character. Our Lord himself was fully at home in the culture in which he preached, yet he and his message were despised and rejected. . . . (Lausanne Committee, 1978, p. 15)

THE MEANING OF CONVERSION

Conversion is one of the words that captures the nature of what the good news demands.[1] It refers to a change in the direction of one's thinking and life. To convert is to experience an inner transformation. It is a turning away from sin and idols and a turning to God by faith through Jesus Christ.

Conversion refers to the events that take place in human experience as God's Spirit brings about the new birth. This may come as a dramatic crisis experience (such as Paul's encounter with Christ). Alternatively, it may be a very subtle but equally profound change that takes place over years of time. Those raised in Christian homes sometimes cannot remember a time Christ was not present and real in their experience.

1. Laubach et al., 1975; Bertram, 1971; Stott, 1975, chap. 5; Green, 1970, chap. 6. See also "Hong Kong Call to Conversion," *World Evangelization* 15 (July-Aug. 1988): 8-13.

STEP 6: ANTICIPATED OUTCOMES

What stimulates conversion varies widely. For one it might be a power encounter between the gospel and the old system of gods (Tippett, 1967, chap. 7). For another it may be the malaise that comes from a life not going well. Yet another may experience a dramatic healing or cure from alcoholism or drug addiction by the power of God. The occasions for conversion are extremely diverse but they all lead to the same process of transformation.

One of the results we look for are people who are converted and are being converted. In cross-cultural settings we need to keep some important matters in mind.[2]

1. Conversion is a change reaching to the roots of human life. The New Testament depicts it as re-creation, resurrection from the dead, transfer from one kingdom to another. We are those who are "crucified with Christ" (Gal. 2:20). We cannot treat conversion as "cheap grace" or character improvement through self-discipline. The Holy Spirit alone can convict and renew the sinner.

2. Conversion is a continuing process, not just an event. We continue to experience conversion whenever we put off the old and put on the new. It takes years to bring many areas of life under the Lordship of Christ. We never stop repenting and turning to God. Conversion is a lifelong process whose fullest meaning is experienced only with the second coming of Christ.

3. Conversion is personal, but it is not individualistic. One person's conversion has an impact on other people. Friends and family feel its reality. Faith often travels along the network of kinship and friendship. Conversion is frequently communal as well. Cornelius became a Christian *with* his household (Acts 10–11). The whole family of the Philippian jailor (Acts 16:31-34) became Christians at the same time. These are examples of multi-individual, mutually-interdependent conversions.

Finally, conversion affects community structures and institutions as Christians become salt and light (Matt. 5:13-16). Individual conversion does not automatically result in social transformation. Yet it provides the dynamic for profound social changes because the power of the kingdom of God is present.

4. Conversion is essentially a change in religious allegiance (C. Kraft, *Christianity in Culture,* chap. 17). The governing principle of life changes from some human idolatry to loyalty to Jesus Christ. Since that which assumes the place of God in one's life differs from person to person, this change will take different forms. We cannot establish ahead of

---

2. Much of this is based on the *Willowbank Report—Gospel and Culture* (Lausanne Committee, 1978, pp. 19-22).

time a set of issues as the true test of allegiance. What that will be is context dependent.

The importance of conversion is that a human life is bound solely to Jesus Christ. A specific list of ethical matters that seem important to the evangelist cannot be made more important than the issue of allegiance. Without the transfer of loyalty to Christ, conformity to or rejection of certain practices or forms will create bad faith. There will be outward reformation without inner transformation.

5. Conversion is not separate from the meanings and forms that govern a people group's life. Conversion even affects the worldview of a people and produces changes at the very heart of a people's cultural inheritance. If life is revolutionized, the principles that govern life are also affected. While an integrated Christian worldview may take years to mature, the first changes are visible at the beginning of the process. Without changes in worldview, the conversion process cannot be sustained. Nor can it produce dynamic changes.

6. Conversion affects the standards and behavior that govern relationships. It gives us new power to obey the demands of the gospel. We are now able to love one another, to give fair measure in our transactions, to respect human life, and so on (Dye, 1976; Lewis, 1947). It also introduces us to new sources of standards found in the Bible and in experience with God. These stand in judgment over our inherited social standards. They fulfill our social aspirations while also correcting them. Yet they do this without deculturizing us. Conversion re-makes. It does not unmake.

7. Conversion does not necessarily divorce us from our kinfolk. Sometimes opposition can be so strong to Christian commitment that relationships break. Conversion means we are spiritually distinct, not socially segregated. Christians should seek to remain an integral and respected part of their family and people.

Conversion anticipates personal transformation and the formation of a community of the people of God. One's life-style will change as it witnesses to new loyalty and priorities. From inner motivation to outward customs these changes will witness to the Lordship of Christ.

THE STARTING POINT

Movement toward Christ is a relative matter. We mark progress by the distance from the beginning point of Christian life and toward Christ

(Kraft, 1979, pp. 239-45). The Søgaard scale portrays this in a two-dimensional way. Movement happens both in knowledge and in attitude.

We can also think of movement in a three-dimensional fashion, related to the three areas singled out for understanding a people. Evangelization attempts to move people toward Christ in each area. It uses the *meaning systems* of a people to produce mature understandings of the gospel and its implications for this particular people. It speaks to the *needs* of people as they perceive them. As Christ's Lordship becomes clear, more and more needs are met in a way that is congruent with the values of the kingdom. Finally, evangelization explores customs, social structures, and institutions to show how Christ fulfills and challenges them. Christians come to enact their *roles* as unto Christ.

The result is movement on several dimensions at differing speeds. In Figure 17.1, the effort is to move people downward into the right, front quadrant.

To the extent that a people or people group become Christian they will grow in each of these dimensions. They will have an increasing clarity and understanding of the revelation of God. They will realize

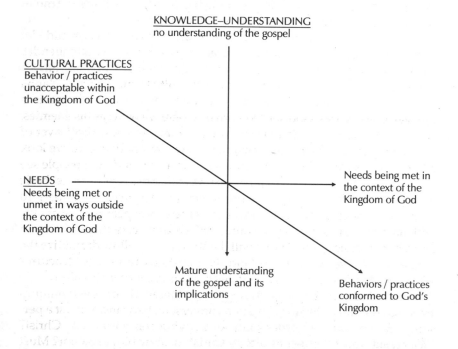

FIGURE 17.1 THE PEOPLE PROFILE AND ANTICIPATED OUTCOMES

how their deepest needs as well as every-day necessities are met by God through Christ. They will experience a continuing transformation of customs and role relationships as they enact old roles with a new dynamic. The net effect of these transformations will increase or decrease the receptivity of the surrounding community to the gospel.

Individuals as well as families and people groups are at different points on these three dimensions. A nominal Christian group (e.g., a middle-class Catholic suburban settlement in Quito, Ecuador) may have much knowledge about Christ. Their attitude may be relatively favorable. Their actual pattern of living, however, may be governed by a Western, materialistic ethic. Movement toward Christ will entail connecting and deepening their knowledge so they sense the incongruity between life and knowledge.

A Thai Buddhist fishing village without a single Christian will experience movement toward Christ differently. Their understanding and knowledge of the gospel is almost nothing. They begin with a set of needs and customs uninfluenced by a Christian tradition. For them movement toward Christ will mean very different changes and consequences than it will for the nominal Catholics of Quito. Both may begin their journey outside of a saving relationship with Christ. Both will move closer to him. But the paths they take will be unique.

We start with people where they are, not where we would like them to be. The purpose of evangelization as a process is to engender changes that help move them toward Christ. Eventually they will have a culturally authentic, spiritually valid opportunity to submit to the claims of Christ. We start with people where they are because we believe this is the way grace works. God started with us where we were: as his enemies.

However, we do not stop at that point. We know the power of God will take them on to new vistas and new ways of living. So we look for results in each of these dimensions. To what extent do the people see Christian faith and Christians as concerned with the struggle to meet basic needs? How will we know a people is relating their needs to Christ? To what extent does the message being presented meet people in their current state of understanding or confusion? Does it carry them further in apprehending the gospel? How will the strategy we follow dramatize the connection between the gospel and their customs and social structure? Will they see Christianity as a destroyer or a fulfiller of their culture?

One question every strategy must contemplate is the minimum starting point for authentic Christian conversion. How much must a person or family know in order to make a saving commitment to Christ? What needs must they see as met by Christ to know him as Savior? Must they feel a sense of guilt or a specific sin that needs forgiveness? What behaviors or customs will a potential convert be asked to repudiate as part of the act of repentance and following Christ? What knowledge, attitude, and behavior changes are intrinsic to the initial events of conversion?

THE ULTIMATE OBJECTIVE

Our final goal is a cluster of congregations with enough Christians and resources necessary to complete evangelization in their own people group. It is admittedly difficult to say when this has happened. We can estimate how many professing Christians are practicing Christians. We can guess the number of those actively evangelizing their own people. We can list the various ministries that have an impact on the unchurched. Each of these will tell us something about establishing the Christian community.

Here the question goes beyond the minimum starting point. How far must the transformation have gone for it to be self-sustaining? How much knowledge? How strong the connection between Christ and the meeting of needs? How changed the customary behavior and action in institutional roles? Do these communities of Christians have what it takes to continue the task of evangelization? If not, what changes must happen for that to be the case?

Part of the problem in defining results is that no transcultural definition is adequate to settle many of these questions. The very variety of Christian interpretation and expression that is a resource in a multicultural world increases the complexity of our task. Not all understandings of Scripture are equally adequate. Nor are all ways of putting Christian faith into practice.

Charismatic Pentecostals, black-robed Coptics, anti-clerical and anti-liturgical Plymouth Brethren, high church Anglicans—these are symbolic of the diversity of the body of Christ. There is no disembodied, supracultural Christianity. The problem is finding the center of Christian faith, a center to which all authentic Christianity is oriented. Center points set the reference for circumferences. What sorts of Christian expression do we include within the circumference of authentic Christianity?

The church is present in adequate measure when motivated by the Spirit of God and molded by the word of God. Yet neither of those is easily measurable. We have to recognize the possibility that evangelism may foster movements in a people group that are *simultaneously* toward Christ and the world (Yamamori and Taber, 1975). Syncretism and a watered-down gospel is an ever present danger.

"Christo-paganism" is the name for syncretism in Latin America and elsewhere. Forcible conversion and inadequate discipling produce a syncretistic faith. Jesus, Mary, the saints, and the ancient gods are all a part of the same Latin American religious universe. Christ is not Lord of the universe. Rather, he is one lord in a panoply of earth lords and devils, ancestral spirits, and magical rites.

North American "Christo-paganism" is no less real. The "American way of life" is for many Christians the operative religion (Herzberg, 1966; Berger 1961; Dayton, 1984; Bellah, 1985). A "Christo-Westernism" is carried to the ends of the earth and offered instead of the Christ of the Bible. Sometimes it is a matter of a "Christo-denominationalism," where elements of a denominational tradition have more importance than the dynamic word of God. Some see the West as a valid mission field not only because of the millions of unchurched, secularized Christians, but because of its own version of "Christo-paganism."

This is the problem. Christianity must be contextualized. Yet when does the context come to determine the content of the faith? When does the content of the faith bring necessary transformations to the context? How do we know when we have an authentic church, a leaven that can leaven the whole lump? What do we do if the leaven loses its fermenting power?

These considerations are why it is important to specify the sorts of results we look for as authentic goals of evangelization. Given our understanding of the center of Christian faith and how we believe God is at work, what are the results our evangelistic strategy seeks? We might begin with the traditional threshold events of Christian faith: decisions, baptisms, new members joining a Christian church. We seek these threshold events.

Yet the Søgaard scale suggests that evangelization is a process with many steps. We can measure movement toward Christ at a number of points, both before and after commitment to Christ. At the least, we will probably want to monitor changes in *knowledge* and *attitude,* and *the rate of change.* What we expect to happen has strong impact on our plan. We can imagine the difference in the plans and actions of two evangelists Al Krass describes:

> One catechist I met told me: "I went to a certain place to preach for the first time on last Sunday. Many people repented. I am now preparing them for baptism." He expected an immediate and total response.
>
> A priest I knew was quite different. He had been preaching in several villages for a number of years. I asked him whether he felt the people were ready to become Christians. "Oh no," he replied. "I don't suppose they ever will. We just go out to let them know what the

Christian faith is all about. Maybe some of their children who go to school will become Christian, but we don't really expect we can convert the fathers." (1974, p. 87)

Later in this book we will deal more specifically with setting goals for evangelization. We set goals for results because we believe it is God's will that some results occur rather than others. By faith we want to set forth what we think God wants *accomplished* in this generation. We must trust God to bring about the miracle of people trusting him for salvation. Even when we have done our best, we still will have a keen sense of our unworthiness as his servants.

Nevertheless, we will not allow such an awareness to justify our own sloth and sloppiness. We are inexcusable when we act without regard for easily anticipated outcomes. We cannot simply "leave the results to God," as though we have no responsibility for any results. One can imagine a modern version of the parable of the pounds (Matt. 25:14-30; Luke 19:11-27). The modern money manager says: "Lord, I invested your money and left the results to God. Unfortunately, I did not do a good job with your investment. The stock market fell and all you gave me was lost." Prudence is an old Christian virtue that is part of wisdom. Wisdom demands that our faith in God lead us to responsible action in seeking the best results. There are results we can anticipate and even control.

God expects us by faith to decide what we are to be and do. We are stewards (1 Cor. 4:1-2) and are to be faithful to our Master. Faithfulness is much more than a dutiful putting in of hours and effort. There is more than enough "good missionary work" that never evaluates itself. Faithfulness is doing the will of the Master, accomplishing the task he sets for us. What counts in the parable of the pounds is not good intentions or long hours of work. Rather, it is the gain made on the money entrusted.

Measurable, carefully specified results are important because the task set for us is important. They allow us to evaluate our methods and efforts to see if we are progressing toward our goals. They keep us from getting bogged down in our means and forgetting our ends. We have no way of guaranteeing the future. Yet by faith we can state what we believe God wants that future to be and go after it.

Proverbs 22:3 says "Sensible people will see trouble coming and avoid it, but an unthinking person will walk right into it and regret it later." God can bless us with the sense to see the coming harvest. We can go and reap it and return with our sheaves rejoicing (Ps. 126:6).

18. The Resulting Church

Our end goal of evangelism is a cluster of vital, dynamic congregations able to evangelize their own people. Evangelistic methods and models strongly affect the sort of church that results.

Evangelization is dialectical. It grows out of the church as a redeemed community. At the same time it creates new churches to be the redeemed community. Thus, any approach to evangelization not dealing with the church is deficient. The church is the agent and the result of evangelization (Snyder, 1977, p. 103). Evangelism brings new churches into being. Then evangelism takes place as a result of the vitality of the churches brought into being.

The church is an agent of the kingdom because of what it *is.* It is the messianic community, existing in love, exercising the gifts of the Spirit. It is an agent of the kingdom also because of what it *does.* It changes the world through evangelism, calling all to repentance and faith. It challenges the world through prophetic ministry, witnessing to God's judgment on all injustice and structures alienating us from God. It cares for the world through diaconate service, extending help to the poor and those in crisis.

Insofar as the church exists and acts according to its true nature, it brings about confrontation with the powers of evil. Acting on behalf of the kingdom of God it transfers people into that kingdom and forms new congregations of the faithful. New Christians need the support and nurture of fellow Christians in communities of faith, hope, and love. The authenticity and adequacy of those congregations for nurture and for continued evangelism are central results desired as a by-product of evangelization.

STEP 6: ANTICIPATED OUTCOMES

THE CHURCH IN THE FREEDOM OF THE SPIRIT

Having the outline of the resulting church in mind simplifies our task of selecting methods and undertaking a strategy. We begin with the freedom of the Spirit for several reasons. The common error in church planting has been imposing familiar patterns from another culture. The home church of the evangelist, with its forms and structures, serves as the model for the church in the new environment. So we find Anglican bishops and surplices in central Uganda, Southern Baptist amens in the jungles of Kalimantan, Wednesday evening prayer meetings in a farming village in the high Andes.

We often impose our Western church models onto a new situation instead of following its unique logic. This has led to a crisis of leadership in areas where the church is growing rapidly. In part this is because churches have adopted the Western ideal of a full-time, seminary-educated, paid clergy.[1] Even if all the graduates from Christian seminaries and Bible schools became pastors, there would not be enough for all the congregations. Theological Education by Extension (TEE) is an effort to meet this problem.

We export our models of church life because our sense of the church as a creation of the Holy Spirit is weak. The Bible sees the church primarily in charismatic terms rather than in institutional or organizational categories. It is more a living organism than a well-ordered organization.

The task in planting a church is allowing the Spirit to create it in the image appropriate to that people group. We must allow the true essentials of the church to have controlling power over the accidental features of organization, institution, and tradition. This means we must distinguish between the exemplary and the mandatory in Scripture. As Michael Harper puts it:

> If the New Testament is our blueprint for ministry in the Church, all one can say is that it is a strange blueprint. There is a certain haphazardness about the appointments to office in the New Testament which only makes sense if you view them as the *ad hoc* prompting of the Holy Spirit, amidst the most taxing of circumstances. The Church was having to make adjustments all the time. It was growing rapidly and spreading widely. It was crossing all kinds of racial, social and cultural frontiers. It was often under fire from its enemies. It had to make, at times, radical adjustments, to rapidly changing situations. . . .

1. Braun, 1971; Read et al., 1971, chap. 22.

242

The New Testament writers . . . are more concerned with "life" than with defining too closely how the Church should be governed and who should do what. For instance, those who attempt to find the origins of the order of deacons in Acts 6 have a hard time proving it. Here is an *ad hoc* situation, and the Church responding sensibly to it. . . . We see no stereotype here, but flexibility to the movings of the Holy Spirit. (1978, pp. 24-25)

The ecclesiastical titles in the New Testament are designations of functions and ministries. There were no bureaucratic structures governed by written manuals of church order. There was no professional clerical class which met a set educational and ecclesiastical criteria. The New Testament designations of pastor, teacher, and bishop simply do not correspond with our church organizational titles. The New Testament gives us examples of what the early Christians did to meet the pressures of their day and continue their evangelizing. It does not intend to give us an organizational chart for deducing church structure.

MODELS FOR THE RESULTING CHURCH

The same flexibility, adaptability, and growth seen in the New Testament should mark the planting of new churches. The church as a community of the Spirit exists in freedom because it exists in the presence of the Lord (2 Cor. 3:17).

A church is not a true church simply because it has a proper hierarchy of offices. Nor does it become the church because it ordains qualified candidates to an organized clergy. Authenticity is not a matter of title, structure, or legal definition. Rather, the gift of the Spirit forming a community of those entering the kingdom of God is the chief criteria.

All the matters of meeting time, place, frequency, liturgy, dress, or the architecture of the building are matters of complete freedom. The legitimacy and authenticity of the church has little to do with these accidental features of church life. All are subject to the freedom of the Spirit and the imperative to be the community of Jesus Christ.

This is not to say that formal organization is the enemy of the Spirit. To suppose that is to misunderstand the point we are making. Life has to have form to sustain itself and to effect changes in the environment. Structure is inevitable. Yet its purpose and meaning is to serve as the tool of indispensable functions. "Particular structures will be legitimate or illegitimate depending not only on what they are intended to accomplish, but on their functions—what they actually do accomplish" (Snyder, 1977, p. 139).

Fish and fowl, lizard and horse, insect and elephant, all fulfill common functions of life: eating, reproducing, adapting to environmental change, defending their young. Yet what a diverse set of structures have evolved to accomplish those common functions! As the church finds itself in each new people group, it will take on new patterns and structures.

Historically, the church has not been the friend of freedom. In most eras it has increased its control over the affairs and diversity of Christian life. It has excommunicated those who would not standardize according to a central pattern. When crossing cultural boundaries, it assumed its standardized forms and structures would be replicated in new people groups. Denominational features are in evidence in Jayapura and Jakarta. American Lutherans and Free Methodists could recognize their own distinctives in Malawi as well as in Memphis.

This lack of freedom is one reason for the more than eight thousand Independent Church movements in Africa. Similar movements exist in all parts of the globe. Each of these churches seeks to find a cultural authenticity and a spiritual freedom not found in its parent bodies.

This lack of freedom is also clearly seen in the church movements that sputter along, only reluctantly transferring authority and requiring leadership to follow Western, bureaucratic patterns. Unfortunately, this is often repeated as Two-Thirds World missions begin cross-cultural evangelism.

Attempts to specify the criteria for the sort of church that is the goal of evangelization have resulted in three images: the "three-self" church, the dynamic equivalence church, and the contexualized church.

1. The "Three-Self" Church

Henry Venn of the Church Missionary Society and Rufus Anderson of the American Board for Foreign Missions developed this model.[2] Churches were to be self-governing, self-supporting, and self-propagating. These qualities were aimed at correcting the dependence and paternalism so evident in the results of nineteenth-century cross-cultural missions. Anderson urged that mission aim at:

1. Converting lost men
2. Organizing them into churches

2. Warren, 1971; Beaver, 1967, 1979; Verkuyl, 1978, pp. 184-88.

3. Producing a competent native ministry
4. Leading the churches to independence and self-propagation.
   (Beaver, 1979, p. 95)

Roland Allen's *Missionary Methods: St. Paul's or Ours?* is a classic statement of this model. His writings circulated widely in the 1920s and 1930s. The "three-self" slogan became the most widely shared formula in Protestant missions, especially since World War II. The appearance of national independence in the majority of the Two-Thirds World encouraged these sorts of indigenous church principles.

However, this formula has faced several sharp criticisms. First, it is rather vague in its meaning. When is a church self-governing or self-propagating? Because it applies to widely variant church situations, its meaning is not clear. China's official Protestant Church is a "Three-self Church," yet it is strongly limited and dictated to by the central government. Is it really self-governing?

Second, the "three-self" formula is not equivalent to indigeneity. A young church can be self-governing in the sense that its parent mission no longer has the controlling voice. Yet it may not express indigenous patterns. It may still receive significant support monies from the mission and sustain policies to keep on good terms with the mission. Its leadership may be Western in their ways of doing things. That is simply what they learned.

On the other hand, a church that receives outside support may be indigenous. The Jerusalem church received outside support (Acts 20–21), but it was not less indigenous simply because it was not self-supporting.

> If the church makes its own decisions, without outside interference, as to how its funds shall be used, and does so on the basis of economic patterns natural to it in its own cultural setting, this church may be considered indigenous, even if funds are provided by an outside source. (Smalley, 1967, p. 149)

The problem with the "three-self" formula is that it does not specify the quality of indigeneity. Consequently, it can be understood in terms of Western individualism and independence rather than being rooted in indigenous patterns.

It also does not include the so-called fourth-self, self-theologizing (Hiebert, 1985). From within each church God will raise up theologians who will develop theologies more relevant to their own culture. Until then, it is difficult to speak of an indigenous theology. The "three-selfs" can be in place and yet the reading and understanding of the Scriptures may still be foreign.

245

Third, McGavran and others claim that this formula is applicable only where the church grows rapidly. In resistant populations where individuals come to Christ slowly and only a few at a time, it is impossible to aim at a three-self church. Churches will not be large enough to carry out these principles or support auxiliary structures (such as hospitals or schools).

Furthermore, the three-selfs do not invariably lead to increased rates of church growth. Some large churches have grown up on the basis of paid pastors and evangelists managed by foreigners. It is true that over time they moved in the direction of the three-selfs. But their beginning and expansion were not due to following three-self principles.

2. The Dynamic Equivalence Church

Several models seek to correct the weaknesses of the three-self formula, looking for a more careful definition of indigeneity.[3] One such model is the dynamic equivalence church (C. Kraft, 1973, *Christianity in Culture*, and "Dynamic Equivalent Churches in Muslim Society").

"Dynamic equivalence" is a theory of Bible translation that breaks with the literal translation model (also called "formal correspondence"). In literal translation, evaluation depends on how closely the translation forms approximate the source language. For example, Philippians 1:8 and 2:1 speak literally of "the bowels" (Greek *ta splanxna* = the viscera). A literal translation such as the *King James Version* renders it "I long after you all in the bowels of Jesus Christ."

The dynamic equivalence model seeks to communicate the *meaning* of the original linguistic forms. The evaluation of the translation depends on the degree to which it has an equivalent impact on the new audience that the original words had on its audience. The *New Inter-*

---

3. Indigenous churches have been defined in various ways. Since it is a complicated concept that requires extended discussion, we will only present some representative definitions. William Smalley: "It is a group of believers who live out their life, including their socialized Christian activity, in the patterns of the local society, and for whom any transformation of that society comes out of their felt needs under the guidance of the Holy Spirit" (1967, p. 150). Daniel C. Hardin: "An indigenous church is a church in which God, Christ, and the Holy Spirit, in contact with people of a particular cultural setting, give rise to a Christian body that is outwardly and uniquely molded by that culture over a fixed framework of fundamental scriptural doctrine" (1978, p. 184). Alan Tippett: "When the indigenous people of a community think of the Lord as their own, not as foreign Christ; when they do things as unto the Lord, meeting the cultural needs around them, worshipping in patterns they understand; when their congregations function in participation in a body, which is structurally indigenous; then you have an indigenous Church" (1969, p. 136).

national Version assumes that most English readers do not know "the bowels" means the seat of the affections. So it translates Philippians 1:8 as "I long for all of you with the affection of Jesus Christ." That is, the dynamic equivalence translation is not concerned with the equivalency of the original and the translation forms but with the response of the hearer. It changes and recombines the linguistic forms to achieve a more immediate communication of meaning. Charles Kraft suggests that this approach might transfer to our goals for church planting.

> A "dynamic equivalence church," then, is the kind of church that produces the same kind of impact on its own society as the early church produced upon the original hearers. In that equivalence the younger church will have need of leadership, organization, education, worship, buildings, behavioral standards, means of expressing Christian love and concern to unconverted people. A dynamically equivalent church will employ familiar, meaningful, indigenous forms, adapting and in-filling them with Christian content. (1973, p. 49)

This model argues that we ought to transcend expectations that new churches imitate the forms and structures of the churches that started them. The focus should be on the functions and impact every church should have in its surrounding context. The forms of liturgy, leadership, education, witnessing, and serving may be very different from our own. Yet if they are equivalent in impact and function to the New Testament church, we are in the presence of an authentic, indigenous church.

The dynamic equivalance model is self-anchoring in the culture of the people group and the New Testament. It does not assume that some specific forms (such as church government or liturgy) are self-definitional for all authentic churches. It provides a corrective for a weak and insipid three-self church that propagates itself solely by biological growth. Like the New Testament church, it grows through conversion.

However, this model has several problems. First, it is difficult to determine the biblically recommended functions of the church. We do not know many of the impacts of the early church in its context. Further, some of the portrait of the early congregations is negative in content (squabbling, sexual immorality, lax discipline, false teaching). We would not want a dynamic equivalence of those inadequate aspects of the apostolic church.

Additionally, the model does not help where there are radical differences in social context. The church today must function in ways unanticipated by the early church or even in ways contrary to its choices. For example, capital formation and interest bearing notes have a very different meaning and function in our social and industrial order than they did in the agrarian societies. The Old and New Testaments both banned such practices. Today an equivalent opposition to such economic practices in capitalist societies would be disastrous. Concern for the poor is no different; in fact, this concern lay behind the banning of usury in the Bible. Rather, the issue is how best in industrial orders to reflect and secure the well-being of the poor. What is often not understood is that "the poor" have a different social location in industrial orders. Biblical mandates and solutions address the poor in agrarian-based societies.

The same is true for the approach the church took toward slavery. The New Testament church was passive, attempting to transform relationships within the institution rather than extinguish it at that point in history. Today we would hardly argue that the church should be equivalently passive.

The early church was a minority movement within an imperialistic state. In many places today it is a majority movement within a democratic state. What differences do the social context make for judging what dynamic equivalence means? This is the issue it must deal with if this model is to be useable.

Even this model can be a cipher whose meaning comes from the particular traditions of the evangelist. Thus, the model needs more spelling out in practice if it is to produce criteria for desired results of evangelization. Without more details as to what needs to be dynamically equivalent, it is hard to evaluate its adequacy as a model.

3. The Contextualized Church

The recent discussion on contextualization is a further attempt to get at the intended meanings of indigenization.[4] It is not so much a model of a church as an analysis of the process by which the gospel is particularized for a given context. We have paraphrased Charles Taber's summary of the distinct advantages of contextualization over indigenization.

(1) Contextualization goes beyond communication and appropriate cultural adaptation to raise social, political, and economic questions. It recognizes that wealth, food conditions, and inner psychic attitudes of security and insecurity condition responses to the gospel. Indigenization tends not to consider these factors.

(2) Contexualization has a more dynamic understanding of culture. It also makes cultural transformation more prominent.

4. See issues of *Gospel in Context* (1978–1982); Hesselgrave, *Theology and Mission*, pp. 71-127; 1988, chap. 7; Donovan, *Rediscovering Christianity* (1978); Kirwen, *The Missionary and the Diviner* (Orbis, 1986).

(3) Indigenization developed more out of experience with small, rather isolated people groups. We now face a globally interrelated world. Contextualization seeks to show how the global system affects all peoples and communities.

(4) Indigenization primarily deals with what is happening "out there" on the mission field. Contexualization looks at the missionary's culture as well and how it might be syncretistic or even nonindigenous within the sending culture. It asserts that the demonic infiltrates all cultures, not just the cultures of those outside the stream of Christian history.

(5) Indigenization views the gospel as "the same" for all contexts. It deals superficially with the way gospel expression might differ in differing contexts. Contextualization argues that what is universal and essential in the gospel is less easily identified than previously thought. It asserts that it exists more remotely from the surface level of verbal and symbolic expression than previously acknowledged.

(6) Indigenization worried in the main about the congregations and denominational structures. Seldom did it think about the indigeneity of hospitals or educational institutions. Contextualization looks at all institutions established or used by missions. It points out the contradiction of indigenous three-self churches surrounded by highly Western health and educational structures.

> Contextualization, then, is an attempt to capitalize on the achievements of indigenization, to correct its errors and biases, and fill in its gaps. It is the effort to understand and take seriously the specific context of each human group and person on its own terms and in all its dimensions—cultural, religious, social, political, economic—and to discern what the gospel says to people in the context. (Taber, 1979, p. 146)

What implications flow from this? First, it means that a given context calls certain themes of the gospel to the forefront. The gospel means one thing for a church living under a totalitarian regime in a situation of affluence and secularism. It will have a different set of imperatives for a rural church living in poverty in a relatively free, democratic society.

As the context varies, the church in each setting faces a different set of challenges to its integrity. Each will incorporate into its life and institutions a unique constellation of meanings so as to manifest the power of the kingdom of God.

To reduce this to the three-self formula is grossly to simplify the range of issues involved. Likewise the dynamic equivalent model will not work because it assumes a functional equivalence between the New Testament and the modern contexts. The first century church was

249

contextualized for *its* setting. What needs to happen is a contextualization under the guidance of the Spirit for *our* settings.

CRITERIA FOR THE RESULTING CHURCH

In anticipating the church that results from our evangelizing, we want to ask a number of questions.

1. What kind of worshiping fellowship would most likely attract other members of this people group?
2. What might be the sort of worship patterns it would find most congenial?
3. How would it show concern for fellow Christians and others in need?
4. Who would lead the church? How would leadership emerge and be equipped?
5. What means might it employ in witnessing to non-Christians?

The answers to these questions are not easy. Furthermore, they will change as the church grows in size and maturity. At the minimum we assume it will face the whole counsel of God and attempt to obey all things Jesus commanded. It will be a leaven within its society, confronting and challenging evil. It will possess for Christ the things that are good, honorable, and true, exhibiting righteousness and justice in its life. It will be an evangelizing agent within its own people.

We realize that the models and criteria we have explored are ideal patterns. The apostolic church was unable fully to practice the patterns laid out for it by Jesus Christ. We should not have unrealistic expectations about the churches we plant. People are only partially converted. Motivations are mixed and commitments limited. The communities of Christians only partially understand and incarnate the values of the kingdom of God.

We continue to work for total conversion and full Christian community. We hope and plan for congregations on fire with the dynamic of the Spirit, reaching out in evangelism and self-sacrificial care. Here, as in conversion, we acknowledge that the starting point is not the place where God stops with a community of Christians. He is willing to start with Christians where they are and move them forward toward greater peace, unity, and love. God is more willing than we often are to start with groups which do not meet his holy standards. He will more and more transform them into the image of his kingdom.

The evangelizing, indigenous church brings our concern full circle. The ultimate result we plan for and seek is a cluster of congregations able to complete the evangelization of their own people. When such an event is before us, we are ready to leave and go to the next unreached people or people group.

19. Ready for Results

Questions to help clarify the future are more important than answers. Our approach believes that *questions are universal while the answers are always unique to the situation.* The details of method as well as the results of the strategy correlate with the details of the people group. By this time it ought to be clear that a simple list cannot summarize the outcomes anticipated.

The *standardized* solution attempts to deal with the problem by providing prescriptions developed outside the situation of evangelism. It comes with a predetermined methodology and a set scenario for results. Yet the more universal and generalized the formulation of results, the less applicable they are to a specific group. The more successful we are in developing an abstract, timeless statement of results, the less it will help in guiding our action. What we need are results as particularized as our methods. Both need to be contextualized in the people group we evangelize.

A good example of this is the unique strategy approach of Phil Parshall. He observed the difficulties standardized solutions have had in the Islamic world. Expecting Muslim converts to pray without prostrating, to worship in mixed sex settings, to come to a church building that looks like an export from Los Angeles is to ask the convert to do more than convert. So Parshall changed the approach and contextualized his expectations about conversion and the resulting church:

- Muslim linguistic forms have been used in place of the more traditional Hindu-Christian vocabulary of the church.
- A facility for washing prior to prayer is provided just outside the worship center.
- Believers remove their shoes and sit on the floor during prayer times.

- Wooden stands are used as Bible holders similar to the ones used for the Koran in the Mosque.
- Prayer is offered with uplifted hands and often with eyes open in Islamic fashion.
- Chanting of the attributes of God, the Lord's Prayer, and personal testimony are performed with great zeal.
- Embracing is done in brotherly Muslim style.
- No particular emphasis is placed on Sunday, for the Muslim considers Friday the holiest day of the week.
- Fasting is encouraged, but it is clearly explained that the thirty-day fast as practiced in Islam does not lead to merit or acceptance with God.
- In the early stage the missionary takes the role of teacher, but within a short time a convert begins to assume this responsibility.
- The name "Christian" is avoided. It is replaced by "Followers of Isa" (Jesus), which has less negative connotation to Muslim society.
- Organization of churches is proposed along autonomous lines much like the loose-knit administrative structures of the mosque.
- Total financial responsibility for church expenses, workers, and buildings is that of the community of believers. From the beginning, no foreign assistance is allowed.
- Development of a homogeneous Muslim convert church. A Hindu, Animist, or "traditional Christian" would be most welcome to worship in the church, but they would be expected to adopt the practices of the convert believers.
- There is no option of flight for the converts. They are expected to remain in their society and maintain a discreet witness to their family and neighbors, which will add to the body of Christ. . . .
- Spiritual dynamics are emphasized. Fasting, prayer, and study of the Word of God are absolute prerequisites of a healthy church. (1979, p. 31)

Conversion brought the Muslim into a community similar to those already found in Bangladesh. The net results were startling.

> In the past four years, over seventy-five Muslims in Bangladesh have become believers. This is almost insignificant when measured against a population of 70 million Muslims. It is important, however,

to realize that this probably exceeds the total number of Muslims converted in Bangladesh during the past fifty years. (Parshall, 1979, p. 31)

Particularizing the methods and results for a people group is more effective than the standard solution approach. We cannot provide generalized lists of expected results since checklists will be as different as people groups are different. What we want to do is to provide some perspectives that are helpful in getting leverage on the future.

FOUR TYPES OF POSSIBLE OUTCOMES

While we cannot predict the future, we can anticipate it. Four possible outcomes come to mind: we can foresee or not foresee results; we can consider results as either negative or positive for our goals. Putting these two axes together produces the diagram in Figure 19.1.

1. *Anticipated positive outcomes* are what we usually call *goals*. They are the results we intend and plan. We pray for them and rejoice when they occur. They are so important in strategies that we devote a whole chapter in this book to them. We believe God will convert sinners and establish worshiping and serving communities of Christians. So we set them forth as our major evangelistic goals.

2. *Anticipated negative outcomes* are what we usually call *problems* (Dayton, 1983). Those which we anticipate we can plan to counteract or counterbalance. A few examples of these sorts of results may be helpful.

a. Studies of campaign evangelism indicate a follow-up gap.

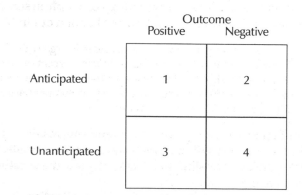

FIGURE 19.1 CLASSIFICATION OF OUTCOMES

Many come forward to make decisions for Christ. Yet only a small percentage wind up active in a Christian congregation (some studies demonstrate as low as 3 percent). Anticipating this, campaign evangelism plans can be modified to cope with this normal result. An example of this modification is the "Rosario Plan" (carried out in Rosario, Argentina), a year-long effort to plant new churches. The mass crusade campaign was only one component of the plan. First, existing churches changed their operation to begin new growth. The planners established as many new house churches as there were preexisting congregations. Campaign converts discovered the house churches especially open and welcoming newcomers. Nearly 60-70 percent of such converts eventually found places in which they became members. This is a dramatic increase in positive results.

b. A radio station in Africa discovered that only a tiny percentage of its potential audience was tuning in. Market research demonstrated that the listeners preferred programming more African and secular than the American music and religious programming on the air. The station decided to use more live programs developed in Africa, as well as pop music and programming on secular subjects.

None of this lessened the station's commitment to evangelism. Its audience zoomed from 2 to 40 percent. However, several missionaries began complaining that the new programming was "worldly." An ensuing struggle within the mission led to the cancellation of the new programming. The old was reinstated and the listenership declined to its former 2 percent.

Not anticipating the rising level of disagreement among fellow missionaries doomed the programming from the start. Had this negative outcome been anticipated, it might have been deflected.

c. Studies show large percentages of people in schools and prisons throw away Bibles or New Testaments handed out indiscriminately.

> Bibles were given to every inmate in a large United States prison. A few days later it was discovered that 90 percent of these found their way into trash cans, thus causing the unnecessary expenditure of more than $250,000 when this program was prematurely spread to other prisons. (Engel, 1977, p. 14)

It is not difficult to anticipate or understand this result. Simple modifications in the method will minimize such massive waste. A program could make Bibles accessible to all who request them rather than distribute them to everyone.

Many more examples exist. Evangelization has numerous side-effects, many of which we can anticipate. We know persecutions will increase with increased conversions in some contexts (such as Indonesia). We also know "premature conversions" can later turn people against Christ ("I tried that when I was younger and it didn't work"). A strategy focused on winning children through education can create the impression that Christianity is only for the young and educated (as did the school method in Africa).

Any plan put into action needs to anticipate the negative by-products of its implementation. Only then can it modify its application and neutralize the negative results.

3. *Unanticipated positive outcomes* are what we usually call pleasant surprises. Sometimes we feel rather ambivalent about them. If we succeed too well, we may suddenly be swamped with no plan to handle the results. When thousands turned to Christ overnight among the highland Dani in Irian Jaya, no one was ready to disciple such numbers of converts. Expecting slow progress but confronted suddenly with 60-70 percent of the people turning to Christ, the missionaries rejoiced and did their best. They had to replan their activity completely.

Of course some unanticipated positive results do not swamp our plan. When Saul suddenly converted and became an ally, it strengthened the early church. Preaching multiplied and Christians breathed easier. But it did not require a whole new plan for evangelizing the eastern Roman world.

4. *Unanticipated negative outcomes* are headaches or unpleasant surprises. They are the sort of problem that can take 80 percent of our energies to cope with them. Because they are unanticipated we are not prepared for them, nor is the church prepared for them. We find ourselves fighting fires instead of giving ourselves to the productive work of reaching our major goals. As Proverbs 22:3 says, "Sensible people will see trouble coming and avoid it, but an unthinking person will walk right into it and regret it later."

In an ideal world we might get to the point where we anticipate most of the negative outcomes. Through experience and research we can come to be more realistic about the results various methods in different contexts produce. We can also approach them systematically through the planning cycle. We cannot control the future, but we need not be surprised by it (Kahn and Wiener, 1967).

Furthermore, we cannot dismiss the negative results by a pietistic response that sweeps them all under the rug of God's providence. True, God can take negatives (like the unjust death of Jesus Christ) and turn them into positives. Yet we cannot say, "Let's sin more so grace can abound more." We believe it is God's desire to win the more and so we seek to learn how to minimize the negatives that may turn the many away.

256

WAYS WE HIDE FROM RESULTS

A lack of concern for results is less and less justifiable in our present world. We have more tools available to us for evaluating the results of our programs and methods. Being good stewards of the gospel means being good stewards of the results of gospel presentation as well. Yet some engaged in evangelization do not seek the knowledge of results. The tragedy is that clear, objective information on how we are doing will enable us to be more effective. If our desire is to glorify Christ, then we ought not be afraid of finding the most fruitful patterns of service. It is worth noting some of the common avoidance patterns in the Christian world.

1. *Measuring activity instead of results* is probably the most common avoidance pattern. Mission agencies often report rates of activity: how many meetings, how many showings of a film, how many pieces of literature distributed, how many hours of broadcasting, how many Bibles distributed, how many patients treated. The message is: judge us by *how much we are doing* not by *how much we are accomplishing.*

Of course activity levels are important, as are the means we are using. Yet the activity is a means to an end. We need to know: did we reach our goal? How many people met Christ as a result of the activity? Were people effectively moved toward Christ by these events? We cannot measure results simply by recounting how carefully or often we used certain means.

A little boy had five nickels to get gum from a gumball machine. He dutifully put each one in and pulled the lever. He was not tall enough to see that the machine was empty. His report to his mother was clear: five times I tried. In evangelization we can legitimately recount our effort. Yet the bottom line, however, is our successes. How many gumballs came out of the machine?

2. *Justifying activities by unknown results* is another common avoidance of results. "Only God knows how many people have come to faith by this great ministry." We all meet Christians with the perverse assumption that God will bless whatever we do so long as we are sincere and zealous. If Christians believe this, then why are they so afraid to find out how much God is blessing? Maybe there is a more effective way to reach our goals.

It is hard to put the question of results to an organization in the full swing of ministry. Often they say they are "leaving the results to God." If this is so, they better be sure they are leaving something pleasing to him. Otherwise it can be no more than a giant excuse for poor methods and slipshod execution.

We may not be able to know all the impacts our ministry is

having, but we can know some of the important ones. How can we consider ourselves good stewards when we never take inventory? We may be deceiving ourselves and others and simply perpetuating failure in unblissful ignorance.

3. *Obscuring the results by propaganda* is also common. Many of us are in organizations that must raise funds. One of the deadliest enemies of strategy is the power of the myths created by fund-raising activities. How do you tell a public their money was ill-spent on an ill-conceived, ineffective strategy?

When methods become movements and causes, it becomes difficult to look at objective results. Testimonials substitute for a broad sample of those affected. Statistics of activities are advertised without analysis of the final results. Selective accounts of what happened are offered as the whole truth.

We recall with amazement a letter early in MARC's existence. The head of a well-known Christian agency approached MARC to do research to prove that his agency's strategy was "ten times more effective than so-and-so." When asked if he wished an unbiased survey to see what was happening, he said his only interest was proof of the superiority of his way.

Propaganda reinforced with selective evidence of positive results can undercut our effectiveness. It can lead to making the means we are using sacred. Then it becomes impossible either to change the method or to evaluate fairly its true effectiveness. More and more unreality enters the system as we remain "faithful" to the original vision and strategy. The method becomes less effective as time passes.

Still we do not drop the method. It has a life of its own and a constituency with a vested interest in its continuance. Sometimes we treat such sacralized methods as "the key" to world evangelization. We can even develop a "messianic complex" about our methods. Who are we fooling?

CHANGES AND THE STRATEGY CYCLE

Anticipated results include impacts upon the various elements of the evangelization strategy and team. Already we know we need to change by growing in wisdom as we understand the results that happen from our approaches. Our organizations also need to be strengthened by the discipline of anticipating and then evaluating the results of the methods used. The results of our strategy will change our attitudes, behavior, and relationships.

258

1. *The Force for Evangelism:* Once the strategy is underway, will those engaged in face-to-face evangelism be able to sustain it? What sorts of things should they look to learn from the process itself? How will the force for evangelism react to various results? Will slow response discourage or extremely rapid response overwhelm? Will the results alleviate any latent doubts about the legitimacy and wisdom of the methods?

2. *Means and Methods:* How quickly can the methods be modified or replaced if it becomes obvious that they are ineffective? What methods will need to be adopted if the results are extremely positive? Will there be the right sorts of personnel to shift from evangelism to discipleship?

3. *Analyzing the Strategy:* What sorts of results will be sufficient to conclude that the overall strategy is valid? Do the positive results outweigh the negative? Can the negative be neutralized? How will the strategy have to be modified if major changes are necessary?

4. *Resources:* If we communicate these results to those supporting the effort, will they continue to support the evangelism? Are there results positive for evangelization in the people group but not likely to be understood (or liked) by the supporting constituency? How can the results be interpreted with integrity so they can understand them? Should we look for alternative sources of support in order to continue evangelization in this target group?

FAILING ON PAPER

By now some readers may feel overwhelmed and frustrated. With so many considerations the temptation is to abandon responsibility for the process and say, "I'll do the best I can and leave the rest to the Lord."

Cross-cultural evangelism is an extremely difficult task and calling. We think it is so difficult we compare it with the medical profession in Chapter 11. It is also a glorious task. The fact that God uses a handful of people to change the course of history indicates what he can do with empowered people.

These are beginning considerations. Only after we move into a situation will we know whether the steps we have planned are appropriate. What we are doing at this point is what we can do before we face the test of real life. It is much better to fail on paper than to fail in practice. As we gain experience in a people group, we will be able to develop much more effective and powerful plans.

Questions

1. What are the major sorts of results we should look for if our strategy is successful?

2. How do we know when a person has become a Christian? What changes or indications are we to look for as "signs" of conversion?

3. What sorts of changes should we expect in terms of movement on the Søgaard scale? How fast do we anticipate such changes?

4. How do we protect the new church from simply replicating the structures and patterns of the originating mission/denomination? How do we allow the new church the freedom of the Spirit to make indigenous decisions about the nature and forms of life of that church?

5. What problems or difficulties can we anticipate from our strategy? What can we do to neutralize or reverse these outcomes?

6. What are the most important results for understanding how much we are accomplishing by the use of our time and energy? How do we protect ourselves and our organizations from only looking for positive results?

7. If we are successful, what sorts of changes will it require in our strategy? In our force for evangelism? In our methods? In our mission? Do we have a plan for leaving? When might our presence no longer be necessary?

8. If we are successful, how will this change the role we see ourselves playing? Can we or our organization switch from church planting and evangelism to church partner and edifier?

STEP 7: YOUR ROLE

Considerations

1. Different people play different roles.

2. Different roles are needed for the missionary task. Different people will play the same roles differently.

3. Just because we have thought and prayed about reaching a people group does not mean we are the ones God is calling to reach them.

4. Ecclesiology can never be separated from methodology.

5. The most difficult change we may have to bring about is change in ourselves.

6. Organizations tend toward stability and thus toward bureaucracy. Bureaucracy tends toward minimizing risk and hence tends to reduce frontier missions.

7. Everyone resists change.

8. Change only takes place where there is discontent.

9. Change takes time.

10. Changing ourselves and changing our organizations is the only way to change the world.

20. Who Are You?

Planning for others always includes planning for ourselves. When we seek to bring about changes in others, we discover we must change ourselves. Who we are and what role we play in the evangelization process are key questions.

The apostle Paul recognizes that different roles exist in the body of Christ. "Each one of us does the work which the Lord gave him to do: I planted the seed, Apollos watered the plant, but it was God who made the plant grow . . . we are partners working together for God, and you are God's field" (1 Cor. 3:5-6, 9). Evangelization involves different roles requiring distinct skills and personalities.

Christians bring a diversity of competencies and interests to the task of world evangelization. Those who can speak with the tongues of angels, those who can befriend even the unfriendliest, those who can research evangelism and write learned tomes, those who can train others in personal witnessing—all are a part of a mosaic of roles that the Spirit is able to put together in a beautiful way. We need to know how God is gifting us and where we fit in with others in reaching the same people.

This step focuses on questions that concern role definition. It involves more than what an individual might be and do. It also deals with what an organization or church might be and do. William Carey said, "Expect great things from God. Attempt great things for God." This chapter is not simply about what we are and can do now, but what God calls us to be and do. Once we plunge into the challenge of the Great Commission we find ourself stretched beyond what we thought possible. We may well find ourselves doing things we never thought possible. We give ourselves to Christ for evangelization. He deepens and expands what we have yielded, fills it with his Spirit, and does marvelous things.

ROLES AND SOCIAL STRUCTURES

All the world's a stage,
And all the men and women merely players:
They have their exits and their entrances;
And one man in his time plays many parts.[1]

The "parts" we play in life are often prearranged for us. We are "child" and then "student," "young adult," "employee," "husband" or "wife," "father" or "mother." We play a number of other roles: scout, soccer goalie, president of the debating team, sales clerk in the health food store, computer programmer, Sunday School teacher, patient in the hospital, broadcaster, journalist, gardener, and so on. We have some idea of the kind of behavior to expect from a person wanting to undertake any of these roles.

Some roles are not easy to identify because they are informal. We speak of the "clown" of a party; the "scapegoat" of a group; the social "bore." None of these are positions for which a person can apply. Yet these informal roles are recognizable in many social groups.

Defining what we mean by *role* is relatively simple. It is a way of describing regular patterns we observe in interpersonal behavior. Most roles come in reciprocal pairs: mother-child, salesclerk-customer, driver-passenger, doctor-patient, teacher-student, brother-sister, husband-wife, criminal-victim. In each of these cases there are some very general, regular ways we expect the partners to behave toward each other.

These ways of behaving are important to people. One quick way to create a disturbance is to start exhibiting different attitudes and behavior than expected when playing a role. Next time you visit the doctor's office, ask the doctor to take off his clothes so you can examine him! Or stand up in the audience and start preaching before the preacher gets up to read Scripture.

Each of these categories is public. We call them "positions." We do not mean that they are paying jobs in an organization. Rather, we mean they are socially defined locations in a social structure. For example, the Western family has the various positions of father, mother, daughter, son, grandparent, uncle, aunt, and various in-laws. Each has a role connected with it. By *role* we mean a set of prescribed attitudes and behaviors that are collectively associated with a position. Expectations guide the enactment of the role. People judge a person by the way he or she carries out the obligations and expectations of the role.

1. William Shakespeare, *As You Like It*, Act 2, Scene 7, lines 139-42.

We expect a medical doctor to be able to analyze various symptoms, diagnose the causes, and prescribe a cure or treatment. We expect a patient to listen to the doctor and to follow his or her directions. A referee monitors the observance and violations of the rules as a game is being played. We do not expect referees to grab the ball and slam-dunk it for the team he or she wants to win.

These are all rather commonsense matters. Yet they have profound ramifications, especially in cross-cultural settings. Each society develops a somewhat different social structure with positions and roles that may be very unlike our own. Consider the position of medical doctor in our own society. What happens when our Western doctor moves to another social context?

India, for example, has a healer's or a doctor's role. In fact, certain parts of India distinguish four classes of healers. One could thus reason that a Western doctor as a healer would readily fit into one or other of these four kinds of healer slots, but this need not be so. Consider the features of the four healer slots:

1. *Saint.* He asks no questions, charges no fees, and cures by prayer. He is very highly respected as a religious person.

2. *Doctor.* He knows everything about the human body so he need ask no questions to diagnose a patient's problem. He charges a high fee, but he guarantees his results—no cure, no fee. He is a highly respected person of much secular knowledge.

3. *Shaman.* He asks no questions but divines the cause of the illness. He makes small charges for his services, but gives little guarantee. His cures usually are highly visible rituals. He rates much lower in the scale of community respect.

4. *Quack.* He is the lowest level doctor with minimal knowledge, so he must ask all kinds of questions while he hunts for the disease and its cause. He often uses bought medicines since he usually is incapable of preparing his own. He charges only small fees, but collects in advance and gives no guarantee of results. His status is very low.

It is easy to see that the missionary doctor emits mostly the cues of a quack. (Loewen, "Roles," p. 220)

This simple example demonstrates some of the issues that face role transfer from a given socio-historical context to another. A number of dynamics that are involved in roles make role transfer complex and often unsuccessful.

Social structures differ. Therefore, cultures have different positions and roles for people to occupy. They also have different expectations for roles that seem similar to our own. Additionally, they view some positions and roles as legitimate and honorable when we view them with disdain or dismay. Social arrangements differ, but this is not usually a matter of right and wrong. However, some meanings and practices associated with a given social structure might be highly objectionable (e.g., racism) and therefore need changing (Abrecht and Smalley, 1959, pp. 140-44).

The many social structures are varying ways of organizing group behavior into regularized patterns for accomplishing tasks and encouraging cooperation. Monarchy remains a contemporary form of political arrangement (and was common in ancient Israel). Many northern hemisphere Christians live under some sort of democracy with a prime minister or president as head of state. Christians are not constrained by Scripture to argue for monarchy or for democracy. One is not right and the other wrong. They are different social arrangements, each with its unique advantages and disadvantages.

The problem comes when we move from one set of social arrangements to a new one. We cannot expect the roles we learned in one context to mesh smoothly with another. We have learned expected behavior for positions that fit one social structure. They may not fit a new one.

Role expectations, rights, and obligations vary. The types of behavior expected from people who hold the "same" positions in different cultures are seldom equivalent. We have already seen that at the level of language, words have ranges of meaning. There is no simple equivalent for the Greek terms *koinonia* (fellowship, community, participation) and *sarx* (body, flesh, principle of evil, etc.). Greek words and English words are not equivalents.

The same is true for roles. Japan is a modern, industrial giant. It has a very powerful and effective education system. The Japanese word for teacher is "sensei." The sensei does many of the same things as an American teacher: gives instruction about subject matters, answers questions, disciplines unruly behavior, administers and grades exams. Yet there is much more:

> The Japanese teacher does not make a sharp distinction between the specific classroom duties and a general responsibility for his pupils. . . . School teachers are expected to be available during vacations, and the school principal has a right to require them to report for work at any time. Even during summer vacation, a teacher will be expected to come to school at least two or three times to evaluate the progress of children's play activities.
>
> The teacher to some extent is held responsible even for the safety and behavior of a child outside school . . . the school does have a responsibility for inculcating basic moral virtues. . . . The teacher sends memos to parents, particularly at vacation times, outlining the proce-

267

dures the parents should follow to insure that their child has a health-
ful vacation and listing places considered inadvisable for the child to
visit. (Vogel, 1963, pp. 58-59; see also Singleton, 1967)

What we see as an invasion of privacy and parental prerogatives, the Japanese take as a customary and valued duty of teachers. It is not that one
is right and the other wrong. It is simply a different way of handling the
matter.

   Role performance is evaluated according to *indigenous standards.*
Our best intentions in an unknown situation can easily go awry. Our behavior is being evaluated by standards and role expectations quite different from those we learned in our primary culture. Until we learn the
role patterns of our adopted culture we will be mystified by the "absurd"
responses people give to us. Nor will the honor they give to "strange"
people make sense to us. We have learned to give prestige to very different positions and role performances.

   Outsiders are assimilated to positions already provided for in
the indigenous social structure, if at all possible. Some of these are "insider" roles, performed by people native to the culture. Some are "outsider" roles, such as merchant, foreign agent, or even missionary. Such
settings provide both opportunity (an outsider can often act in novel
ways that set off change) and danger (an outsider can be completely misunderstood). Misunderstandings often happen in the following ways:

   1. The outsider is assimilated to a particular indigenous position. This happens without the outsider's knowledge or awareness.

   2. The insider makes demands and looks for indigenously expected attitudes and behaviors. Yet the outsider does not know what
those expectations are or considers some of them inappropriate.

   3. The outsider responds in ways inappropriate, offensive, or
confusing to the insider. Some demands are resisted by the outsider so
as to retain a sense of integrity as defined by the outsider's culture. Some
responses given are appropriate in the outsider's culture but offensive
within the insider's culture.

   4. The insider's expectations are not fulfilled. The outsider be-
haves in strange and offensive ways. Basic obligations are not met.
Hence, the outsider is seen by the insider as hypocritical and uncaring,
obviously not a person of integrity and worth.

   As in his or her own culture, the outsider receives prerogatives
according to the role assigned by the insiders. The behavior expected and
the rights assigned are consistent with the insider's interpretation of that
role.

   Building trust and credibility is largely a matter of learning and

268

performing the roles indigenously assigned and tacitly accepted by the outsider. This normally happens as a bi-culture develops. Exchanges occur in which the outsider is able to perceive cultural gaffs. Dialogue develops with insiders about better ways of behaving and interacting within the culture.

Much distrust happens because of the contradictory cues outsiders give off. On the one hand they play the role of "religious expert" or "teacher–godly person." On the other, their behavior is such that it is perceived in indigenous categories as contrary to what truly religious people do. Loewen has written of this problem in Southeast Asia:

- Holy men wear one dirty, yellow robe.
- Missionaries have a wardrobe of stylish clothes.
- Holy men have a begging bowl and beg for a living.
- Missionaries have bank accounts and endless foreign income.
- Holy men are celibate.
- Missionaries indulge in sex. (If you doubt it, just count the number of missionary women in relation to men on any mission station.)
- Holy men are totally dedicated to the gods.
- Missionaries say so too, but they have cars and go on furlough. (Loewen, "Roles," p. 221)

Obviously, the question of role is not a simple one. In our own culture, many of our roles are not ones we choose. Similarly, in alien settings the host culture assigns them to us. We have little choice in the matter. But we do have other choices. We can choose to understand and appreciate the differences between our own social roles and those of which we are now trying to be a part. We can consciously choose to work at learning our new roles. We can also seek to keep from being assigned roles that restrict our credibility or ability to act in ways that further evangelization.

Insensitivity to this issue is not a little matter. China offers a particularly dramatic example of this. Coming in as teachers of a "new philosophy," missionaries found themselves in competition with the traditional *literati* of China. These Confucian scholars held the most respected position in the social order. Because of their influence and power, they were able to mount a very effective and devastating anti-foreign/anti-Christian propaganda effort (Cohen, 1963). The situation was exacerbated because government officials themselves came from the top Confucian literati. Frequently missionaries who felt mistreated appealed over the heads of local literati to the extra-territorial rights of foreigners, rights guaranteed by the power of the Western military. The Boxer Rebellion of 1900 had deep roots in the hostility of the Chinese literati to the "Christian literati foreigners." The role assigned to and accepted by missionaries had fateful consequences for Christianity in China.

PERSONAL ROLE DEFINITION

How we come to assume a particular role is more than the result of a larger social group imposing it upon us. Personal factors play an important role as well. Who we are is in part a result of the roles we play and the relationships we experience in those roles. Yet which roles groups allow us to play is a function of the skill and style with which we play our roles.

How people come to see themselves as well suited to engage in certain roles is complicated matter. We know that the availability of role models is an important incentive. We also know that motivation is a powerful factor. Special aptitudes show up early in some people. Parents and teachers encourage the development of a selected range of traits and habits that they see as desirable. Somehow it all fits together in a complex way to form the person who decides to master certain role skills. Groups then allow this person to play certain roles. Rewards and punishments come in response to how well the role is played.

We also know the Spirit gives gifts (*charismata*), special attributes that every member of the body of Christ possesses (1 Cor. 12:7; 1 Pet. 4:10-11). Without these gifts, the church cannot achieve the results it seeks. We have no idea why one gift comes to one member and not another. What we know is that all the gifts necessary for the proper functioning of the body and the ministry of the church are potentially available.

When people discern their gifts, it influences their role definition. How this discovery happens is a very personal matter, though the community of Christians can be important in confirming it. Further, we cannot say that gift identification is a one-time-for-all experience. Gifts may vary over the lifetime of an individual, different ones emerging at different stages of life. Some gifts (such as teaching, wisdom, pastoring) seem not to descend in full bloom. They go through a process of development. Experience significantly enhances them. They grow and mature as people exercise them.

This book is not on discerning one's spiritual gifts. Neither is it on how they relate to personality and natural abilities. Other books provide suggestions along those lines.[2] The broad issue of forging a self-

2. C. Peter Wagner, 1979.

identity to undergird a basic vocational choice and role performances involves more than gifts.[3] Yet the question of role for the Christian always means coming to terms with gifts within the body of Christ. In the Bible we read:

> There are different kinds of spiritual gifts, but the same Spirit gives them. There are different ways of serving, but the same Lord is served. There are different abilities to perform service but the same God gives ability to everyone for their particular service. The Spirit's presence is shown in some way in each person for the good of all. (1 Cor. 12:4-7)

First, Paul tells us that people will do different things. No single gift is adequate for all the needs of the body of Christ.

Second, there is an underlying unity or harmony. In every case it is the same Lord who is at work in giving ability, gifts, particular services. We can recognize the way God fits us together to do his work in spite of very different ways of doing things—even with the "same" gifts.

Third, there is no single uniformity in the ways in which a gift or service is carried out. There are different ways of serving the Lord. Two people may have the same gift of evangelism. Yet they may have radically different ways of expressing that gift, each with fruitful results. This should not be an occasion for controversy or prideful comparison. Rather, it is for the praise of one Spirit who makes each work for his glory.

It may be that for each people group there is a distinctive manner in which a gift is best expressed. The aggressive, public, mass evangelism of the Western world (as exemplified by Billy Graham or Luis Palau) may not be appropriate among a Muslim people. There a more interpersonal, quiet, face-to-face evangelism may be more fruitful.

Fourth, there are different levels of ability with which people can express their gift and service. Two piano players will play with differing degrees of skill. Spiritually gifted people show a range from average to outstanding. Some bring in a twentyfold harvest, others a hundredfold. These differences are also from God and are not a basis for prideful distinction in the body of Christ.

Fifth, Paul speaks of particular service. This means a number of things. We believe one of them is the calling to a particular target group. Paul's particular service was to the Gentiles, just as Peter's calling was to the Jews. The gifts, the way of serving, the ability needed—all vary according to the target group we seek to bring to confess Christ as Lord.

Cross-cultural evangelism is a very demanding and difficult

3. Dayton and Engstrom, 1976; Bolles, 1976.

type of service to render to the Lord. It requires high levels of gifts and skills. We cannot assume ahead of time that a person who is a successful evangelist, counselor, administrator, or pastor in one culture would be the same in another.

We properly answer the question of personal role definition only within a particular service and a given fellowship of believers. In the light of what we have set forth as the particular ministry needs of the target group, what role are we to play?

In answering this we bring to bear all we know about ourselves—our gifts, the faith we have in God for this situation, our experience, our skills and training, our personality and interests, the opinions of others about our strengths and weaknesses, our relationships to family, church, and organizations. Where do we fit in the overall approach defined for reaching the target group?

OUR PRIMARY ROLE IDENTIFICATION

Primary role identification refers to the one or two roles a person plays that more than all other roles define who they are. Primary role identifications relate to maleness and femaleness, age, status, occupation, and life situation. All other roles are secondary and carried out in harmony with the primary role.

When we ask most people who they are, they respond with a personal or family name. If they have to give a second answer, they will usually respond with some important or primary role identification: I am a tennis player, a feminist, a theologian, a housewife, a lawyer. People who do not have a primary role identity usually have a sense of malaise. Their life does not have the zest of people who have found a niche or a cause to which to give themselves.

As evangelists and Christians we need to be in touch with our primary identifications. Whatever they are, they will influence the way we play any of our other roles. Certainly the indispensable modifier of our primary role identification ought to be "Christian." The fruits of the Spirit should make a tangible difference whether we are athlete, executive, day care supervisor, salesclerk, or missionary.

Of course the form and ways the fruits of the Spirit are expressed vary from person to person and culture to culture. Nonetheless, the Christian healer, patron, merchant, teacher, or candlestick maker will carry out the role in a qualitatively different way from those whose primary role identification is not integrally connected with the Spirit.

272

Jesus as Messiah gave us a model by which to gauge our own performance. We will know a renunciation of self and an identification with our target group that transcends our natural human selfishness. The manner in which we carry out our roles in love and humility may have more impact than the precision with which we learn new roles in strange cultures. As the Willowbank Report puts it, we will know a renunciation of status (because we come to serve, not to dominate), a renunciation of independence (recognizing we are part of an interdependent body), and a renunciation of immunity from the hurts and temptations of the people among whom we serve.[4] Just as Jesus renounced his prerogatives and became a servant, so will we as the ones he sends.

Ultimately, the answer to our question of role is answered by Jesus Christ in his incarnation and death. We are those who belong to the crucified and risen Savior who has demonstrated how to live in all roles of life. In the midst of all our cultural sensitivity we must also have a deep and spiritual centering of our being that brings a qualitatively new dynamic to the way we live out all roles.

4. *Lausanne Occasional Paper #2:* "The Willowbank Report" (LCWE, 1978).

21. *Where Do You Fit?*

A decision about involvement with a target group can mean many things. It ranges from rejecting any further interaction with a people group to moving ahead to be part of their complete evangelization. Individually and organizationally we have a wide scope for choice.

First, we can decide to do nothing more than pray. Our examination of who we are in the light of the ministry needs and force for evangelism might indicate our unsuitability for direct involvement. We can still pray.

Second, we can use what we have learned in investigating this target group to discover another group more suitable for our capabilities. We need to remind ourselves that our planning process is an integral part of the *total process* of mission. In gaining experience on paper, we may well avoid learning "the hard way" by carrying out unwise ventures. We may well discover avenues of service with higher likelihoods for success.

Third, we can respond to our analysis by passing on what we have learned. Discussions with other churches or agencies can further the actual evangelization of a people group.

Fourth, we may conclude that we can move forward only with the cooperation of other Christians, even if we take the lead. We may call a conference of other agencies or churches to build bridges leading to evangelization of the target group.

Fifth, we may conclude that we know too little to decide what our role should be. Our decision in this case would be for more research before making any decision.

Sixth, we may conclude that at this point no one, including ourselves, can carry out the task. Yet we may believe that if our organization obtained more training and did further research, we could become qualified. This conclusion would lead to a new training and research program.

Seventh, we may conclude that we are the best organization, but we need additional people and resources to go further. Our next step might be to find these people and resources.

Eighth, we may see ourselves as having only one part in the overall process. Perhaps finding funds and developing basic research are our strengths. Others may have the experience and personnel to carry out first evangelization. If we build a joint venture where each agency contributes what it has, we can reach the people group. Our next step would be to bring together such a coalition and develop mutual agreements.

Ninth, we could conclude that ours is the agency to take on the total task. We would move forward with the completion of planning. We would then gather the resources and put the plan into action.

QUESTIONS TO ASK

It is helpful to discover what sorts of organizations have experienced success in situations similar to the one we are considering. Agencies specialize in various sorts of ministry and target peoples. Gifted people and the development of a network of connections and resources lead agencies into particular competencies.

First, if our strategy calls for saturation evangelism as a central means, we want to look for other agencies known for that strategy. Latin America Mission (In-Depth Evangelism) and SIM International (New Life for All) are both experts in the use of this approach. The United Bible Society, Lutheran Bible Translators, and Wycliffe have a long track record with Bible translation. Arab Ministries has spent many decades in evangelizing North African Muslims. Their insights might well be helpful to a new ministry targeting unreached Mauritanians.

Second, each of us also lives and works within a given tradition of Christian faith. We do so out of a mixture of conviction and compromise. Some of the distinctives that we believe reflect Scriptural priorities are not adequately realized in other traditions. Some elements or emphases of our own tradition, however, make us uncomfortable. Ecclesiastical traditions permit more or less freedom in personal religious lifestyle, cooperation with other traditions, doctrinal definitions, liturgy, style of ministry, and selection of methods. Part of understanding ourselves involves coming to terms with our own tradition and the tradition of our mission agency.

In evaluating strategies we can never separate ecclesiastical profile from methodology. How a potential convert perceives the gospel

275

depends, in part, on how he or she perceives us and our ecclesiastical profile. Much the same methodology and strategy may be used by a Pentecostal agency and a Lutheran mission. Yet the difference of focus may be dramatic because of the difference in Christian tradition.

When we scan the world church we discover that different traditions have both success and failure stories. The Anglican Church is dynamic and dominant in Uganda. The Presbyterians are the largest church group in Korea. The evangelical African Inland Church has more members in Kenya than any traditional denominational group. In Latin America the Presbyterians stagnate at the same time that the various Pentecostal groups are exploding with growth. The Baptists and Methodists are the largest denominations in the United States of America. The Roman Catholic Church overshadows both of them in Zaire.

If we are able to see ourselves as part of a worldwide body of Christ, then we can rejoice in the success of the gospel in other traditions. We can also admit that our tradition may not be the most effective in evangelizing and planting churches among particular target peoples.

We may conclude that a particular target people will require a significant focus on faith healing as part of the gospel communication. The indigenous culture may have many traditional healers with intense concern at the popular level with health and sickness. As people come into the church, we might wish to inaugurate a corps of spiritually gifted Christian healers. We might train them to lay hands on the sick and minister to them as God gifts them. Over time they would provide a functional substitute for the traditional healer's rituals and paraphernalia. Some Christian traditions are very uncomfortable with emphases on miraculous gifts of the Spirit such as prophecy or healing. To conclude that our target group needs a clear emphasis on healing and that the force for evangelism could be a group banning divine healing is nonsensical.

These matters are rather delicate. We do not want to minimize the *theological* issues involved. They need full airing. Yet it is rather un-Pauline not to rejoice in the spread of the gospel (Phil. 1:15-18). We know from experience that good, sincere Christians from traditions with whom we have disagreements carry the love and message of Christ. We may not be happy that they speak in tongues (or that they do not speak in tongues). We may wish they taught a pretribulational rapture (or didn't teach such a doctrine). We cannot wish Christ were not taken to an unreached people.

We must be honest with our information. Our target group may consider the simultaneous praying in tongues (part of our tradition) as confusing or even offensive. They may consider such behavior as bizarre or only for the mentally disturbed. A formal, highly ritual, rather staid approach may have the most appeal. What is our role if our ecclesiastical tradition does not allow us to explore alternative ways of incarnating Christian life and worship? Do we doggedly insist that new converts conform to an expression of faith exported from a Norwegian Pentecostal community?

There is real tension here. We are part of a sending community that is somewhat ethnocentric.[1] It demands we reproduce a Baptist, Presbyterian, Lutheran, Methodist, Anglican, or Independent church. Yet we also realize that freedom of the Spirit means the freedom for a new church to forge its own indigenous forms. Our loyalty and unity with our sending community pulls us in one direction. The priority of those who need to be evangelized and need to develop their own indigenous Christian traditions pulls us in another. Where we fit in the evangelization process depends on the compromises we can and must make in this tension.

Third, we need to ask about our own experience. Have we ever evangelized a target group like this before? If we do not have the experience, do we believe we can gain it? Where have we been successful in the past? Does this new situation appear similar in its makeup to those within which we have been successful?

One way of understanding this further would be to make profiles of all the situations where we have been successful. We would attempt to describe the people as they were when we first contacted them. We would then plot the various steps that brought them to their current status. This information would serve as a comparison case to the target group for which we are now developing a strategy.

We need also to be sure that we still have the experience gained from those past successes. The turnover of personnel in an organization can result in the loss of ten or fifteen years of prior experience. An organization can also change from its original focus. Fifteen years ago an agency may have been in frontier or pioneer mission work. Now in the wake of success it has become a church-supporting agency.

Fourth, we need to ask about our own resources. Do we have the management capability, the people, and the resources (especially finances) to do what is needed to reach the target people? A negative response to this question does not automatically rule us out. It does face us with the realization that more will need to happen than just getting on with the task.

---

1. Ethnocentrism is the tendency to evaluate other traditions by the practices and ideals of our own tradition. It is a defensive reaction by which we conclude that the ways of our own people are superior to those of others.

Fifth, we need to ask about our organizational structure. We may discover that we need a different structure than we have used in the past. We may find, as Overseas Crusades did in the mid-1970s, that we need to send teams rather than individual couples.

Sixth, we need to question our ability to communicate what we are about to undertake to our present or future constituency. What is our reputation with them? How will they view our attempts to reach this target group? If we begin a new and innovative approach, will they continue to support us? Perhaps we are going into community development as part of an overall church planting strategy. Will our constituency see that as integral to gospel communication or might they conclude that we are losing our evangelistic purpose?

Seventh, do we have the vision to reach this target group? What changes and sacrifices will such an endeavor require? In order to exact high levels of commitment or significant changes from the status quo, we need a high and holy vision of what could be only if. . . . Does this vision exist within the organization? Is it flexible enough to change?

Eighth, do we have the faith to believe that this is what God wants us to do? Do we believe that this people group can be reached? We are not talking blind faith. We are talking about informed faith, faith that understands the risks of failure and *still* believes that God is sending us forward.

Ninth, do we have the courage to move forward? Vision, faith, and courage are all closely related. Here we ask whether the *organization* has the experience and history that creates the "can do" feeling. Is it willing to risk for the sake of the gospel?

BRINGING ABOUT CHANGE

In reaching the unreached we are in the business of change. We seek to change the trajectory of a people group so it moves from ignorance to knowledge of Christ. We seek to move it from whatever attitude it holds toward Christ to a positive attitude of submission and worship.

We also seek changes in ourselves and our organizations. We want to enter the life of a new people, to learn their culture and language, to form new relationships. We have to change in the process of being assimilated into a new way of life. Our organization will at least have to change to relate to a new church if our endeavor is successful. Even before that it may have to change in order to undertake a strategy to reach the new target group.

Change is difficult. All organizations tend toward stability. As we find effective ways of doing things, we become confirmed in those ways. They are then codified into policies and procedures. As time passes they become "the way we do things around here." We are comfortable with them because they give us a sense of control.

The analysis of who we are and where we fit may turn up areas that need to change if we are to see the target group evangelized. How do we go about it? What kinds of considerations will help us discover whether changes can happen sufficient to carry out the strategy?

Look for Needs

One of the axioms of management is, "Find out what people want and make a deal with them." If you can meet a desire I have, then I may be willing to think positively about some of the desires you have. A deal is something from which both parties hope to profit. Find allies whose needs *you* can meet.

Take a Long-Range View

It is much easier to plan your way backwards from an ideal future than to analyze how to change the situation you are now in. Picture the kind of organization you would like to have five or ten years from now in order to meet what you believe are the goals God has given you. Use these to find discrepancies in the present organization.

Take Your Time

Most of us greatly overestimate what we can do in one year and greatly underestimate what we can do in five or ten. People in organizations do not change quickly. If you are a recognized change agent or a leader in your organization, you will find that one way forward is to allow your followers to push you.

Involve as Many People as Possible

According to an old saying, "Good goals are my goals and bad goals are your goals." Most of us are interested in the things we have planned. We all have difficulty following someone else's agenda. We need to involve an ever-growing circle of people in bringing about change. The ideal situation is when everyone in the organization feels that he or she has participated in whatever changes are needed.

Be Open to New Ideas

None of us has all the wisdom we need. What we perceive to be the ideal could very well be improved with others' ideas. As Christians we have a unique gift: each one of us is indwelt and empowered by the Holy Spirit. We should not be surprised that the same Holy Spirit brings ideas to the minds and hearts of others that are just as potent as our own. The *Christian* change agent needs to be willing to submit to the same type of process that is being expected of others.

Break It Down into Steps

Do not try to do everything at once. Reduce the changes that need to be taken to bite-size and chewable pieces.

Use Examples

Rather than try to change everything at once, try to change just one part. This may be a kind of pilot project. For example, an "experiment" to reach a particular target group might serve as a model for the whole organization. Involve the rest of the organization members in the pilot project so they can become owners as well as observers. To the extent the project succeeds they can participate in the success. To the extent it fails, they do not have to be directly involved. "After all, it was only an experiment."

Build on Success

What is it you or your organization does well? Do not ask, "How can we be rid of this bad thing we are doing?" Rather ask, "How can we use the success that God gave us in this area to broaden ourselves into new areas?" It is always better to build close to your strengths than to shore up weaknesses.

Affirm Progress

We all need to be told that we are moving in a positive direction. If we have set out on an experiment or pilot project, if we are in the business of trying to change our organization, we need to communicate to people that progress is being made.

Uncover the Future Slowly

Your vision may result from hundreds of hours of thought and years of experience. You need to assess how much of your vision people will accept as their own. Do not push ahead with the next step until the first is accepted by an adequate number of innovators. Bringing about change is identical to the process found in the Søgaard scale. At this moment people in your organization are at different points in their knowledge and attitudes about your desired changes. They need to move through a process that brings them to the point where they become committed advocates of the new.

Expect To Be Led by the Holy Spirit

It amazes us how often we act as though we do not believe that the Holy Spirit will lead. Expect the Holy Spirit to lead in your thinking, planning, and discussions. Paul tells us that it is God who works in us the "wanting to and the doing according to his good purpose" (Phil. 2:13). We must trust God to do that. Without the inner motivation, the "want to," our plans go no where. Others, too, have ideas and visions. We must expect the Holy Spirit to lead us together as a *body*. Expect the Holy Spirit to operate in those who are "less honorable" in the organization as in those who are "more honorable" (1 Cor. 12:22-25).

Questions

1. Who are *you*? How do your roles and gifts fit together? What is your primary role identification?

2. What sorts of skills/knowledge do you need to acquire if you are to perform your role with excellence? What about your organization? How does it need to change to be a vital part of reaching the target group?

3. Is your ecclesiastical tradition suited to the target group? To the churches already present?

4. What sorts of resources and experiences tell you that you have what it takes to reach the target group?

5. Who are the change agents in your organization or church? How much time will it take for the desirable changes to occur? How can you break the changes into a number of different steps?

STEP 8: PLANNING

Considerations

1. If you do not care where you are going, any road will get you there.

2. If one draws the bull's-eye after the bullet is fired, anyone can hit the target.

3. What we are doing is not as important as what we get done.

4. Most people have not decided what it is God wants them to accomplish in measurable terms.

5. Measurable goals have awesome power to change us.

6. Clear goals attract clear plans.

7. No one can forecast the future. To state a goal or to make a plan is to make a statement of faith.

8. Good goals are our goals. Bad goals are your goals.

9. Planning for people is extremely difficult.

22. *Goals for Evangelization*

If you don't care where you are going, any road will get you there. If you draw the bull's-eye after you fire the bullet, anyone can hit the target. What we are doing is not as important as what we get done.

These three simple sentences focus on one of the major problems of Christian endeavors: the failure to set measurable goals for the future. In this section we will attempt to define the differences between purposes and goals. We will set forth procedures for writing goals for missions. Planning begins with writing a statement of purpose followed by statements of goals.

THE DIFFERENCE BETWEEN PURPOSES AND GOALS

We need high and noble purposes. The Shorter Catechism of the Westminster Confession gives a wonderful purpose statement: "The chief end of man is to glorify God and enjoy him forever." It is hard to think of a better purpose statement for Christians.

But *how* do we glorify God? What does that look like when it is happening? We might say it means to worship God, to witness to his great love, to care for one another, and to express Christ's compassion to all of humanity. These four purposes support the highest or primary purpose of glorifying God.

We might say that the purpose of our mission is to proclaim God's love among people who do not know him. Although this is a well-understood and acceptable purpose for us, it is very difficult to express what *actions* we will take as a result of the purpose. High and holy purposes must be supported by measurable goals.

286

Unfortunately, the English language has many different words that may mean the same thing. For example, what we define as a purpose others call an aim, an objective, or even a goal. We define a *purpose* as an aim or description of *why* we are doing what we are doing. We define a *goal* as a measurable and (in the mind of the person setting it) accomplishable *future event*. It is measurable both by time (when it will become a past event) and by performance (how we know it has happened).

In this sense "to share Christ with the refugees from Southeast Asia" is a purpose statement. "To have a worshiping church of twenty-five people among the Kampuchean refugees in Los Angeles by the end of this year" is a clear-cut goal. Both talk about the same activity, but with very different degrees of concreteness.

Since goals lie in the future, they are statements of faith. James 4:13-15 reminds us:

> Now listen, you who say, "Today or tomorrow we will go to this or that city, spend a year there, carry on business and make money." Why, you do not even know what will happen tomorrow. What is your life? You are a mist that appears for a little while and then vanishes. Instead, you ought to say, "*If it is the Lord's will*, we will live and do this or that."

The Bible is full of people who made such statements of faith. Nehemiah asked the king if he might go and rebuild the walls of Jerusalem. In his mind he pictured the way the world might be, the way God wanted it to be. He had faith to believe that given adequate resources, God would use him to rebuild those walls.

Paul had the goal to move on past Rome to Spain:

> But now that there is no more place for me to work in these regions, and since I have been longing for many years to see you, I plan to do so when I go to Spain. I hope to visit you while passing through and to have you assist me on my journey there, after I have enjoyed your company for a while. (Rom. 15:23-24)

Neither Nehemiah nor Paul knew whether he would accomplish his goal. By saying clearly what they wished to do, they were making statements of faith about what God would have them do. This is why our definition of evangelism needed three parts. The aim and purpose are *intentional*. The goal is *measurable*. Without a measurable goal we are at sea without a compass.

Purposes can inspire us, but goals have the power to push us forward. The Holy Spirit uses a clear picture or statement of faith of what could and should be to push us on. This is well understood even outside the church. Dr. Ari Kiev (1973) of the Cornell Medical Center wrote:

> With goals, people can overcome confusion and conflict over incompatible values, contradictory desires and frustrated relationship with friends and relatives, all of which often result from the absence of rational life strategy.
>
> Observing the lives of people who have mastered adversity, I have repeatedly noted that they have established goals and, irrespective of obstacles, sought with all their effort to achieve them. From the moment they fixed an objective in their mind and decided to concentrate all their energies on a specific goal, they began to surmount the most difficult odds.

Paul understood it well:

> Not that I have already obtained all this, or have already been made perfect, but I press on to take hold of that for which Christ Jesus took hold of me. Brothers, I do not consider myself yet to have taken hold of it. But one thing I do: Forgetting what is behind and straining toward what is ahead, I press on toward the goal to win the prize for which God has called me heavenward in Christ Jesus. (Phil. 3:12-14)

One of the best illustrations of the power of setting goals can be found in the Church Growth movement. At the center of their theory is the idea of making growth projections, statements about future growth. When local churches set such specific goals it has a tremendous motivating power on the members of the congregation. They begin to act for church growth.

The same thing has been happening in mission agencies. By shifting the emphasis from sending (a process activity) to reaching (a definable, measurable goal), they are beginning to find new life and vitality.

THE RELATIONSHIP OF GOALS TO ONE ANOTHER

Since goals are future events, they are related to one another. They can be arranged into higher and lower goals, greater goals and lesser goals. In doing so we can speak of primary, intermediate, and immediate goals.

For example, our personal goal might be to graduate from a university with a particular major on a given date. Before this primary goal can happen there are a number of intermediate goals. We must have enough money to pay the tuition and fees. We need to meet residency requirements as well as pass enough courses. We must write the dissertation or senior thesis. Yet even before these intermediate goals, there are a number of immediate goals. We must sustain our health and sanity, get enough sleep, and have enough food each day. Maintaining our relationships with our family can also affect our goal accomplishment. Today we might have to work well enough to maintain the job that is providing funds for our tuition.

The same is true for organizations. If you set out to plant a twenty-five-member congregation among the ethnic Chinese refugees from Vietnam, you will have a variety of intermediate and immediate goals. You will have to identify the location of these refugees in France, recruit missionaries, secure housing and resources.

THE POWER AND ADVANTAGES OF GOALS

When goals are fuzzy or nonexistent or when we try to live only by purposes, it is difficult to keep an organization alive. Clear goals convey real advantages.

Clear goals create ownership and motivation. Earlier we quoted the saying "Good goals are my goals; bad goals are your goals." The truth in this statement is that goals need to be owned by someone. They are abstract statements without an advocate. By sharing goals and allowing many to participate in setting goals, we can spread ownership of those goals and motivate many more people into obedient action in evangelism.

Clear goals strengthen communication. "Can two walk together unless they be agreed?" (Amos 3:3). When I tell you my goals you know the direction I am moving. You also know that I do not intend to move in some other direction.

Clear goals are basic to good planning. Planning needs to begin with purposes. We need to know why and where we are going. Yet without accompanying goals we begin to plan for *process.* We get all wrapped up in what we are *doing.* Committees often fall prey to this. The first question at the first meeting of a committee should not be, "What should we do this year?" Rather, it should be, "What should we get *done* this year?"

Clear goals help show the direction of progress. They are like stopping-off points on a journey, like intermediate cities on a map. Since we can tell when they have become a past event, we can know that we are moving past one and on to another. This enhances motivation and gives us a sense that we are going somewhere.

STEP 8: PLANNING

Clear goals strengthen and test our faith. As statements of faith, goals put us on the edge of discovery. The greater our faith, the greater our goals should be. As we "fail" or "succeed" in reaching goals, we can see the Holy Spirit directing our lives and teaching us the measure of our faith. Without goals we often drift and are without the insight to draw the lessons of experience.

WRITING CLEAR GOALS AND PURPOSES

All goals should be related to their purposes. One of the tests of a good goal is the question, "Does it relate to our (my) purpose?" We need to begin by writing an overarching purpose statement and the supporting purposes for the organization. Once we have written them, we can develop clear goals.[1]

Well-written goals are stated in terms of end results rather than a process or an activity:

> *Good:* **Ten missionary candidates successfully pass their oral evaluation by August 1.**

> *Poor:* **Ten missionary candidates begin their training on July 1.**

Well-written goals should be achievable within a definite time. Poorly written goals are never fully achievable, or have no specific target date.

> *Good:* **The church in Barrville has grown to sixteen members by July 1, 19__.**

> *Poor:* **There is a growing church in Barrville.**

Well-written goals are definite as to what is expected, while poorly written goals often are ambiguous.

> *Good:* **A three-thousand-word sermon is typed for delivery by June 15.**

> *Poor:* **A good sermon is preached.**

Well-written goals are practical and feasible. We should avoid goals that are theoretical or idealistic.

1. See Charles Hughes, *Goal Setting* (1965); Ed Dayton, *God's Purpose/Man's Plans* (1972); Robert Mager, *Goal Analysis* (1972).

Good: **Twenty invitations are given to local civic leaders by March 15.**

Poor: **As many outstanding civic leaders as possible are involved in the meeting.**

Well-written goals need to be precisely stated in terms of quantities where applicable.

Well-written goals also need to be limited to one goal or statement. Avoid writing two or more goals where only one is needed to explain what needs to happen (Dayton and Engstrom, 1979).

GOALS FOR PEOPLE

In the past most evangelistic and mission efforts had only two types of measurable goals: (1) the number of decisions or recommitments to Christ; (2) the number of people who actually joined a local fellowship. In recent years the second goal has been particularly effective in helping local congregations make statements of faith about what they believe God would do with and through them. The Church Growth movement brought this goal into prominence.

However, we can and should also write goals for the intermediate points on the Søgaard scale. In each case we want people to move upward in the knowledge and understanding of Christ and the gospel. At the same time we want that movement to make them increasingly positive in their attitudes about Christ and the church.

The difficulty in writing goals for attitudinal changes is that we have to specify what might indicate such a change for a people group different from our own. Sometimes this is easy and at other times it is very difficult. To illustrate, suppose we have a group at the bottom of the scale. No one in their midst knows anything about Christ or his gospel. Let us assume that they are hostile to all outsiders. Our primary goal is at least one congregation of forty-five worshiping Christians in their midst who are continuing to evangelize their own people. The first step is to write a measurable, accomplishable goal. It might be: **The chief of the _____ clan has extended an invitation for two missionaries to live in his village by August 1.** Accomplishing such a goal would be strong evidence that at least people were ready to communicate with missionaries.

On the other hand, if the attitude toward outsiders was favorable, our goal might be more ambitious: **By February 20, the chief** of the _____ clan tells the members of his subgroup that the four missionaries living in their midst worship a God called Jesus who they believe created the world. In this case we are envisioning movement from no knowledge to awareness of the gospel.

We could then write goals for moving people to the point of understanding the basic characteristics of the gospel and the point of seeing it as a way of salvation. Changes in attitude also need goals. We would have to decide what sorts of attitudes are exhibited toward the gospel as it is initially heard. Then what sorts of changes would manifest a shift in a more positive direction? Here we would want to describe the sorts of things a person would *do* as an indication of an increasing positive attitude.

Then when the commitment to Christ has been registered, we would set goals for the continued process of growth. During the early period after an affirmation of faith, people reassess the decision they have made. A goal for this time might be: **Those making an affirmation of faith as a result of _____ are to complete the Christian discipleship program within three months.**

We would need other concrete goals for developing the support system and capability of new Christians coming to the place of sharing their faith with others of their people group. Our goal is a worshiping *and* witnessing congregation. Simply getting them into the circle of committed Christians is not enough.

Of course we must say that target people encounter Jesus Christ in very unique ways. People may come very rapidly and en masse to a favorable attitude toward Christ, knowing almost nothing about him. For them goals to teach and increase their knowledge would be crucial. Others may have a relatively large amount of information, yet be indifferent or resistant to its implications. For them the goals would have to focus strongly in building relationships and changing attitudes.

23. *Plans for Evangelization*

In many ways this chapter is the crux of the book. All the best intentions, all the careful research, and hours of prayer can easily shipwreck on the rocks of the future. History is littered with the hulks of mission efforts that ran aground because planning was too narrow, too limited, or altogether missing.

WHAT DO WE MEAN BY PLANNING?

Planning has many meanings and uses. In the sense that planning is contemplating the future, everyone "plans." Yet that is not what we mean by planning. Few college or seminary courses include teaching the skills of planning. If we mention the word, it often conjures up in people's minds the picture of a blueprint for a building. Indeed, we often talk about "a blueprint for the future." Upon examination, this phrase sounds rigid, with little room for flexibility. When we use a blueprint for erecting a new building, we normally do not expect to change the design halfway through construction.

Unfortunately, we have taken this technological model and too easily applied it to human relationships. There is something in us that rightfully is repelled by the idea of blueprints for people. Christ's church is much grander than that. The human mind cannot comprehend his kingdom. No wonder we shy away from planning for *people*.

We need to disavow immediately this mechanistic view of planning. Planning should be thought of as a bridge between where we are now and the future we believe God desires for us. It is true that planning usually includes a series of well-thought-out steps of how we will proceed in order to achieve our goal. What people often fail to see, however, is that plans for people need to be revised continually. We take the first step forward, look backward, look forward, and then replan as necessary.

Planning is an attempt to produce surprise-free futures, to anticipate as much as possible what the future is likely to hold and how we will respond to it (Kahn, 1976).

David Ewing (1969) points out that organizations overlook the *people* dimension of planning at their peril. It is likewise a mistake to attempt to transfer the type of planning that has been learned in the generation of *things* to the business of communicating the gospel.

Still there is much we know about planning that needs to be put to work by those seeking to reach the unreached. The literature on planning is voluminous. We will not attempt to repeat it here. Rather, we will show why plans for evangelization are a key part of world evangelization and then point the reader to some of the more useful literature.

THINKING CHRISTIANLY ABOUT PLANNING

We have already suggested that goals are statements of faith. We make them before one another and before our Lord. Plans are also statements of faith. They are our attempt to sketch out what we believe is the will of God for the future. Understanding this is crucial as we seek to bring others into the planning phase of evangelization.

Planning is corporate. As Christians we claim to be part of a fellowship that is well described as a body. In ways we do not fully comprehend we are intimately interconnected with other Christians. Each member of the body is animated by the same Spirit. For this reason we can expect ideas to come from within the group as well as from its leaders. By sharing our dreams and visions widely, we make it possible for the body to function smoothly.

Planning may be a gift of the Spirit. Some people are more skilled in visualizing the future. They can take what appears to others as disjointed and unconnected and fit it together in a whole. People thus gifted are not necessarily the ones with the vision of the future or even the best ones to execute the plan.

In his helpful book, *Your Spiritual Gifts Can Help Your Church Grow,* Peter Wagner (1979) indicates that we have a lot to learn about spiritual gifts. He believes that the Bible does not give us a definitive list of all the gifts. Even if we believe it is definitive, some of the gifts listed involve what we mean by planning.[1] In Romans 12 the gift of administration includes the ability to interrelate many things that need to be done to accomplish a major endeavor.

Planning is a necessary part of good stewardship. If our resources are to be invested and expended wisely, then we have to make wise decisions. It is impossible to make decisions for the future. We can only make decisions now that will *affect* the future.

Planning means taking risks, not avoiding risk. That is, it is the calculating of risk. Planning assumes an unknown future. It assumes that the problems we face will be unlike those we have faced previously.

Planning challenges us to see where our "standard operating procedures" apply and where they will have to be modified or created anew. The rules of thumb or proverbs we often quote take a wise person for them to work. "A stitch in time saves nine." "Haste makes waste." It does not tell us what "in time" means nor when we are hasty instead of efficient. Planning helps us to act wisely.

BASIC PLANNING CONCEPTS[2]

1. Describe the Goal

Almost every goal requires a plan. The larger the goal, the more extensive the plan. As we will see, most plans are nothing more than a series or a string of subgoals fitted together. Effective planning can succeed or fail right here. Fuzzy or inadequate goals lead only to fuzzy or inadequate plans.

Often there will be different goals for different phases of a program.

2. Describe the Present Situation

In addition to a description of the people group, an examination of helping and hindering forces is very useful for planning. Psychologist Kurt

---

1. Romans 12:7 refers to the gift of "serving" (Gk. *diakonia*) and is taken by some to mean the supervision of the giving of aid to the needy (see New English Bible and Jerusalem Bible). Romans 12:8 refers to the gift of "leadership" (Gk. *proistamenos*). It comes from a word meaning to "stand before others," as do rulers in a community.

2. Much more help is found in Engstrom and Dayton, *The Art of Management for Christian Leaders* (1976) and *Strategy for Leadership* (1979).

Lewin (1935) initially proposed the idea of using the force field model for analysis of social situations. A given pattern can be understood as the result of a balance between the various forces acting on a situation. Some of those forces can be seen as helping or hindering change in the direction of the goal we have before us. Movement toward the goal will occur when the helping forces are increased or the hindering forces are reduced.

Here one might consider the factors that hinder knowledge and understanding of Christianity or that incline people to be negative about Christ. Our plan will have to take aim at the hindering forces as well as enhance whatever helps people to understand Christ and be positive about him.

Thus, any time we consider changing a situation we must make a list of these opposing forces. We choose the ones that will be easiest and have a greater impact in producing movement in the direction we seek.

3. Choose Methods

Having described the goal, we now decide the best way to reach it. Very seldom will there be a perfect fit between the human situation and a previous solution. We have to reinforce the idea that each situation is, to some degree, unique. Out of all we have learned and others have learned we need to discover new means and methods.

4. Lay Out the Sequence of Events Needed

With goals and methods chosen, we need to decide the sequence of events. Here such tools as PERT (Program Evaluation Review Technique), flow charts, Gantt charts, and other devices described in planning literature are useful. The primary reason for making plans is to coordinate the work of many people. Demonstrating these plans graphically is an important tool for communication.

Entering a new people group involves many things. People have to be recruited and trained for the mission, government permissions obtained, logistics of support laid out, means of raising funds settled, and means for communication and evaluation designed. When some of these begin will depend on when others finish. If one of them fails, all may fail. In many ways it is like a relay race in which one person cannot begin until he or she has received the baton from someone else.

Each of these events can be viewed as a subgoal. This means

that each needs to have a goal owner and a date by when it will be accomplished. In Figure 23.1 we show a fairly simple PERT chart for planning an evangelistic program. By following the diagram from left to right, the great interdependency of people and events immediately becomes apparent.

5. Calculate the Resources Needed

Resources include time, people, facilities, finance, and cooperation. Unfortunately, too much planning *begins* here. We should not sit down to build the tower without first counting the cost. Yet we had better design the tower before we try to figure out if we can afford it. Often one of our goals is to find the people or the money for the task.

A few hints here. There are two ways to calculate time: (1) the elapsed or calendar time, or (2) people time or people hours. For example, the amount of time to obtain a visa may be one month. This is calendar time and no amount of expenditure of people hours will speed up the process. The number of people hours needed may be only four or five hours, considering the time needed for filling out the forms, getting pictures, and mailing them. We must not confuse these two types of time.

In thinking about people we have a natural tendency to assume that six different people should be assigned to six major goals. One of the advantages of the PERT technique is that it shows us not only how long it may take to reach a particular goal, but the interrelationship of goals. Often six goals can be shared by only two or three people. The work needed for them can be carried out at different times.

We need to have the faith to believe that God wants us to use the best tools we can. Too often we equate good stewardship with the use of the poorest or least adequate facilities. It is not always good planning to substitute a less expensive tool for another. Suppose we have planned to produce teaching materials using a small offset press supplied with in-country materials. The substitution of a mimeograph machine, with stencils that have to be imported, might greatly hinder our whole plan. Of course, the most valuable resource we have is people. There is no replacement for trained and experienced people.

Finances are the bugaboo of mission endeavors. The time to cut back on finances is *not* during the planning stage. We may ultimately have to change our plans because of lack of finances, but do not *plan* this out at the beginning! Honestly assess what you believe will be needed and then add 10 or 15 percent to cover contingencies.

We do not often think of *cooperation* as a resource. Yet success

PLANNING FOR EVANGELISM

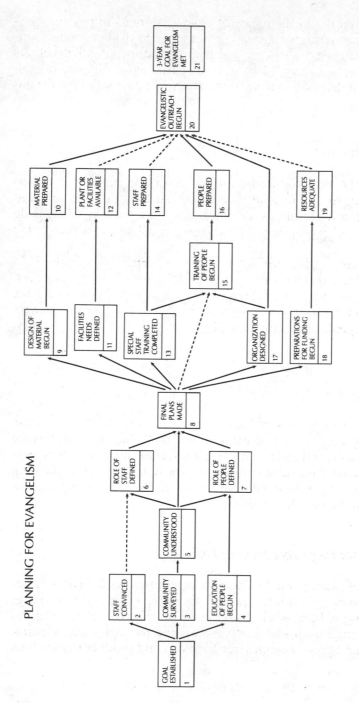

FIGURE 23.1   PERT DIAGRAM

or failure often lies in the hands of others. We need to pay for some cooperation, as when we depend on someone to deliver needed supplies. We also need to work for and maintain cooperation with others working in the same area. Make sure you list all of the different organizations and individuals whose cooperation will be needed for the endeavor.

6. Analyze Resources

When all of the resources needed are added up, do your faith and plans match? If they do, you are ready to move ahead. If they do not, you need to seek alternative solutions. Do not be discouraged if your plans do not appear workable at first. It is far better to fail on paper than to fail in practice.

A simple plan form we have used repeatedly is reproduced in Figure 23.2. Note that this form includes all the ingredients we have discussed, from purpose to cost. This form will seldom be large enough for most tasks. However, it does communicate in a fairly compact manner all of the elements of effective planning.

THE DYNAMICS OF PLANNING

Plans need constant revision. The further plans stretch into the future, the less likely they are to describe what will really happen. Yet even the early stages will need review and revision. Certainly we need to review an overall plan for the future every year. The dynamics of the planning process help us to understand what God is teaching us through our experience and the experience of others.

1. Planning for People Is Extremely Difficult

People are infinitely variable. The more people involved, the more complex their tasks. This is not meant to discourage, but to acknowledge that planning is hard work. In order to be effective, plans must be owned. Through the use of group process and the ownership of plans, people can bring their energies into harmony and produce tremendous effects.

GOAL NAME _____ GOAL NUMBER _____

PURPOSE   For this reason: _____
_____
_____
_____
_____

GOAL   We plan to   _____
accomplish this: _____
_____
_____
_____
_____
_____

by this date: _____
we will know it   _____
has happened   _____
because:
_____
_____
_____
_____
_____
_____

STEPS   We plan to take   _____
these steps: _____
_____
_____
_____
_____

PEOPLE   These people are   _____
responsible: _____
COST   It will cost this   _____
amount: _____

FIGURE 23.2   ORGANIZATIONAL PLANNING CHART

300

2. Plans Are Difficult to Coordinate

People in the home office and in the field office bring very different perspectives to the planning process. We need to *share* our plans. We need organizational strategies. Effective organizations *plan to plan*.

World Vision International begins its planning two years ahead. In December it asks each of its field leaders to make up ten-year plans for what they feel God wants to see happen in their areas. These are reviewed in January at the home office and an overall analysis is sent back to the field. Then this is used as a basis for one- to five-year forecasts that are returned to the home office. These are reviewed in May and compared with the forecasted income expected from the support countries. With this information in hand the field offices can present detailed plans and budgets. These are approved in August. The process begins again the following December.

Obviously, this is a great deal of work. Yet it pays off in that there are fewer mistakes. It also means a heightening of the communal process whereby the Holy Spirit can take all the parts of the body and use them to shape the direction of the ministry. Communication is enhanced and together the various parts of World Vision grow in understanding.

3. Planning Gives Us a Better Understanding of Why We Succeed or Fail

When we state ahead of time what we intend to accomplish, then we can see how far we miss our target. We sometimes don't set goals because of our fear of failure. Yet most of life itself is failure. Even the best baseball players only bat .400 (meaning they do not succeed at getting a hit 60 percent of the time). Failures can be great teachers. We need to learn from more than just our successes.

4. Planning Takes Time

Our experience tells us that while it is time-consuming, in the end, effective planning will reduce the total amount of time and energy needed to reach the goal. It is an investment with large dividends in the future.

301

STEP 8: PLANNING

SHORT- AND LONG-RANGE PLANNING

Short-range planning, usually encompassing less than a year, is essentially problem solving. The problem is to reach a particular goal. All of the techniques of problem solving and decision making are important here.

Short-range planning should always be done within the context of long-range planning. A major weakness of many organizations is that they plan year by year without contemplating where they are going. This is all too easy for not-for-profit organizations whose income depends on future giving. Yet even such organizations, when they have set high goals for four- or five-year financial campaigns, have usually found excellent results.

It is unfortunate that the faith needed to put an "$80 million challenge" in front of our constituency cannot be extended to the challenge to reach ten unreached people groups in five years! Too often we hear, "If only we had the money. . . ." Our response is, "If only we had the challenging goals!"

Long-range planning normally covers one to five years. Some call planning beyond five years "forecasting." Again we suggest you consult other literature for the details of how this is done effectively. The techniques are no different for the Christian organization, even though Christians have the advantage of knowing the ultimate outcome!

The basic elements we have met before are still important for long-range planning. We begin with a clear statement of our purpose. We must have a clear understanding of our mission so that we know where we want to go and what we will not do in the future. In this case we must do long-range forecasting: what will the world be like in which we will be working? Our assumptions about trends and likely events become even more important here than in short-range plans. The further we project into the future, the less reliable our forecasts become. Many roads exist between now and the desired future. We must examine the alternatives so that as one fails or is excluded, we have others at hand. We need also to define what our means and methods will be.

Once we have these in place we need to (re)design the organization. Organization follows and serves the goals and needs of our mission. Often the existing organization will fit the need. At other times we will have to plan for major modifications in order to realize our long-term goals.

One of the great values of long-range planning is that it gives us time to raise the money we will need. It is unlikely that the details of our long-range plan will be more than 50 percent accurate at best. However, the overall cost of the plan may not be so far off.

302

Long-range planning exhibits the repetitive nature of planning more clearly than short-range planning. Planning has to be built into planning. It is the *process* of planning that is of greatest value. The plans may change and they may be wrong, but what we learn in the planning process is of inestimable value.

METHODS FOR PLANNING

There are many methods to help you plan. Dayton and Engstrom's *Strategy for Leadership* (1979) offers some good suggestions. The important thing is to tailor the planning methods to the need. Avoid over-planning. Too many organizations are over-managed and under-led. If you are planning to build a building, a great deal of detailed planning will be necessary. Each window, doorframe, pipe, and wire will need to be specified. But as we have said before, planning for people is very different from planning for things. Buildings will sit quietly and wait to be built. People will not. Plans for buildings will look very much the same three years later as the buildings are completed. Detailed plans for people are much more dynamic and changing.

For the Christian the techniques of planning are always placed in the context of God's sovereign workings. Jesus often called his disciples to come apart and pray. He knew they had to be drawn out of their "everydayness" of ministry and needs to be met. For a body of Christian believers, planning is a corporate act of faith. Like prayer, planning calls a halt to the everyday activity and brings us aside to evaluate, to rethink, and to take new steps of faith. As we pray and plan we make new statements of faith as to what we believe is God's will for us.

Like prayer, planning is hard work. Both need to be directed by the Holy Spirit and both require an act of the will to bring all thoughts into captivity to Christ. In both we are seeking to bring ourselves into harmony with the will of God. Prayer is the act of actively waiting for God's action for us. Planning is the act of actively setting out the actions we believe God wants from us. In both cases we are making ourselves available to God's great purposes and plan.

Questions

1. What are the differences between your organization's purposes and goals? How do the two relate to each other?

2. Does your organization have clearly defined goals?

3. In thinking about reaching an unreached people group, what is your purpose? What are your goals?

4. Does your organization have a planning system? Does it have a planning cycle?

STEP 9: ACT

Considerations

1. Thinking, planning, acting, and evaluating can never be separated from one another. They all go on at the same time.

2. The primary problem is not money. It is people and organizations. Every missionary team is unique and has its own distinct needs.

3. Most mission organizations do not plan to succeed.

4. One thing you can always expect is the unexpected.

24. Taking Action

Our ability to make detailed plans for the future is severely limited. The future is the one thing over which we have the least control. We cannot do all of our planning, stop, and then start acting out our plans. The moment we start to act, we have to start evaluating where our actions are not conforming to our plans and make the necessary corrections.

This is true in all parts of life. When an aircraft is coming in for a landing, the pilot is constantly measuring the sideways movement of the airplane that may be due to a crosswind. Lining up with the runway is dependent on compensating for such movement. If, at the last minute, the plane cannot be lined up with the runway, the pilot aborts the approach and tries again.

It is important to see that this is the natural order of events. We should not be surprised that things do not turn out exactly as we planned. Rather, if we *anticipate* that things probably will be different than we imagined, then we are ready to make corrections and replan.

The pilot *knows* that there is a possibility that a crosswind will blow the plane off course. It is the knowledge and anticipation that things may be different than the plan that makes an effective pilot. It is this same kind of knowledge that makes an effective missionary.

We can reduce our ten-step circle and summarize it in four processes, as shown in Figure 24.1.

The processes that we need to go through are: think, plan, act, evaluate, think, plan, act, evaluate, think, etc. We need to do this both on a grand scale and on a small scale.

For each of the phases of our short-range plans we need to evaluate the results of our actions and rethink, replan, and act in a more effective manner. For example, we may try to establish a relationship of trust with the chief of a village only to discover that the task involves

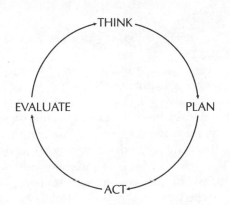

FIGURE 24.1 ABBREVIATED PLANNING CYCLE

much more time and cultivation than we expected. We may have to stretch that part of the plan out and rethink what must be done to strengthen the tie.

The purpose of this brief section is to put the necessary action into the context of planning and evaluating. There is an extensive literature on the various aspects of cross-cultural communication. Many excellent books dealing with the missionary vocation are now available. These all give concrete guidance for the action facets of evangelization and church planting.

RESOURCES, MEANS, GOALS

When we plan, we begin with purposes and goals, not resources. The sequence is goals, means, resources (see Figure 25.1, p. 321 below). However, once we begin to act, the reverse sequence is followed. We first must come up with the resources, use them to carry out the means and methods, and, in the process, achieve our goals.

We have subgoals here as well. We have a goal for obtaining resources. We also have a goal for carrying out means and methods. These different events are actually a chain that is linked together. If one of these links fails, the entire enterprise is jeopardized. Therefore the repetitive cycle of think, plan, act, evaluate, think, plan, act, evaluate applies at each of the steps of finding resources, supplying means, and reaching goals.

1. Gathering Resources

Almost always we begin with finance and people. We cannot raise finances unless someone is committed to doing so. Traditionally in the faith mission system the missionary has been directly responsible for raising support. While this has the advantage of personalizing missions for many people, it has the disadvantage of discouraging missionaries not adept at raising finances. Furthermore, project funds above missionary support is usually difficult to raise in this fashion. The problem often is that there is no direct connection between the gifts and skills necessary to be a communicator of a need and those needed to be a cross-cultural communicator of the gospel. This approach also reinforces the impression that the job of the local church and of missions is sending missionaries overseas. It is questionable whether there is long-range wisdom in putting missionaries through a regimen with the primary purpose of appealing for funds.

The task of carrying the good news to people who have never heard it is a glorious one, incomparable in its scope and potential impact. Christ has called the church to this task. Many churches are responding to the call for financing frontier and pioneer missions.

In the same way that it takes time and effort to communicate cross-culturally, it takes time and effort to communicate what we are about. Fund-raising has received heavy criticism in recent years—and rightfully so. There are too many instances in which those raising funds are living high while the benefits for those they claim to be serving have been minimal.

Yet this is not the whole picture. If we send an improperly trained and/or supported missionary team to reach the unreached, they may be completely ineffective in achieving that goal. Then the cost of fund raising is 100 percent. In effect, we have nothing to show for the funds invested except lives and years wasted. What is the cost of fund raising when a missionary family spends nine to twelve months visiting churches for that purpose? We recognize that more happens in those visits than fund raising. Yet we do need to see that the costs of such visits are not insignificant.

We can learn from Christian agencies that have attempted to raise funds *on behalf of* their staff rather than *through* their staff. They have discovered that they can be quite successful when the cost of fund raising varies between 8 and 12 percent. When compared with the 25 to 35 percent that most secular agencies invest in fund raising, this is commendable. It is heartbreaking to see Christians who claim that their Lord owns the cattle on a thousand hills acting as though God barely has a lease on one pasture.

Likewise, local churches need to spend a reasonable amount of the money collected for missions on missionary education. We live in a culture with a huge communication overload. Advertising agencies research their target groups carefully and spend huge amounts of money to communicate specific messages. The local church cannot hope to compete on the same level with the vast array and sophistication of the advertising media. Yet it can recognize that the importance it gives to what is being communicated will be the importance associated with that communication. Important programs are ones that people are talking about, looking forward to. An *important* mission conference would be one that people have been looking forward to for four months.

We ascribe importance to events on the basis of how well they are planned and how well they are executed. We do not expect to find Hollywood quality audio-visual presentations within our local church. Yet the larger the church, the higher the standards for presentations. Furthermore, people do interpret the importance of any presentation on the basis of how much *comparative* effort goes into it.

All of this says that it is not only necessary but appropriate for the local church to invest time, energy and money in communicating the needs of a broken and lost world. Is it wrong to think that a church should spend five percent of its missions budget on missions education within its constituency? Would not such an effort both demonstrate the church's commitment to missions and produce responsive prayers, contributions, and commitments from the congregation?

2. The Right People Mix

In Chapter 11 we suggested the need for different levels of missionaries in terms of training and experience. Good planning includes planning for the kind of people needed for the sort of mission we are planning. If the plans change, then the people may well need to change. If the only people we have bring little or no field experience, we may need to add a phase of "on-the-job-training."

It does not sound glamorous for an agency to spend two or three years and employ several people to "do research." It is often difficult to maintain the motivation of the missionaries and those supporting the project when it is in a research phase. Yet to move ahead without good information may lead to results that are particularly unglamorous.

311

If we are going to reach unreached people, we often will need mature veterans to lead the group. The idea that one is committed to a particular field for life sounds noble on paper. In practice it is often less effective than moving a person with a great deal of experience into a new area. This will require new language learning, a difficult task. With the right missionary and skills, the knowledge of how a culture and language is learned will facilitate the transition and make that person an even more effective communicator.

In most pioneer situations utilizing a missionary team of both mature and less experienced missionaries is the best way to go. Such a mix requires that there be a good design for communication and lines of authority. There also need to be regular times of evaluation. Whenever possible this team should train together. The team building and training should begin even before they move to the field. The initial planning with the study of the target group and the setting of the initial approach and its phases should be thought through and discussed by those actually going.

The lines of communication between the ministry team and the support bases also will need to be well designed. Communicating across thousands of miles is difficult. Once the team plunges into the business of language and culture learning, it becomes emotionally separated from those "back home." There is a natural tendency to let communications slide because of the need "to get on with the work." We need to resist this tendency. Outside leadership is of real value here: another person can look objectively at what the team is doing. Monthly evaluation and review of goals is extremely useful here.

Here again we need to return to the question of expending funds. Most mission agencies resist building up large numbers of home personnel. Such are seen as "overhead," as a necessary evil. Yet all effective organizations have significant numbers of staff involved in supporting the frontline producers. Even in the most modern armies we find three to four people on the home front to support one person in the field.

Missions are in the business of profit: profit for the Lord. The question is not how much is spent on overhead and how much on frontline ministry, but did we accomplish what God wanted us to accomplish? Whatever that takes is an expenditure we should not be reluctant to make.

3. Applying Means and Methods

The task of missions is the task of the whole church. Specific people groups need specific members of Christ's body assigned to reach them. Yet they are all linked to the support base and to those who enfold them in prayer. Prayer support is as much a part of the connecting links between the body as are the finances.

When there are larger distances to travel, and/or the people to be reached are more remote, then means and methods have to be applied all along the line. Means and methods are needed to keep in communication. Means and methods are needed to insure that the appropriate logistics are maintained for those on the field. Means and methods are needed to provide ancillary services such as medical care. Of course, means and methods will be utilized in the communication of the gospel and the planting of churches.

In the same way that the needs of a particular people are unique, the needs of a particular missionary team are unique. Uniformity in policies and procedures should always be tempered with the purpose of the agency. Uniformity *does* often lead to reduced expense. Yet uniformity can also increase the eventual cost to the particular missionary team.

In *The Homeless Mind*, Peter Berger et al. (1973) point out that bureaucracy is one of the unforeseen outcomes of democracy. Democracy implies that everyone is equal. When everyone is equal, no one is special. In these conditions the bureaucracy begins to think of itself as the object of primary importance. In the end the bureaucracy operates like a machine. People are relegated to a product.

This desire to be treated equally is in constant tension with the specialties we all have. We have no neat solutions to this dilemma. We would only suggest that for each unreached people we must think back and see what means and methods need to be applied to the entire mission organization so we can do the best we can to meet the specific need.

A word needs to be said here about becoming too comfortable in a foreign land. Many missions appear to be operating on a shoestring budget. Yet, paradoxically, missionary compounds and institutions all over the world exist primarily for the benefit of the people running the institutions. Thus we find schools originally intended to educate missionaries' children in the field with as many as three-quarters of its students coming from nonmissionary families. When one considers the large expenses and investment of missionary time to run such schools, it is more cost effective to fly the children to school in the home country.

The reason many of these institutions exist is that the mission and the missionaries did not *plan* to succeed. They did not set a deadline as to when the job would be done and they could withdraw. If these missionary bases were in countries where there were still numbers of unreached people and if the missionaries at these institutions were seeking to reach them, this criticism could easily be modified. However, the very presence of such institutions often strengthens the "settled-downness" of the entire missionary community. We need to give adequate support. We need also to plan to end that support.

COURSE CORRECTION—REPLANNING

Think, plan, act, evaluate, think, plan, act, evaluate. Once we begin to act, it is often very difficult to stop to evaluate. This is particularly true if we believe we are succeeding. We need to stop occasionally and see whether what we are doing fits into our total plan.

Some time each week should be set aside to review what actually has been done during the week. What will be done next week should likewise be considered. A monthly written review, even if it is written only to ourselves, is a disciplined exercise that will help us understand how we are moving.

Planning takes time. If we face a situation dramatically different from the one anticipated such that an entirely new plan is required, then we need to take the time to replan. Evaluation will often uncover areas where we need to rethink and replan. This is never comfortable. We do not like to discover that we are not doing what we anticipated or that we are succeeding not so much due to our own efforts but because of external circumstances.

In general, missionaries are very much like school teachers. They do not like to evaluate one another. Consequently, many annual or semi-annual field meetings of missionary staffs within a country are times of sharing blessings and recounting *activities*. They are seldom times of evaluation. What a difference it might make if a group of missionaries shared with each other what they hoped God was going to do with them in the coming year. Then a year later they could compare what actually happened and discuss together what they might do to reach their goals.

To identify change, we have to compare what we are doing with what we intend to do. When change comes, we need to estimate what impact it will have and how we will have to change our ability to do what we plan for the future.

Planning helps us anticipate the different kinds of futures we may face. Our skill in handling the unexpected and the wisdom that comes from experience can be gained only after we act.

Questions

1. Is your organization's primary concern with raising money or reaching people?

2. Does your organization have a long-range planning system that includes definable goals?

3. Does your organization have built into it the necessary communication system to inform people?

4. Does your organization have the right mix of people for the task it is attempting?

5. Does your organization usually do its homework?

6. Do you have good lines of communication between those in the field and those at the home base?

7. Does your organization normally have a plan to *leave* a field?

STEP 10: EVALUATION

Considerations

1. Evaluation takes place only when we plan to evaluate.
2. Evaluation begins with goals, not with resources.
3. The most difficult evaluation is personal evaluation.

25. *Evaluation*

L ife is wondrously complex. If we have a major goal for a year and it
 is supported by fifty-two weekly goals, and if each weekly goal is
supported by daily goals, then we sense how complex life is. The marvelous thing is that we not only survive, but thrive in such a complex
world.

As we close the circle, we come to an area to which most organizations give the least attention. Evaluation looks at whether we
reached our goals, whether the way we went about them was appropriate, whether we still believe our goals are appropriate.

In one sense we are always evaluating. We always must draw
on past experience to solve current problems. So we draw lessons from
history. This is what experience is all about. Yet history also tells us that
the future will not be the same as the past. Though our experiences of
the past can help us through the future, we also need to gain new experience through our immediate situation. Evaluation is a conscious means
of doing that.

Success itself can be a trap. Something that worked in the past
may become a standard solution. We may stop evaluating, stop seeking
a better way to do what we set as our key goals. We can so easily think
we have found *the* solution. The trouble is that problems keep changing.
One friend of ours has described this situation as trying to paint a freight
train while standing on another moving freight train. We have to keep
moving and changing in order to stay abreast of our moving and changing world.

SET UP AN EVALUATION PROCEDURE

An evaluation procedure should be a natural part of the planning process. To review a plan means in part to evaluate. Specific times should be set aside to evaluate performance and effectiveness. (A word of caution: we will *never* do everything we set out to do, nor will we do it in just the way we planned.) It is of paramount importance that we evaluate performance, not persons. The reason most people fear evaluation is that they view it as a mechanism to place blame.

Evaluation needs to be continuous. In understanding how to carry out evaluation, it is useful to think of it in terms of goals, methods, and resources. Planning, acting, and evaluating involve all three of these. We plan in one order, act in the opposite, and then evaluate in the same order in which we plan. Figure 25.1 helps us see how this works.

	PLANNING	ACTING	EVALUATING
GOALS	1	3	1
METHODS	2	2	2
RESOURCES	3	1	3

FIGURE 25.1   PLANNING, ACTING, EVALUATING

GOALS EVALUATION

The first question is: "Did we reach the goal?" We may have come by a different route than we expected. We may have spent more resources than anticipated. Yet did we reach the goal? Regardless of the outcome, we need to take time to look back and see what God (and Satan!) has been doing. What we are discussing here are our major goals, not our daily and weekly goals.

If we met the goal we originally set, why was it accomplished? We may discover that we reached the goal through a series of entirely unplanned circumstances. In Chapter 15 we talked about reaching the

Turkana of Kenya. The goal of one of the approaches was to befriend a diviner. This in fact happened. The young Kenyan involved met the wife of a diviner quite unexpectedly. She subsequently introduced him to her husband, and the friendship began. The particular way the goal was reached was not planned. It just happened that way.

If we did not reach our goal, why did we not reach it? Was the goal unrealistic? Is there a possibility that we could still reach it if we gave it more time or more energy? Was the goal inappropriate? Did we abandon it? What can we learn because of not reaching the goal?

If we did reach the goal, did it have the desired result? All of our goals are linked together. The one in the future depends on the one we are attempting to meet now. Will the meeting of this goal lead us to a better opportunity? Or will it have a bad effect? Will it ultimately help us to realize our purposes? Were they really the goals we wanted? Have we learned something in the process of working them out that would cause us to restate them if we were to begin again? Are there some goals that should have been dropped?

For example, our goal might have been to launch a new publication. This was part of a larger purpose, which was to move a people group to a more positive attitude about Christianity. Perhaps the goal was reached: the magazine is launched. However, research indicates it is not having the desired effect. It is so easy to rejoice in the goal accomplished that we forget *why* we originally wanted to reach the goal.

Finally, as we examine our success or failure, we need to ask what we can learn for the future as a result of trying to reach this goal. How can we share what we have learned with others? How can we utilize this approach or avoid it in the future?

EVALUATING MEANS AND METHODS

Whatever happened in terms of goal achievement needs to be evaluated in terms of the means and methods. Did we use the ones we planned to use? Were they effective? Did their effectiveness (or lack of it) have something to do with us individually? Was it a matter of circumstances being different from what we anticipated?

Did we use the means *when* we said we would? Were they used in a timely manner? Did we adapt our methods to the situation as we found it? As we developed new methods, what did we learn? What did we learn from the people we are trying to reach? What did we learn about ourselves? What did we learn about these particular procedures?

Did the means and methods produce some unexpected outcomes, goals we did not aim at accomplishing? Were these outcomes good or bad?

Were the means and methods we used viewed as Christian and humane? As we look back on them, how do we feel about them? Were they culturally sensitive? Did they properly portray the body of Christ? What did our organization or agency think about the means and methods? Were they opposed to certain policies or procedures of the organization? Do the policies and procedures need revision in the light of the effectiveness of the methods?

How did other Christian groups view our means and methods? We are often working side-by-side with Christians from other churches or agencies. Did they feel our means and methods honored the Savior?

Finally, and most importantly, how did these means and methods appear to the target group? Were we manipulative? Did we model means and methods they could use? Did these means and methods leave this people more able to find their own selfhood within Christ or did they become more dependent on outsiders?

EVALUATING RESOURCES

Missionaries and agencies in general have a great tendency to use whatever resources are at hand. There is always the feeling that there are never enough resources. At the other end of the scale, we often do not attempt things because we do not think we have adequate resources. We need to evaluate resources, but only after we have evaluated goals, means, and methods.

Time is a crucial resource to evaluate. Did we use the amount of time we said we would? Why? Did we use the *number of people* we said we would? Did we use the number of people hours we expected to use? *People's* time is money. There is a definite cost associated with every hour someone serves in an organization. This is why it is correct to take the total income of an agency and divide it by the total number of people working for the agency. The result is the amount of money required for each person, on average, to do his or her job.

What does your evaluation tell you about the *people* themselves? Hopefully, all of the goals relate to someone's accountability. What was learned about their strengths and weaknesses? Were they motivated by what they did? From what you learn, you will be able to reassign responsibilities or even replace people.

323

STEP 10: EVALUATION

Did we use the *amount of money* we said we would? More? Less? Why? Our plans are based upon a given amount of resources. If we could not raise the funds, we should have changed the plans and thus the goals.

Finally, what did your evaluation tell you about your *organization?* Did you form some new organization subsets, such as a task force, that should be continued? Are there some formerly excellent organizational components that should be disbanded?

Overall, was our expenditure of resources good stewardship? If we had to do it again would we believe that this investment of time and people and money was a good use of God's gifts?

EVALUATION AS A PROCESS

This element of planning needs to be built in as a regular event. It needs to be the beginning and ending of every Christian endeavor. Its purpose is not to demean or control people but to evaluate *work.*

Evaluation enables us to set "posteriorities," that is, what we are *not* going to do next year. Organizations are like an alligator whose tail keeps growing. We keep adding new components, goals, and procedures and seldom drop any of the old ones. As a consequence, the tail gets so large we can hardly move.

How does the process of evaluation work? We would suggest a number of practical elements.

Evaluation should be planned. Just as important as deciding *when* is setting the *standard for measurement.* Sometimes this is the same as the goal. If our intermediate goal is to have two significant leaders in the target group develop a positive attitude, our specific goal might be to have them home for a meal on such-and-such a date. In this case the measurement would be the same as the goal. At other times the measurement is not equivalent to the goal. Eventually we will have to decide what counts as a positive attitude on the part of the two leaders.

Means and measurements should be designed. If our goal is to move 10 percent of the target group to an understanding of the characteristics of the gospel, we will need to design a culturally acceptable way of measuring that. Whatever our goal is, the earlier we design the measurement, the earlier we will discover ways of measurement not open to us.

Report against goals and milestones. One of the most effective ways of evaluating is to write regular reports to ourselves and others. A report should state how many of our goals and milestones have been reached. Reporting in itself often causes us to pause and evaluate.

Self-evaluation. This is one of the most profitable disciplines to acquire. To have regular personal times of evaluating one's performance and activities against one's intentions is extremely valuable.

Joint evaluation. Missionaries can join together to evaluate each other's individual and common goals. This is a very powerful tool. Once the initial reticence of sharing one's failures is over, times of evaluation can be great spiritual events. How can we pray for one another effectively if we do not understand each other's needs?

Regular planning and forecasting. By setting up an annual planning cycle that includes a five- to ten-year forecast, we have an excellent vehicle for evaluation. When we compare what we now believe will happen in the next five to ten years with what we stated a year ago, we gain very good insight into successes and failures.

PERSONAL PERFORMANCE EVALUATION

The Bible has a great deal to say about not judging one another. That is not the issue before us here. We are not to judge people, but we are to evaluate *work.*

Each of us needs appreciation and affirmation. We need to be appreciated for our effort, as well as for what we have accomplished. Yet true appreciation is based on understanding both the difficulty of the task and what was expected. A friendly smile and pat on the back are meaningless if the person affirming us does not really understand what we have done. We need to believe that someone knows what we are doing and how well we are doing. We need to know that what we are doing is important enough for someone to want to understand it. We need to have our performance evaluated.

Only in this way can we help people grow. The ultimate purpose of evaluation is that the organization might perform better and its people grow in technical performance and relationships with each other. It is never easy to hear that we have performed poorly. All growth has painful sides to it.

Effective evaluation must begin with an agreement between the subordinate and the superior as to what is to be done and the limits within which it is to be done. This is basic. A good job description and negotiation will spell out the behaviors and results expected. Yet there are two steps beyond this. They must also agree on how they will *measure* this performance. There is a difference between knowing that something has been done and knowing how it will be measured.

STEP 10: EVALUATION

In effect, what is needed is a formal procedure for providing a description of each position or job. Although job descriptions usually include the purpose, responsibility, and tasks of a job, often they do not contain the specific goals that are to be accomplished. Such goals should be defined with the position holder. Goals will tell both the organization and the person how they will know that the position purpose is being fulfilled.

Each of those goals should in turn have standards of performance, the specifics of how the goal is to be measured. The superior and subordinate should then jointly agree on both the standards and the time by which these standards will be met. Since a quarterly, or at least a semi-annual, evaluation is a must, it is helpful to relate the standards to the evaluation time.

This type of negotiating will not only clarify a person's understanding of the job, it will greatly strengthen the superior's understanding of the subordinate. It also lays the foundation for subsequent evaluation and informs the subordinate that the organization is concerned and interested in that person and his or her performance.

Appraisal is part of a much larger system of getting things done. Most books cover it as a subsection. Robert Dubin's *Human Relations Administration* (4th edition [1974]), is an excellent resource in this area.

CLOSING THE CIRCLE

So we end—and so we begin again. For those already doing cross-cultural ministry the first step is evaluation. We need to understand who we are and our history. We need to face up to our successes and failures. All of this will lead to a new understanding of the mission God sends us to accomplish.

The process we have described in this book is not an easy one. It is more difficult to carry out than it is to explain. It is hard to change and give up ways of doing things we understand. It is hard to begin again. It is much more comfortable to assume that the future will be like the past, to think that if we continue doing things the same way, only a little better, then this will honor God. But of all people Christians should be for change. Our past is forgiven. Our future is secure. If God be for us, who can be against us?

Questions

1. Do you have goals in your plan for evaluating performance?
2. Do you have a way of evaluating means and methods?
3. Do you have a way of evaluating the effectiveness of the money you are spending?
4. What are you doing now that you ought to stop doing next year?
5. How do you evaluate yourself against what you are doing? What should you do about it?

Bibliography

Abrecht, Paul, and Smalley, William. "The Moral Implications of Social Structure." *Practical Anthopology* 6, no. 3 (1959): 140-44.

Accad, Fouad. "The Qur'an: A Bridge to Christian Faith." *Missiology* 4, no. 3 (July 1976): 331-42.

Ahrens, Theodor. "Concepts of Power in a Melanesian and Biblical Perspective." *Missiology* 5, no. 2 (April 1977): 431-42.

Allen, Louis A. *Professional Management.* New York: McGraw-Hill, 1973.

Allen, Roland. *Missionary Methods: St. Paul's or Ours?* Grand Rapids: Eerdmans, 1962.

Andersen, Wilhelm. "Further Toward a Theology of Mission." In *The Theology of Christian Mission,* ed. Gerald Anderson. Nashville: Abingdon Press, 1961.

————.*Towards a Theology of Mission.* London, SCM Press, 1955.

Anderson, Gerald, ed. *The Theology of Christian Mission.* Nashville: Abingdon Press, 1961.

Arrington, Leonard J., and Bitton, Davis. *The Mormon Experience.* New York: Alfred A. Knopf, 1979.

Babbie, Earl. *The Practice of Social Research.* Belmont: Wadsworth, 1975.

Balch, David. *Let Wives Be Submissive: The Domestic Code in 1 Peter.* Chico, CA: Scholars Press, 1981.

Barker, Eileen. *The Making of a Moonie.* New York: Basil Blackwell, 1986.

Barrett, David. "Annual Statistical Table on Global Missions: 1988." *International Bulletin of Missionary Research* 12, no. 1 (January 1988): 17.

————. *Evangelize! A Historical Survey of the Concept.* Birmingham: Woman's Missionary Union, New Hope, 1987.

————. "The Expansion of Christianity in Africa in the Twentieth Century." *Church Growth Bulletin* 5, no. 5 (May 1969): 362-66.

————. "In Defense of Mono-ethnic Churches." *Church Growth Bulletin,* May 1979, p. 276.

————. *Schism and Renewal in Africa.* Nairobi: Oxford University Press, 1968.

————. *The World Christian Encyclopedia.* Nairobi: Oxford University Press, 1980.

Bassett, Glenn A. *Management Styles in Transition.* New York: American Management Association, 1966.

Beach, H. P., and Fahs, C. H., eds. *World Missionary Atlas.* New York: Institute of Social and Religious Research, 1925.

Beaver, R. Pierce. *The Gospel and Frontier Peoples.* Pasadena: William Carey Library, 1973.

————. "The Legacy of Rufus Anderson." *Occasional Bulletin* 3, no. 3 (July 1979): 94-97.

————. *To Advance the Gospel: Selections from the Writings of Rufus Anderson.* Grand Rapids: Eerdmans, 1967.

Becker, V. "Gospel, Evangelize, Evangelist." *Dictionary of New Testament Theology,* ed. Colin Brown, pp. 107-15. Grand Rapids: Zondervan, 1976.

Behm, Johannes. *"glōssa heteroglōssa."* *Theological Dictionary of the New Testament,* vol. 1, ed. G. Kittel, pp. 719-27. Grand Rapids: Eerdmans, 1964.

Bell, Daniel, ed. *Toward the Year 2000.* Boston: Houghton Mifflin, 1968.

Bellah, Robert, et al. *Habits of the Heart: Individualism and Commitment in American Life.* Berkeley and Los Angeles: University of California, 1985.

Benko, Stephen, and O'Rourke, John J., et al., eds. *Catacombs and the Colosseum.* Valley Forge: Judson Press, 1971.

Berger, Peter L. *The Capitalist Revolution.* New York: Basic Books, 1986.

————. *The Noise of Solemn Assemblies.* New York: Doubleday, 1961.

————. *Pyramids of Sacrifice.* New York: Basic Books, 1974.

Berger, Peter L., et al. *The Homeless Mind.* New York: Vintage Books, 1973.

Berkouwer, Gerrit C. *The Church.* Grand Rapids: Eerdmans, 1976.

Bertram, Georg. *"strephō."* Theological Dictionary of the New Testament, vol. 7, ed. G. Friedrich, pp. 714-29. Grand Rapids: Eerdmans, 1971.

Beyerhaus, Peter. *Missions—Which Way?* Grand Rapids: Zondervan, 1971.

————. *Shaken Foundations: Building Mission Theology.* Grand Rapids: Zondervan, 1972.

Bierstedt, Robert. *The Social Order.* 3d ed. New York: McGraw-Hill, 1970.

Bietenhard, H. "People . . ." *Dictionary of New Testament Theology,* ed. Colin Brown, vol. 2, pp. 788-805. Grand Rapids: Zondervan, 1976.

BIBLIOGRAPHY

Bodley, John H. *Victims of Progress.* Menlo Park: Benjamin-Cummings, 1975.

Bolles, Richard N. *What Color Is Your Parachute?* Rev. ed. Berkeley: Ten Speed Press, 1976.

Bowen, Elenore S. *Return to Laughter.* Garden City: Natural History, 1964.

Bowles, Gordon. *The People of Asia.* New York: Charles Scribner's Sons, 1978.

Braaten, Carl E. *The Flaming Center.* Philadelphia: Fortress Press, 1977.

Bradshaw, Malcolm. *Church Growth Through Evangelism-in-Depth.* Pasadena: William Carey Library, 1969.

Braun, Neil. *Laity Mobilized: Reflections on Church Growth in Japan and Other Lands.* Grand Rapids: Eerdmans, 1971.

Brewster, E. Thomas, and Brewster, Elizabeth S. *Language Acquisition Made Practical.* Colorado Springs: Lingua House, 1976.

Brierly, Peter, ed. *Beyond the Churches.* Monrovia: MARC, 1984.

Bright, John. *The Kingdom of God.* Nashville: Abingdon Press, 1953.

Bruce, F. F. *The Defense of the Gospel in the New Testament.* Rev. ed. Grand Rapids: Eerdmans, 1977.

Brunner, Emil. *The Misunderstanding of the Church.* Philadelphia: Westminster Press, 1953.

Büchsel, Friedrich. *"genea."* *Theological Dictionary of the New Testament,* vol. 1, ed. G. Kittel, pp. 662-65. Grand Rapids: Eerdmans, 1964.

Candsdale, George. *All the Animals of the Bible Lands.* Grand Rapids: Zondervan, 1970.

Carey, William. *An Enquiry Into the Obligations of Christians to use means for the Conversion of the Heathen.* New facsimile edition. London: The Carey Kingsgate Press, 1961.

Cho, Ki Sun Joseph. "Rural Evangelism in Asia." In *Let the Earth Hear His Voice,* ed. J. D. Douglas, pp. 624-33. Minneapolis: World Wide Publications, 1975.

Chua, Wee Hian. "Evangelization of Whole Families." In *Let the Earth Hear His Voice,* ed. J. D. Douglas, pp. 968-76. Minneapolis: World Wide Publications, 1975.

Clark, Dennis E. *The Third World and Mission.* Waco: Word, 1971.

Clark, Stephen B. *Building Christian Communities: Strategy for Renewing the Church,* Notre Dame: Ave Maria Press, 1972.

Cohen, Paul A. *China and Christianity.* Cambridge: Harvard, 1963.

Coleman, Robert E. *The Master Plan of Evangelism.* Old Tappan: Revell, 1963.

Conn, Harvie. *Theological Perspectives on Church Growth.* Philadelphia: Presbyterian and Reformed, 1976.

Cook, Harold R. *Historic Patterns of Church Growth*. Chicago: Moody Press, 1971.

Corwin, Charles. "Japanese Bonsai or/and California Redwood." *Missiology* 6, no. 3 (July 1978): 297-310.

Costas, Orlando. *The Church and Its Mission*. Wheaton: Tyndale, 1974.

———. "Depth in Evangelism—An Interpretation of 'In-Depth Evangelism' Around the World." In *Let the Earth Hear His Voice*, ed. J. D. Douglas, pp. 675-97. Minneapolis: World Wide Publications, 1975.

———. "Missiology in Contemporary Latin America: A Survey." *Missiology* 5, no. 1 (January 1977): 89-114.

Cowan, Marion. "A Christian Movement in Mexico." *Practical Anthropology* 9, no. 5 (Sept.-Oct. 1962): 193-204.

Crosby, Philip. *The Art of Getting Your Own Sweet Way*. New York: McGraw-Hill, 1972.

Dale, Ernest. *Organization*. New York: American Management Association, 1967.

Dale, Kenneth J. *Circle of Harmony*. Pasadena: William Carey Library, 1975.

Daneel, M. L. *Old and New in Southern Shona Independent Churches*. Hawthorne: Mouton Publications, 1971.

Davis, Raymond H. "Church Growth and Cultural Change in Turkana." Unpublished Thesis, Fuller Theological Seminary, 1978.

Dayton, Edward R. "Current Trends in North American Protestant Ministries Overseas," *Occasional Bulletin* 1, no. 2 (1977).

———. *God's Purposes/Man's Plans*. Monrovia: MARC, 1972.

———. *Planning Strategies for Evangelism: A Workbook*. 6th ed. Monrovia: MARC, 1978.

———. *Resources for Christian Leaders*. 2d ed. Monrovia: MARC, 1978.

———. *That Everyone May Hear: A Workbook*. Monrovia: MARC, 1986.

———. *What Ever Happened to Commitment?* Grand Rapids: Zondervan, 1984.

———, ed. *Mission Handbook: North American Protestant Ministries Overseas*. 11th ed. Monrovia: MARC, 1976.

Dayton, Edward R., and Engstrom, Ted W. *Strategy for Leadership*. Old Tappan: Revell, 1979.

———. *Strategy for Living*. Glendale: Regal Books, 1976.

DeRidder, Richard R. *Discipling the Nations: A Biblical Basis for Missions*. Grand Rapids: Baker Book House, 1971.

Derwacter, Frederich M. *Preparing the Way for Paul*. New York: Macmillan, 1930.

Dickson, David. *The Politics of Alternative Technology*. New York: Universe Books, 1974.

BIBLIOGRAPHY

Directory of Christian Work Opportunities. Seattle: Intercristo, 1978.

Donovan, Vincent. *Rediscovering Christianity*. Maryknoll, NY: Orbis, 1978.

Douglas, J. D., ed. *Let the Earth Hear His Voice*. Minneapolis: World Wide Publications, 1975.

DuBose, Francias M. *How Churches Grow in an Urban World*. Nashville: Broadman Press, 1978.

Dunn, James D. G. *Unity and Diversity in the New Testament*. Philadelphia: Westminster Press, 1977.

Dye, T. Wayne. "Toward a Cross-cultural Definition of Sin." *Missiology* 4, no. 1 (1976): 26-41.

Edwards, Christopher. *Crazy for God*. Englewood Cliffs: Prentice-Hall, 1979.

Elkins, Phil. *Church-Sponsored Missions*. Austin: Firm Foundation Press, 1974.

Elliott, John. *A Home for the Homeless: A Sociological Exegesis of 1 Peter*. Philadelphia: Fortress Press, 1981.

Ellul, Jacques. *The Ethics of Freedom*. Grand Rapids: Eerdmans, 1976.

————. *The Political Illusion*. New York: Alfred A. Knopf, 1967.

————. *Propaganda*. New York: Random House, 1965.

————. *The Technological Society*. New York: Alfred A. Knopf, 1964.

Engel, James F. *Contemporary Christian Communications*. Nashville: Thomas Nelson Publishers, 1979.

————. *How Can I Get Them to Listen?* Grand Rapids: Zondervan, 1977.

Engel, James F., and Norton, Wilbert. *What's Gone Wrong With the Harvest?* Grand Rapids: Zondervan, 1975.

Engel, James, et al. *Consumer Behavior*. 5th ed. Hinsdale, IL: Dryden Press, 1986.

Engstrom, Ted W. *The Making of a Christian Leader*. Grand Rapids: Zondervan, 1976.

Engstrom, Ted W., and Dayton, Edward R. *The Art of Management for Christian Leaders*. Waco: Word, 1976.

————. *The Christian Executive*. Waco: Word, 1979.

Erikson, Erik H. *Identity, Youth and Crisis*. New York: W. W. Norton, 1968.

Evans-Pritchard, E. E. *Peoples of the Earth*. 20 vols. Suffern, NY: Danbury Press, 1973.

Ewing, David. *The Human Side of Planning*. New York: Macmillan, 1969.

Fee, Gordon. *The First Epistle to the Corinthians*. Grand Rapids: Eerdmans, 1987.

Fisher, Ron. "Why Don't We Have More Church Planting Missionaries?" *Evangelical Mission Quarterly* 14, no. 4 (October 1978).

Fitzmeyer, Joseph A. *The Gospel According to Luke X-XXIV.* New York: Doubleday, 1985.

Forrester, Jay W. *Urban Dynamics.* Cambridge: MIT Press, 1969.

Fowler, J. Andrew. "Towards Wholeness in Ministry Among the Iban." *Missiology* 5, no. 3 (July 1977): 275-84.

Fraser, David A. "An 'Engel Scale' for Muslim Work?" In *The Gospel and Islam,* ed. Don McCurry, pp. 164-81. Monrovia: MARC, 1979.

Freilich, Morris, ed. *Marginal Natives at Work: Anthropologists in the Field.* New York: Halsted Press, 1977.

Freyne, Sean. *Galilee from Alexander the Great to Hadrian, 323 B.C.E. to 135 C.E.* Wilmington, DE: Michael Glazier, 1980.

Friedrich, Gerhard. *"euangelizomai."* *Theological Dictionary of the New Testament,* vol. 2, ed. G. Kittel, pp. 707-37. Grand Rapids: Eerdmans, 1964.

————. *"kērux," Theological Dictionary of the New Testament,* vol. 3, ed. G. Kittel, pp. 683-718. Grand Rapids: Eerdmans, 1965.

Gager, John G. *Kingdom and Community: The Social World of Early Christianity.* Englewood Cliffs: Prentice-Hall, 1975.

Gardner, John W. *Excellence.* New York: Harper & Row, 1961.

————. *Self-Renewal.* New York: Harper & Row, 1964.

Gerber, Vergil. *A Manual for Evangelism/Church Growth.* Pasadena: William Carey Library, 1973.

Gibbs, Eddie. *I Believe in Church Growth.* Grand Rapids: Eerdmans, 1985.

Gottwald, Norman. *The Tribes of Yahweh.* Maryknoll, NY: Orbis, 1979.

Grant, Michael. *The World of Rome.* New York: New American Library, 1960.

Grant, Robert. *Early Christianity and Society.* New York: Harper & Row, 1977.

Green, Michael. *Evangelism in the Early Church.* Grand Rapids: Eerdmans, 1970.

————. "Methods and Strategy in the Evangelism of the Early Church." In *Let the Earth Hear His Voice,* ed. J. D. Douglas, pp. 165-72. Minneapolis: World Wide Publications, 1975.

Grimes, Barbara. *Ethnologue.* Dallas: Summer Institute of Linguistics, 1979.

————, ed. *Index to the 10th Edition of the Ethnologue.* Huntington Beach, CA: Wycliffe Bible Translators, 1984.

Grundmann, Walter. *"dēmos." Theological Dictionary of the New Testament,* vol. 2, ed. G. Kittel, pp. 63-65. Grand Rapids: Eerdmans, 1964.

Gulliver, P. H. "A Preliminary Survey of the Turkana." South Africa: University of Cape Town, 1951.

Hahn, Ferdinand. *Mission in the New Testament*. Naperville: Alec R. Allenson, 1965.

Hall, Edward T. *Beyond Culture*. New York: Doubleday, 1977.

———. *The Hidden Dimension*. New York: Dubleday, 1966.

———. *The Silent Language*. New York: Doubleday, 1959.

Hardin, Daniel C. *Mission: A Practical Approach to Church Sponsored Mission Work*. Pasadena: William Carey Library, 1978.

Harnack, Adolf von. *The Mission and Expansion of Christianity in the First Three Centuries*. Magnolia: Peter Smith Publishing, 1972.

Harper, M. *Let My People Grow*. Plainfield: Logos, 1977.

Hengel, Martin. *Judaism and Hellenism*. 2 vols. Philadelphia: Fortress Press, 1974.

———. *Property and Riches in the Early Church*. Philadelphia: Fortress Press, 1974.

Herberg, Will. *Protestant, Catholic, Jew*. New York: Doubleday, 1960.

Herzberg, Frederick. *Work and the Nature of Man*. New York: Thomas Y. Crowell, 1966.

Hesselgrave, David J. *Communicating Christ Cross-culturally*. Grand Rapids: Zondervan, 1978.

———. *Dynamic Religious Movements*. Grand Rapids: Baker Book House, 1978.

———. *Theology and Mission*. Grand Rapids: Baker Book House, 1978.

———. *Today's Choices for Tomorrow's Mission: An Evangelical Perspective on Trends and Issues in Missions*. Grand Rapids: Zondervan, 1988.

Hian, Chua Wee. *The Making of a Leader*. Downers Grove, IL: InterVarsity, 1987.

Hiebert, Paul G. *Anthropological Insights for Missionaries*. Grand Rapids: Baker Book House, 1985.

———. *Cultural Anthropology*. Philadelphia: J. B. Lippincott, 1976.

Hile, Pat. "Communicating the Gospel in Terms of Felt Needs." *Missiology* 5, no. 4 (October 1977): 499-506.

Hillman, Eugene. *Polygamy Reconsidered*. Maryknoll: Orbis Books, 1975.

Hocking, William E. *Living Religions and a World Faith*. New York: Macmillan, 1940.

———. *Re-thinking Missions*. New York: Harper & Row, 1932.

Hodges, Melvin L. *A Guide to Church Planting*. Chicago: Moody Press, 1973.

Hoekendijk, J. C. "A Call to Evangelism." Reprinted in *The Conciliar-Evangelical Debate*, ed. Donald McGavran, pp. 41-55. Pasadena: William Carey Library, 1977.

Hoffman, George. "The Social Responsibilities of Evangelization." In *Let the Earth Hear His Voice,* ed. J. D. Douglas, pp. 698-712. Minneapolis: World Wide Publications, 1975.

Holland, Clifton L. *The Religious Dimension in Hispanic Los Angeles.* Pasadena: William Carey Library, 1974.

"Hong Kong Call to Conversion." *World Evangelization* 15, no. 53 (July-August 1988): 8-13.

Hornstein, Harvey A., et. al. *Social Intervention.* New York: Free Press, 1971.

Horsley, Richard, and Hanson, John. *Bandits, Prophets, and Messiahs.* New York: Harper & Row, 1985.

Howells, William. *The Heathens: Primitive Man and His Religions.* New York: Doubleday, 1948.

Hughes, Charles. *Goal Setting.* New York: American Management Association, 1965.

Hwang, Bernard. "Ancestor Cult Today." *Missiology* 5, no. 3 (July 1977): 339-65.

Hyde, Douglas. *Dedication and Leadership.* Notre Dame: University of Notre Dame Press, 1966.

Interchurch World Movement of North America. *World Survey, American Volume.* New York: Interchurch Press, 1920.

Janis, Irving, and Mann, Leon. *Decision Making.* New York: Free Press, 1977.

Jeremias, Joachim. *Jerusalem in the Time of Jesus.* Philadelphia: Fortress Press, 1969.

Judge, E. A. *The Social Patterns of the Christian Groups in the First Century.* Wheaton: Tyndale, 1960.

Judson, David J. C. "Evangelism Among the Blind, Deaf and Handicapped." In *Let the Earth Hear His Voice,* ed. J. D. Douglas, pp. 776-89. Minneapolis: World Wide Publications, 1975.

Junker, Buford H. *Field Work: An Introduction to the Social Sciences.* Chicago: University of Chicago Press, 1960.

Kahn, Herman. *Thinking About the Unthinkable.* New York: Avon Books, 1964.

Kahn, Herman, and Wiener, Anthony J. *The Year 2000.* New York: Macmillan, 1967.

Kasdorf, Hans. "Luther's Bible: A Dynamic Equivalence Translation and Germanizing Force." *Missiology* 6, no. 2 (April 1978): 213-34.

Kee, Howard. *Christian Origins in Sociological Perspective.* Philadelphia: Westminster, 1980.

Kelley, Dean M. *Why Conservative Churches Are Growing.* New York: Harper & Row, 1972.

Kelly, David C. "Cross-cultural Communication and Ethics." *Missiology* 6, no. 3 (July 1978): 311-22.

Kennedy, James. *Evangelism Explosion*. Wheaton: Tyndale, 1983.

Keyes, Larry. *The Last Age of Missions: A Study of Third World Mission Societies*. Pasadena: William Carey Library, 1983.

Khair-Ullah, Frank S. "Linguistic Hang-ups in Communicating with Muslims." *Missiology* 4, no. 3 (July 1976): 301-16.

―――. "The Role of Local Churches in God's Redemptive Plan for the Muslim World." In *The Gospel and Islam*, ed. Don McCurry. Monrovia: MARC, 1979.

Kiev, Ari. *A Strategy for Daily Living*. New York: Free Press, 1973.

Kirwen, Michael. *The Missionary and the Diviner*. Maryknoll, NY: Orbis, 1986.

Kraemer, Hendrik. *The Christian Message in a Non-Christian World*. Grand Rapids: Kregel, 1938.

―――. *Religion and the Christian Faith*. Luke House, Farnham Rd., Gilford, Surrey: Lutterworth Press, 1956.

Kraft, Charles H. *Christianity in Culture*. Maryknoll, NY: Orbis Books, 1979.

―――. "Cultural Concomitants of Higi Conversion: Early Period." *Missiology* 4, no. 4 (October 1976): 431-42.

―――. "Dynamic Equivalence Churches." *Missiology* 1, no. 1 (January 1973): 39-57.

―――. "Dynamic Equivalent Churches in Muslim society." In *The Gospel and Culture*, ed. Don McCurry, pp. 114-28. Monrovia: MARC, 1979.

Kraft, Marguerite G. *Worldview and Communication of the Gospel*. Pasadena: William Carey Library, 1978.

Krass, Alfred C. "A Case Study in Effective Evangelism in West Africa." *Church Growth Bulletin* 4, no. 1 (1967).

―――. *Five Lanterns at Sundown: Evangelism in a Chastened Mood*. Grand Rapids: Eerdmans, 1978.

―――. *Go . . . And Make Disciples*. Naperville: Alex R. Allenson, 1974.

Kümmel, Werner G. *The Theology of the New Testament*. Nashville: Abingdon Press, 1973.

Küng, Hans. *The Church*. New York: Doubleday, 1967 (reprint 1976).

Ladd, George E. *A Theology of the New Testament*. Grand Rapids: Eerdmans, 1974.

―――. *Jesus and the Kingdom*. Waco: Word, 1964.

Larson, Donald N. and Smalley, William. *Becoming Bilingual*. Pasadena: William Carey Library, 1972.

Lasch, Christopher. *The Culture of Narcissim*. New York: W. W. Norton, 1979.

Laubach, F., et al. "Conversion, Penitence, Repentance, Proselyte." In *Dictionary of New Testament Theology,* ed. Colin Brown, vol. 1, pp. 353-62. Grand Rapids: Zondervan, 1975.

Lausanne Committee for World Evangelization. *The Pasadena Consultation—Homogeneous Units.* Wheaton: LCWE, 1978.

————. *The Willowbank Report—The Gospel and Culture.* Wheaton: LCWE, 1978.

LeBar, Frank M. *Ethnic Groups of Insular Southeast Asia.* Snyder: Human Relations Area File, 1972.

————. *Ethnic Groups of Mainland Southeast Asia.* Snyder: Human Relations Area File, 1964.

Levinson, Harry. *The Exceptional Executive.* Cambridge: Harvard University Press, 1968.

Lewin, Kurt. *Dynamic Theory of Personality.* New York: McGraw, 1935.

Lewis, C. S. *The Abolition of Man.* New York: Macmillan, 1947 (reprint 1962).

Liao, David. *The Unresponsive: Resistant or Neglected?* Chicago: Moody Press, 1972.

Liefield, Walter L. "Theology of Church Growth." In *Theology and Mission,* ed. David J. Hesselgrave, pp. 173-87. Grand Rapids: Baker Book House, 1978.

Loewen, Jacob A. *Culture and Human Values: Christian Intervention in Anthropological Perspective.* Pasadena: William Carey Library, 1975.

————. "Mission Churches, Independent Churches, and Felt Needs in Africa." *Missiology* 4, no. 4 (October 1976): 405, 425.

————. "Roles: Relating to an Alien Social Structure." *Missiology* 4, no. 2 (April 1976): 217-42.

Lofland, John. *Doomsday Cult.* Enlarged ed. New York: Irvington Publications, 1977.

Long, Norman. *An Introduction to the Sociology of Rural Development.* Boulder: Westview Press, 1977.

Luzbetak, Louis J. *The Church and Cultures.* Pasadena: William Carey Library, 1963.

Mager, Robert F. *Goal Analysis.* Belmont: Fearon Publishers, 1972.

Malherbe, Abraham J. *Social Aspects of Early Christianity.* Baton Rouge: Louisiana State University Press, 1977.

Malina, Bruce. *The New Testament World: Insights from Cultural Anthropology.* Atlanta: John Knox Press, 1981.

Malinowski, Bronislaw. *Magic, Science, and Religion.* New York: Doubleday, 1954.

Maloney, Clarence. *The Peoples of South Asia.* New York: Holt, Rinehart and Winston, 1974.

Mandelbaum, David G. *Society in India.* 2 vols. Berkeley: University of California Press, 1970.

MARC (Missions Advanced Research and Communication Center). *To Reach the Unreached.* Monrovia: MARC, 1978.

———. *World Christianity: East Asia.* Monrovia: MARC, 1979.

———. *World Christianity: Middle East.* Monrovia: MARC, 1979.

———. *World Christianity: Southern Asia.* Monrovia: MARC, 1980.

———. *You Can So Get There from Here.* Monrovia: MARC, 1979.

Marshall, I. Howard. *The Gospel of Luke: A Commentary on the Greek Text.* Grand Rapids: Eerdmans, 1978.

Maslow, Abraham. *Motivation and Personality,* 2d ed. New York: Harper & Row, 1970.

Maurer, Christian. *"phulē." Theological Dictionary of the New Testament,* vol. 9, ed. G. Friedrich, pp. 245-50. Grand Rapids: Eerdmans, 1974.

May, Rollo. *The Courage to Create.* New York: Banton, 1975.

Mayberry-Lewis, David. *The Savage and the Innocent.* Scranton: Beacon Press, 1968.

Mayers, Marvin K. *Christianity Confronts Culture.* Grand Rapids: Zondervan, 1974.

McCullough, W. S. "Fish." *Interpreter's Dictionary of the Bible,* ed. George Buttrick, vol. 2, pp. 272-73. Nashville: Abingdon Press, 1962.

McCurry, Don. *The Gospel and Islam,* Monrovia: MARC, 1974.

McFarland, H. Neil. *The Rush Hour of the Gods.* New York: Macmillan, 1967.

McGavran, Donald. *Bridges of God.* New York: Friendship Press, 1955.

———. *The Clash Between Christianity and Cultures.* Grand Rapids: Baker Book House, 1974.

———. *Ethnic Realities and the Church.* Pasadena; William Carey Library, 1979.

———. *How Churches Grow.* New York: Friendship Press, 1959.

———. *Understanding Church Growth.* Grand Rapids: Eerdmans, 1970.

———, ed. *The Conciliar-Evangelical Debate: The Crucial Documents 1964-1976.* Pasadena: William Carey Library, 1977.

McGavran, Donald, and ARN, Win. *How to Grow a Church.* Glendale: Regal Books, 1973.

McLoughlin, William. *Modern Revivalism.* New York: Ronald Press, 1959.

McNee, Peter. *Crucial Issues in Bangladesh.* Pasadena: William Carey Library, 1976.

Meadows, D. H., and Meadows, D. L. *Limits to Growth.* New York: Universe, 1974.

Meeks, Wayne. *The First Urban Christians: The Social World of the Apostle Paul.* New Haven: Yale University Press, 1983.

Mellis, Charles J. *Committed Communities*. Pasadena: William Carey Library, 1977.

Meyer, Donald. *The Positive Thinkers*. New York: Doubleday, 1965.

Meyer, Rudolf. *"ochlos." Theological Dictionary of the New Testament*, vol. 5, ed. G. Friedrich, pp. 582-90. Grand Rapids: Eerdmans, 1967.

Miller, Donald G. *The Nature and Mission of the Church*. Atlanta: John Knox Press, 1957.

Minear, Paul. *Images of the Church in the New Testament*. Philadelphia: Westminster, 1960.

————. "The Vocation of the Church: Some Exegetical Clues." *Missiology* 5, no. 1 (January 1977): 13-37.

Mobley, Harris. *The Ghanaians' Image of a Missionary*. Long Island City: E. J. Brill, 1970.

Montgomery, James. *Dawn Two Thousand: Seven Million Churches to Go*. Pasadena: William Carey Library, 1989.

Morgan, Gareth. *Images of Organization*. Beverly Hills: Sage Publications, 1986.

Mounce, Robert H. "Gospel." *Baker's Dictionary of Theology*, ed. Everett F. Harrison, pp. 254-57. Grand Rapids: Baker Book House, 1960.

Murdock, George P. *Africa*. New York: McGraw-Hill, 1959.

Murdock, George P., et al. *Outline of Cultural Materials*. 4th rev. Fort Meyers, FL: Human Relations Area File, 1971.

Murphree, Marshall. *Christianity and the Shona*. Atlantic Highlands: Humanities Press, 1969.

Murphy, Edward F. *Spiritual Gifts and the Great Commission*. Pasadena: William Carey Library, 1975.

Naisbitt, John. *Megatrends*. New York: Warner Books, 1982.

Neill, Stephen. *A History of Christian Missions*. New York: Penguin Books, 1964.

Nelson, Marlin L. *The How and Why of Third World Missions*. Pasadena: William Carey Library, 1976.

————. *Readings in Third World Missions*. Pasadena: William Carey Library, 1976.

Nevius, John. *Planting and Development of Missionary Churches*. Phillipsburg: Presbyterian and Reformed, 1958.

Newbigin, Lesslie. *The Open Secret: Sketches for a Missionary Theology*. Grand Rapids: Eerdmans, 1978.

Nida, Eugene A. *Learning a Foreign Language*. New York: Friendship Press, 1957.

————. *Message and Mission*. Pasadena: William Carey Library, 1960.

————. "The Other Message." *Occasional Bulletin* 3, no. 3 (July 1979): 110-12.

————. *Toward a Science of Translating*. Long Island City: E. J. Brill, 1964.

————. "Why Are Foreigners So Queer? A Socio-Anthropological Approach to Cultural Pluralism." Paper presented to the American Society of Missiology, June 16, 1979.

Nida, Eugene A., and Taber, Charles. *The Theory and Practice of Translation*. Long Island City: E. J. Brill, 1974.

Nock, Arthur D. *Early Gentile Christianity*. New York: Harper & Row, 1964.

O'Connor, Elizabeth. *Journey Inward, Journey Outward*. New York: Harper & Row, 1968.

O'Dea, Thomas F. *The Mormons*. Chicago: University of Chicago Press, 1957.

Olson, Bruce. *Bruchko*. Altamonte Springs, FL: Strang Communications, Creation House, 1989.

Ortlund, Raymond C. *Lord, Make My Life a Miracle*. Glendale: Regal Books, 1974.

Osiek, Carolyn. *What Are They Saying about the Social Setting of the New Testament* (Paulist Press, 1984).

Packard, Vance. *The Hidden Persuaders*. New York: David MacKay: 1957.

Padilla, C. René. *The New Face of Evangelicalism*. Downers Grove, IL: InterVarsity, 1976.

Palmer, Donald C. *Explosion of People Evangelism*, Chicago: Moody Press, 1974.

Parshall, Phil. *Beyond the Mosque: Christians Within Muslim Community*. Grand Rapids: Baker Book House, 1985.

————. "Evangelizing Muslims: Are There Ways?" *Christianity Today* 23, no. 7 (January 5, 1979): 28-29, 31.

————. *New Paths in Muslim Evangelization*. Grand Rapids: Baker Book House, 1980.

Pate, Larry D. *From Every People: A Handbook of Two-Thirds World Missions with Directory/Histories/Analysis*. Monrovia: MARC, 1989.

Paul VI, Pope. *On Evangelization in the Modern World*. Washington, DC: United States Catholic Conference, 1976.

Peters, George. *A Biblical Theology of Missions*. Chicago: Moody Press, 1972.

————. "Contemporary Practices of Evangelism." In *Let the Earth Hear His Voice*, ed. J. D. Douglas, pp. 199-207. Minneapolis: World Wide Publications, 1975.

————. *Saturation Evangelism*. Grand Rapids: Zondervan, 1970.

Peters, Thomas J., and Waterman, Robert, Jr. *In Search of Excellence: Lessons from America's Best-Run Companies*. New York: Harper & Row, 1982.

Peters, Thomas J., and Austin, Nancy. *A Passion for Excellence: The Leadership Difference.* New York: Randon House, 1985.

Pickett, J. W. *Christian Mass Movements in India.* Lucknow Publishing House, 1933.

Pickett, J. W., et al. *Church Growth and Group Conversion.* 5th ed. Pasadena: William Carey Library, 1973.

Ponsi, Frank. "Contemporary Concepts of Missions." *Missiology* 6, no. 2 (April 1978): 134-53.

Powdermaker, Hortense. *Stranger and Friend: The Way of an Anthropologist.* New York: Norton, 1967.

Price, Frank, and Orr, Clara E. *Occasional Bulletin,* 23 Novermber 1960. New York: Missionary Research Library.

Quebedeaux, Richard. *The Worldly Evangelicals.* New York: Harper & Row, 1978.

Rabinow, Paul. *Reflections on Fieldwork In Morocco.* Berkeley: University of California Press, 1977.

Randall, Max W. *Profile for Victory: New Proposals for Missions in Zambia.* Pasadena: William Carey Library, 1970.

Read, William. *New Patterns of Church Growth in Brazil.* Grand Rapids: Eerdmans, 1965.

Read, William, and Ineson, Frank. *Brazil 1980.* Monrovia: MARC, 1973.

Read, William R., Monterroso, V. M., and Johnson, H. A. *Latin American Church Growth.* Grand Rapids: Eerdmans, 1969.

Richardson, Don. *Peace Child.* Glendale: Regal Books, 1974.

Ridderbos, Herman. *Paul: An Outline of His Theology.* Grand Rapids: Eerdmans, 1975.

Robb, John. *The Power of People Group Thinking.* Monrovia: MARC, 1989.

Roberts, W. Dayton. *Revolution in Evangelism.* Chicago: Moody Press, 1967.

―――. *Strachan of Costa Rica.* Grand Rapids: Eerdmans, 1971.

Roberts, W. Dayton, and Siewert, John A. *Mission Handbook: USA/Canada Protestant Ministries Overseas.* 14th ed. Monrovia: MARC; Grand Rapids: Zondervan, 1989.

Rogers, Everett M. *Diffusion of Innovation.* New York: Free Press, 1962.

Rogers, Everett M., and Shoemaker, F. Floyd. *Communication of Innovations: A Cross-cultural Approach.* New York: Free Press, 1971.

Rostovtzeff, M. *The Social and Economic History of the Roman Empire.* 2d ed. Revised by P. M. Fraser. 2 vols. London: Oxford University Press, 1957.

Royal Anthropological Institute. *Notes and Queries on Anthropology.* New York: Humanities Press, 1951. Reprint. Boston: Routledge & Kegan, 1971.

Safrai, S., and Stern, M. *The Jewish People in the First Century.* Vol. 1. Philadelphia: Fortress Press, 1974.

————. *The Jewish People in the First Century.* Vol. 2. Philadelphia: Fortress Press, 1976.

Schaeffer, Francis. *The Church at the End of the 20th Century.* Downers Grove, IL: InterVarsity, 1970.

Schaller, Lyle. *The Change Agent.* Nashville: Abingdon Press, 1972.

Schlette, H. R. *Toward a Theology of Religions.* New York: Herder, 1963.

Schmidt, Karl L. *"diaspora." Theological Dictionary of the New Testament,* vol. 2, ed. G. Kittel, pp. 98-104. Grand Rapids: Eerdmans, 1964.

————. *"ethnos, ethnikos." Theological Dictionary of the New Testament,* vol. 2, ed. G. Kittel, pp. 364-72. Grand Rapids: Eerdmans, 1964.

Schneider, Louis, and Dornbusch, Sanford. *Popular Religion: Inspirational Books in America.* Chicago: University of Chicago Press, 1958.

Schreck, Harley, and Barrett, David B., eds. *Unreached Peoples: Clarifying the Task.* Monrovia: MARC, 1987.

Schrenk, Gottlob. *"patria." Theological Dictionary of the New Testament,* vol. 5, ed. G. Friedrich, pp. 1015-22. Grand Rapids: Eerdmans, 1967.

Schürer, Emil. *The History of the Jewish People in the Age of Jesus Christ.* Vols. 1-3. New English edition, revised and edited. Edinburgh: T. & T. Clark, 1973-1987.

Schwartzberg, G. *Atlas of India.* Chicago: University of Chicago Press, 1977.

Seaton, Ronald, and Seaton, Edith. *Here's How: Health Education by Extension.* Pasadena: William Carey Library, 1976.

Shenk, Wilbert R., ed. *The Challenge of Church Growth.* Scottdale: Herald Press, 1973.

Sherwin-White, A. N. *Roman Society and Roman Law in the New Testament.* London: Oxford University Press, 1963.

Shewmaker, Stan. *Tonga Christianity.* Pasadena: William Carey Library, 1970.

Sider, Ronald J. *Rich Christians in an Age of Hunger.* Downers Grove, IL: InterVarsity, 1977.

Singleton, John. *Nichu: A Japanese School.* New York: Holt, Rinehart and Winston, 1967.

Skivington, Bob. *Mission to Mindanao.* Box 1594, Manila: Conservative Baptist Publications; also available through Church Growth Book Club, Pasadena, CA.

Smalley, William, ed. *Readings in Missionary Anthropology.* New Canaan, CT: Practical Anthropology, 1967.

————. *Readings in Missionary Anthropology II.* Rev. and enlarged ed. Pasadena: William Carey Library, 1979.

Smelser, Neil J. *Theory of Collective Behavior.* New York: Free Press, 1962.

Smith, James. *Without Crossing Barriers.* Unpublished thesis, School of World Mission, Fuller Theological Seminary, 1976.

Smith, W. Douglas, Jr. *Toward Continuous Mission.* Pasadena: William Carey Library, 1978.

Snyder, Howard. *Community of the King.* Downers Grove, IL: InterVarsity, 1977.

————. *The Problem of Wineskins: Church Structure in a Technological Society.* Downers Grove, IL: InterVarsity, 1975.

Søgaard, Viggo. "Applying Christian Communications." Ph.D. dissertation, University Microfilms, Ann Arbor, MI, 1986.

————. *Everything You Need to Know for a Cassette Ministry.* Minneapolis: Bethany Fellowship Press, 1975.

Soper, Edmund D. *The Philosophy of the Christian World Mission.* Nashville: Abingdon-Cokesbury, 1943.

Spindler, George D. *Being an Anthropologist: Fieldwork in Eleven Cultures.* New York: Holt, Rinehart and Winston, 1970.

Stambaugh, John, and Balch, David, *The New Testament in Its Social Environment.* Philadelphia: Westminster Press, 1986.

Stenning, D. J. "Salvation in Ankole." In *African Systems of Thought,* ed. M. Fortes, et al. London: Oxford University Press, 1964.

Stewart, James C. *American Cultural Patterns: a Cross-Cultural Perspective.* La Grange Park, IL: Intercultural Network, 1971.

Stoesz, Edgar. *Beyond Good Intentions.* Newton: United Printing, 1972.

Stott, John R. W. *Basic Introduction to the New Testament.* Grand Rapids: Eerdmans, 1967.

————. "The Biblical Basis of Evangelism." In *Let the Earth Hear His Voice,* ed. J. D. Douglas, pp. 65-78. Minneapolis: World Wide Publications, 1975.

————. *Christian Mission in the Modern World.* Downers Grove, IL: InterVarsity, 1976.

Strathmann, H. *"laos." Theological Dictionary of the New Testament,* vol. 4, ed. G. Kittel, pp. 29-57. Grand Rapids: Eerdmans, 1967.

Subbamma, B. V. *New Patterns for Discipling Hindus.* Pasadena: William Carey Library, 1970.

Sundkler, Bengt. *Bantu Prophets.* 2d ed. London: Oxford University Press, 1961.

————. *The World of Mission.* Luke House, Farnham Rd., Gilford, Surrey: Lutterworth Press, 1965.

Swank, Gerald O. *Frontier Peoples of Central Nigeria and a Strategy for Outreach.* Pasadena: William Carey Library, 1977.

Swanson, Allen J. *Taiwan: Mainline vs. Independent Church Growth.* Pasadena: William Carey Library, 1971.

Taber, Charles. "Contextualization: Indigenization and/or Transformation." In *The Gospel and Islam,* ed. Don McCurry, pp. 143-54. Monrovia: MARC, 1979.

————. "Evangelizing the Unreached Peoples." In *Gospel and Frontier Peoples,* ed. R. Pierce Beaver, pp. 118-35. Pasadena: William Carey Library, 1973.

————. "The Limits of Indigenization in Theology." *Missiology* 6, no. 1 (January 1978): 53-79.

Talbert, Charles. *Reading Corinthians.* New York: Crossroad, 1987.

————. *Reading Luke: A Literary and Theological Commentary on the Third Gospel.* New York: Crossroad, 1982.

Theissen, G. *Sociology of Early Palestinian Christianity.* Philadelphia: Fortress Press, 1977.

Thomas, Winburn T. *Protestant Beginnings in Japan.* Rutland: Charles E. Tuttle, 1959.

Tidball, Derek. *The Social Context of the New Testament: A Sociological Analysis.* Grand Rapids: Zondervan, 1984.

Tillapaugh, Frank. *Unleashing the Church: Getting People Out of the Fortress and Into Ministry.* Glendale: Regal Books, 1982.

————. *Unleashing Your Potential: Discovering Your God-Given Opportunities for Ministry.* Glendale: Regal Books, 1988.

Tillich, Paul. *Christianity and the Encounter of the World Religions.* New York: Columbia University Press, 1963.

Tippett, Alan. "Conversion as a Dynamic Process in Christian Mission." *Missiology* 5, no. 2 (April 1977): 203-21.

————. *People Movements in Southern Polynesia.* Chicago: Moody Press, 1971.

————. *Verdict Theology.* Lincoln Christian College, 1967.

Toch, Hans. *The Social Psychology of Social Movements.* Indianapolis: Bobbs-Merrill, 1965.

Toffler, Alvin. *Future Shock.* New York: Random House, 1970.

Triandis, Harry C. *Attitude and Attitude Change.* New York: John Wiley & Sons, 1971.

Trueblood, Elton. *The Company of the Committed.* New York: Harper & Row, 1961.

Tuggy, A. L. "Philippine Inglestani CHRISTI." Unpublished thesis, Fuller Theological Seminary, 1974.

Tuggy, A. L., and Toliver, R. *Seeing the Church in the Philippines.* Robesenia, PA: O.M.F. Books, 1972.

Turner, Harold W. *African Independent Church.* 2 vols. London: Oxford University Press, 1967.

Vander Werff, Lyle L. *Christian Missions to Muslims.* Pasadena: William Carey Library, 1977.

Verkuyl, Johannes. *Contemporary Missiology.* Grand Rapids: Eerdmans, 1978.

Verner, David. *The Household of God and the Social World of the Pastoral Epistles.* Chico, CA: Scholars Press, 1983.

Vicedom, George. *The Mission of God.* St. Louis: Concordia, 1965.

Voelkel, Janvier. *The Eternal Revolutionary: Evangelical Ministry to the University Student in Latin America.* Unpublished thesis, School of World Mission, Fuller Theological Seminary, 1971.

Vogel, Ezra. *Japan's New Middle Class.* Berkeley: University of California Press, 1963.

Vogt, Evon. *Handbook of Middle American Indians: Ethnology.* Vols. 7 and 8. Austin: University of Texas Press, 1969.

Wagner, C. Peter. *Frontiers in Missionary Strategy.* Chicago: Moody Press, 1971.

————. *Our Kind of People.* Atlanta: John Knox Press, 1978.

————. *Stop the World, I Want to Get On.* Glendale: Regal Books, 1973.

————. *Strategies for Church Growth: Tools for Effective Mission and Evangelism.* Glendale: Regal Books, 1987.

————. *Your Spiritual Gifts Can Help Your Church Grow.* Glendale: Regal Books, 1979.

Wagner, C. Peter, and Dayton, Edward R. *Unreached Peoples '79.* Elgin: David C. Cook, 1978.

————. *Unreached Peoples '80.* Elgin: David C. Cook, 1979.

Warren, Max. *To Apply the Gospel: Selections from the Writings of Henry Venn.* Grand Rapids: Eerdmans, 1971.

Watson, David. *I Believe in Evangelism.* Grand Rapids: Eerdmans, 1976.

Wax, Rosalie H. *Doing Fieldwork: Warnings & Advice.* Chicago: University of Chicago Press, 1971.

Webber, Robert. *Common Roots.* Grand Rapids: Zondervan, 1978.

Weber, Max. *Economy and Society.* 3 vols., Berkeley: University of California Press, 1968.

Weekes, Richard. *Muslim Peoples.* Westport: Greenwood Press, 1978.

Wells, David. *God the Evangelist: How the Holy Spirit Works to Bring Men and Women to Faith.* Grand Rapids: Eerdmans, 1987.

Wheeler, Alwyne. *Fishes of the World.* New York: Macmillan, 1975.

White, Hugh V. *A Theology for Christian Mission.* Willett, Clark and Company, 1937.

BIBLIOGRAPHY

Whiteman, Darrell. *Melanesians and Missionaries: An Ethnohistorical Study of Social and Religious Change in the Southwest Pacific.* Pasadena: William Carey Library, 1983.

Willems, Emilio. *Followers of the New Faith.* Nashville: Vanderbilt University Press, 1967.

Williams, Thomas R. *Field Methods in the Study of Culture.* New York: Holt, Rinehart and Winston, 1967.

Williamson, John, et al. *The Research Craft.* New York: Little, Brown, 1977.

Wilson, J. Christy. *Today's Tentmakers.* Wheaton: Tyndale, 1979.

Wilson, Samuel, ed. *Mission Handbook: North American Protestant Ministries Overseas.* 12th ed. Monrovia: MARC, 1980.

Wilson, Samuel, and Siewert, John, eds. *Mission Handbook: North American Protestant Ministries Overseas.* 13th ed. Monrovia: MARC, 1986.

Winter, Ralph D. *The Unfinished Task.* Pasadena: William Carey Library, 1978.

Wonderly, William. *Bible Translations for Popular Use.* New York: American Bible Society, 1968.

Wong, James, et al. *Missions From the Third World.* Singapore: Church Growth Study Centre, 1973.

Yaker, Henri, et al. *The Future of Time.* Garden City: Doubleday, Anchor Books, 1971.

Yamamori, Tetsunao. *Church Growth in Japan.* Pasadena: William Carey Library, 1974.

————. *God's New Envoys: A Bold Strategy for Penetrating "Closed Countries."* Portland, OR: Multnomah Press, 1987.

————. "Toward the Symbiotic Ministry: God's Mandate for the Church Today." *Missiology* 5, no. 3 (July 1977): 265-74.

Yamamori, Tetsunao, and Taber, Charles. *Christopaganism or Indigenous Christianity?* Pasadena: William Carey Library, 1975.

Index